Defending the Japanese State

Defending the Japanese State

Structures, Norms and the Political Responses to Terrorism and Violent Social Protest in the 1970s and 1980s

Peter J. Katzenstein
and
Yutaka Tsujinaka

East Asia Program
Cornell University
Ithaca, New York 14853

The **Cornell East Asia Series** publishes manuscripts on a wide variety of scholarly topics pertaining to East Asia. Manuscripts are published on the basis of camera-ready copy provided by the volume author or editor.

Inquiries should be addressed to Editorial Board, East Asia Series, East Asia Program, Cornell University, 140 Uris Hall, Ithaca, New York 14853.

TABLE OF CONTENTS

LIST OF TABLES

LIST OF FIGURES

LIST OF ABBREVIATIONS

AMPO	Nichibei Anzen Hosho Jyoyaku (The U.S. and Japan Mutual Security Treaty)
AWDF	Anti War Domestic Front (Hansen Minshu Sensen)
BUND	Communist League (Kyosando)
CHUKAKU	Revolutionary Communist League the Core Faction (Kakukyodo Chukaku-ha)
CR	Community Relations
EAAJA	East Asian Anti-Japan Armed Front (Higashi Ajia Han-Nichi Buso Sensen)
EPC	European Political Cooperation
GHQ	General Headquarters of the Supreme Commander for the Allied Powers
IACP	International Association of Chiefs of Police
JCP	Japan Communist Party
JICA	Japan International Cooperation Agency (Kokusai Kyoryoku Jigyo-dan)
JRA	Japan Red Army (Nihon Sekigun)
JSP	Japan Socialist Party
LDP	Liberal Democratic Party
MITI	Ministry of International Trade and Industry (Tsusho Sangyo-Sho)
MOAFF	Ministry of Agriculture, Fishing and Forestry (Nosui-sho)

MOF	Ministry of Finance (Okura-sho)
MOFA	Ministry of Foreign Affairs (Gaimu-sho)
MOHA	Ministry of Home Affairs (Jichi-sho)
MOI	Ministry of the Interior (Naimu-sho)
MOJ	Ministry of Justice (Homu-sho)
MOL	Ministry of Labor (Rodo-sho)
MPD	Metropolitan Police Department in Tokyo (Keishi-cho)
NPA	National Police Agency (Keisatsu-cho)
PAB	Police Affairs Bureau (Keiho-kyoku)
PFLP	Popular Front for the Liberation of Palestine
PSIA	Public Security Investigation Agency (Koanchosa-cho)
SCAP	Strategic Commander for the Allied Powers
SDF	Self Defense Forces (Jieitai)
UNAFEI	United Nations Asia and Far East Institute for the Prevention of Crime and the Treatment of Offenders

PREFACE

This monograph focuses on a subject that has been relatively neglected by Japanese specialists and political scientists alike. Yet in a world in which terrorism and violent social protest has become a permanent feature, political assumptions about how states defend their security both at home and abroad are no longer well served by an exclusive focus on the role of the military. Police powers have undergone dramatic changes during the last forty years, in Japan as in other industrial states. Japan's modern history makes an analysis of these changes both politically important and intellectually rewarding. Politically a study of the security police can teach us much about the organization of power in contemporary Japan and the kind of democracy that has evolved in Japan since the end of World War II. A study of the Japanese security police should also help us to gauge more accurately the character of the Japanese state, a controversial subject among specialists and policymakers alike.

This monograph offers a description of the organizational structures and norms that shape Japan's policy of internal security. It traces the institutional and political relations that link various governmental actors within the state, with domestic society, and with a variety of transnational structures; it analyzes the domestic and international norms that help political actors define the interests that inform policy; and it describes Japan's domestic and international policies of internal security during the last two decades.

The description in this monograph will eventually be part of a broader set of studies that seek to explain Japanese security policy in recent years. This explanation will be based on two comparisons: with Japan's policy of external security on the one hand and with Germany's policies of internal and external security on the other. A comparison with Japan's external security policy will be a useful complement to this monograph's focus on the police and internal security. And it should help us relate our conclusions about Japan to those reached in numerous studies of Japan's political economy. The comparison with Germany may reveal those elements that are distinctive of Japan's approach to security as well as telling us something about the two states that, having won the Cold War, will have a growing influence in world politics.

Our work has been helped immeasurably by a large number of individuals -- government officials, scholars, and journalists -- who were willing to provide us with data and insights on a subject largely neglected by existing scholarship on Japan. We are also much in debt to a number of colleagues who read and commented on earlier drafts of this study: David Bayley, Ronald Dore, Robert Farrell, Haruhiro Fukui, Hirobumi Hatakeyama, Ellis Krauss, Hiroaki Matsuzawa, Setsuo Miyazawa, Masayuki Murayama, Michio Muramatsu, Nobuo Okawara, Hideo Otake, T.J. Pempel, Susan Pharr, Richard Samuels, Robert Smith, Patricia Steinhoff, Keiichi Tsunekawa, and Ezra Vogel. Their critical comments were very useful for us even when, at our own peril, we chose to disregard them.

This research was made possible by a grant of the German Marshall Fund of the U.S. to Peter Katzenstein and by grants of the Fulbright Commission Japan) and the American Council of Learned Societies to Yutaka Tsujinaka.

We are grateful for the research assistance of David Choi, Miho Kawahatsu, Masumi Shimoji and, in particular, Bronwyn Dylla as well as the help we received from Kenna March, Holly Rice, and Karen Smith in helping us prepare the manuscript for publication. Finally, we would like to thank Cornell's East Asia Program for its willingness to include this monograph in Cornell's East Asia Series.

Ithaca   Peter J. Katzenstein
July, 1991   Yutaka Tsujinaka

INTRODUCTION

This monograph examines how Japan has reacted to the rise of terrorism and violent social protest that has affected its internal security [Apter and Sawa, 1984, p.228]. Japanese terrorism has centered around the Japan Red Army (JRA). After a brief period of operation in Japan in the late 1960s and early 1970s the police forced the JRA to relocate to the Mideast which became the base for its operation during the next two decades [Steinhoff, 1988a, 1989a]. Internal security was also challenged by social movements in the 1970s and 1980s that opposed, for example, the construction and subsequent enlargement of Tokyo's Narita Airport and that embraced a host of other left-wing causes [Apter and Sawa, 1984]. Although the JRA and violence-prone social movements have been largely unconnected, they are typically discussed by police officials and the media under the same label of kageki-ha or radicals. Police estimates the strength of violence-prone groups on the Left at about 35,000 members in the 1980s including 14,000 activitists; but everyone agrees that the JRA enjoys virtually no active support inside Japan [National Police Agency, 1982, p.89. Advanced Course, 1989, p.421. Clifford, 1976, p.25. Tashiro, 1985, p. 135].

Terrorism has triggered political responses in Japan that have been remarkably consistent. These responses derive from the structure of Japan's state and the context of social and legal norms in which political choices on questions of internal security are being made. The organizational structure of the Japanese police is a blend of centralization and decentralization. Its operative mission is no longer informed exclusively by the notion of state service through social surveillance aiming, as it did in the 1930s and 1940s, at the eradication of political dissent. Instead since 1945 Japan's police has been revamped. While it retains a largely centralized structure for protecting Japan's internal security, its mission has also been redefined to respond to broader social needs. The societal orientation of Japan's police is effective. It evokes a sense of traditional community in the service of modern police technologies. "The police have not been molded in a vacuum. Rather, they fit Japanese society like a glove fits the hand, and the societal hand has determined the form of the glove" [Ames, 1981, p.1]. And when, on rare

1

occasions, that hand forms a fist, as is true of some aspects of Japan's internal security policy, so does the glove.

The normative context in which the police seeks to defend internal security derives primarily from the social acceptance of informal police surveillance. This contrasts with the strong statist ideology sanctioning intrusive police practices and the eradication of political dissent before 1945. By the same token, despite Japan's strict adherence to international law, that social acceptance is not extended easily beyond the water's edge. International cooperation on questions of internal security appears to be largely interest-driven.

Internal security policy has been shaped by these organizational structures and social as well as legal norms. In a very short time in the early 1970s the police succeeded in forcing Japan's terrorists offshore. The grim reality of the "embarrassingly violent and defiant activities of Japanese [sic] Red Army political radicals abroad in the service of other causes," suggested to one student of the Japanese police in the mid-1970s that "one might be excusably tempted to observe facetiously that Japan is able to control its crime at home simply because it exports its violence and terrorism abroad. Certainly there can be no doubt that it is this contaminated world image that preoccupies the Japanese more than any crime control problems at home" [Clifford, 1976, pp.3,23].

Political concern over the activities of the JRA continue both in Japan and abroad. In May 1988 Yasuhiro Shibata was arrested in Japan. He had entered illegally from North Korea to where he and a group of the JRA had hijacked a plane in March 1970. In November 1987 the Japanese police arrested the number two man of the JRA, Osamu Maruoka, in Tokyo after he had travelled throughout Asia for several months. After Maruoka's arrest traces of two other members of the JRA were found in the Philippines. Two other JRA members, Junzo Okudaira and Tsutomu Shirosaki, have been linked to a series of bombing and rocket attacks in Asia and Europe. The NPA has gradually come around to the view that the Wakaoji hostage case (the manager of the Philippines branch of the Mitsui Trading Company was taken hostage in November 1986 and released in March 1987 in exchange for three million dollars) was directly related to the JRA. Circumstantial evidence, including records in Maruoka's passport and the confession of a suspect arrested on January 7, 1991 in the Philippines, suggests the JRA's involvement [Nikkei, January 8, 1991. Asahi, January 8, 1991. Yomiuri, January 8, 1991]. The woman leader of the JRA, Fusako Shigenobu, has reportedly been at the site of a powerful bomb attack at an US facility in Naples which killed five people and injured seventeen others in April 1988. And only a few days earlier another member of the Red Army, Yu Kikumura, was arrested on the New Jersey turnpike with three pipe bombs in his car, apparently planning an attack in New York city or on a meeting of international finance ministers in

Washington D.C. [Steinhoff, 1988a, p.1. Farrell, 1990. Keisatsucho, 1989a, pp. 284-87]. At the outbreak of the war in the Mideast in January 1991, seven members of the Red Army were reported to have promised their support to Iraqui President Saddam Hussein; meanwhile the National Police Agency (NPA) organized a 50-member task force to gather additional information on international terrorism, including on the JRA headquartered in Syria [The Japan Times, January 17, 1991, p. 2. Nikkei, January 17, 1991].

Violent social protest inside Japan on the other hand has remained a main staple of Japan's domestic politics. A recent episode illustrates that protest around Narita Airport, though less frequent, has not abated. In December 1989 about 6,500 policemen used large steel cages and an armored box suspended from several cranes to dislodge about a dozen protesters, armed with firebombs and slingshots as well as arrows abd bows, who were opposing the expansion of Narita Airport [Sterngold, 1989]. The protesters occupied a shack and four steel towers built on a newly proposed runway. The police sprayed the protesters incessantly with powerful water cannons and lowered two huge steel cages from cranes which deflected firebombs and stones hurled at them from the towers. And the police used a steel gondola, also suspended from a crane, from which five crouching policemen eventually leaped to take over one of the towers. After a day of fighting the police had arrested three protesters. There were no injuries.

Since this battle was waged, several similar incidents have occured in 1990. They were directed against the initiative of the Ministry of Transport and the police to prepare for an expansion of the airport [Mainichi, November 29, 1990]. In addition, in October 1990, the Airin riot shook Osaka for about a week. The riot was prompted by local police corruption, specifically the involvement of the police with the Yakuza (Japan's organized crime) in the exploitation of day laborers (Weisman, 1990c). And more than 60 guerrilla actions and bombing attacks occured in the course of the Emperor's enthronment ceremony in November 1990. These incidents illustrate the continued importance of violent social protest and the challenge it poses to the internal security of the Japanese state.

The existing literature on Japan's policy of internal security is very sparse in both English and Japanese. We have some excellent scholarly analyses of the Japanese police system written in English by Walter Ames, David Bayley, William Clifford and Setsuo Miyazawa which have served as a source of inspiration and information for other writers such as Craig Parker [Ames, 1981. Bayley, 1978. Clifford, 1976. Parker, 1984. Miyazawa, 1991a]. And we also have the distinguished and authoritative writings on Japanese terrorist organizations and violent social movements by David Apter and Nagayo Sawa, William Farrell and Patricia Steinhoff, as well as a short article by Robert Angel, which offer important insights into how the Japanese police and court system has responded to threats to Japan's internal security during the last two decades [Apter and Sawa, 1984. Farrell, 1990. Steinhoff, 1988, 1989a and 1989b. Angel, 1990]. But information on the security police is scant, and the topic of internal security has been neglected compared to the fascination with Japan's economic success. Furthermore, the lack of data explains why existing scholarship is largely based on field research methods that combine participant observation with community studies. The analytical categories that inform these writings combine structural and cultural categories. In the words of David Bayley "culture as well as social structure are now seen as comprising independent sets of variables in criminological theory, with such structural factors nestling inside, as it were, the patterning of Japanese culture" [Bayley, 1984, p.185. Kühne and Miyazawa, 1979, p.91].

The scholarly literature in Japanese is also small. Miyazawa's study of the behavior of detectives [1985. 1990, pp. 36-42] and Murayama's study of the patrol police in Tokyo [1990] constitute the bulk of the few scholarly analyses that we have. Virtually all scholars writing in Japanese on the police are lawyers interested primarily in legal change or legal cases [Hogaku Semina, 1980, 1987]. Political analyses have been written largely by journalists, such as Takagi's study on the left-wing radicals [Takazawa, Takagi, Kurata, 1981. Takagi, 1988], Suzuki's report on the security police and police leaders [1978, 1980, 1985], Tahara's numerous accounts of the role the police plays in the national bureaucracy [1979, 1986a, 1986b, 1990], and Nishio's analysis of the new internal security policy from the perspective of an anti-nuclear activist [1979, 1984]. Like the writings of lawyers, journalistic accounts of the police tend to be explicitly evaluative in judging the police by the standards of universal human rights. Hironaka's historical-institutional analysis of the security police [1973] is a notable exception. It is the only scholarly account that offers a detailed and informative analysis of the security police from 1945 to 1970.

The very definition of the concept of internal security is of course not invariable. Police officials, social movement activists and terrorists are likely to differ in their assessment and evaluation of the extent and need for policies designed to defend the security of the state against its internal enemies. But like other states, Japan too has faced some serious domestic challenges to state authority. Its policies of internal security tell us much about the broader political regime that maintains domestic order in Japan.

This monograph will focus on two such challenges, the rise of terrorism and violent social protest in the 1970s and 1980s. These challenges have been politically very important and, arguably, central in how key decisionmakers have defined Japan's problem of internal security. Except where it is relevant to our analysis, we are not dealing with social and political protests in the 1950s and 1960s. And other problems, such as ordinary crime, the threat of right-wing political extremism and the pervasiveness of organized crime, are touched on only briefly and less systematically. This is not to argue that they are unimportant. But Japan's political and bureaucratic elite simply has not considered right-wing extremism and organized crime as direct a threat to the Japanese state as the threat from the Left. This by itself is a very important fact about Japan.

There are two political questions that command attention in a study of Japan's internal security. First, since along numerous dimensions police powers have increased very substantially during the last two decades, what explains the caution with which that power normally has been exercised in numerous informal ways, occasionally with massive public displays, and always with a minimum use of physical force? Secondly, with Japanese terrorism quickly moving offshore in the early 1970s, why have transnational police structures been so unimportant to Japan, and why have the efforts to coordinate policies of internal security with other states been so halting until very recently? The answer to both questions rests in a proper understanding of the norms that have informed how Japan's bureaucratic and political elites have defined the requirements of internal security policy.

Striking about these norms is their concrete social character which encompasses abstract legal rights. Japan's social norms do not contradict its legal norms, but they animate these legal norms and give them a standing that legal norms do not necessarily have on their own. The divergence between growing police powers and a surprising degree of caution in the exercise of those powers lies in the strength of Japan's social norms as illustrated by the keen attention that the police pays to the restraints that public opinion imposes on police action as well as the police's astute seizing of the opportunities that public and published opinion creates for police action. This importance of social norms entails, and here lies the answer to the second question, a relative weakness in the appeal of abstract legal norms that make international law a framework that for countries with more legalistic cultures, such as Germany, offers a compelling framework for building transnational links and seeking greater policy coordination. To put it differently, on questions of internal security the social embeddedness of Japan's legal norms make more difficult the attempts to internationalize Japan that are increasingly forced upon it and to which it must respond.

The structures that define interest, this monograph assumes, do not in themselves explain policy. For interests are plastic and can be conceived in numerous ways, depending on the normative context in which they are put. Interest-based explanations are not wrong but incomplete. Without a proper appreciation of the normative context that helps inform Japan's policy choices, our understanding of Japan's internal security policy would miss an essential insight into Japanese politics. The undeniable growth of informal police powers, and the abundant evidence that the police lacks the resources to characteristic feature of Japanese politics. Japan lacks a center of political accountability. "In a political system where the various power groups refuse to give anyone a mandate for making binding decisions, institutions with the means of physical coercion -- the police and the military -- . . . are essentially in charge of themselves" [Van Wolferen, 1990]. And the internationalization of Japan's internal security policy is not so much the result of a political decision to implement an important set of changes as one aspect of a process of social and political change that, at the margin, is affecting most major Japanese institutions during the last two decades.

This monograph analyzes both the domestic and the international politics of Japan's internal security policy. After providing data on the incidence of terrorism, violent social protest and various types of crimes (Part 1) and establishing a historical baseline for some of the most important features of Japan's police system before 1945 (Part 2), the monograph describes police and other organizational structures most relevant for Japan's internal security (Part 3) and analyzes the normative context in which policy is formulated and implemented on issues of internal security (Part 4). The monograph concludes by analyzing the domestic and international aspects of Japan's internal security policy (Part 5) and summarizing briefly its main findings (Part 6).

I.
AN OVERVIEW OF TERRORISM AND VIOLENT PROTEST

In response to a crime wave in 1988-89 the Japanese were reported to be fearing a spreading of an 'American disease' [Darlin, 1989. Weisman, 1989. Kambara, 1989]. Yet despite the public anguish reported in the press any discussion of Japan's reaction to terrorism and violent social protest must begin with underlining the country's extremely low crime rate which makes Japan an international anomaly. This has little to do with Japan's national character. Until the early 1960s Japan's record with violent crime was no better than that of the other major advanced industrial states. But since then Japan's crime rate has declined, in sharp contrast to the United States and Western Europe. Between the early 1950s and the mid-1970s Japanese crime decreased in a society undergoing rapid urbanization and industrialization. And between 1962 and 1972 all crime, excluding minor traffic violations, decreased by 20 per cent while serious crime dropped by 40 per cent.

Although overall crime rates have increased since the mid-1970s, serious crime (murder, robbery, rape, arson and felonies) have continued to decline [Advanced Course, 1989, pp.136-37, 149, 158. Miyazawa, 1990. Vogel, 1979, pp.204-07. Hoshino, 1984, pp.199-205. Bayley, 1978, pp.5-7. Ames, 1981, pp.57-62. Clifford, 1976, pp.1-4,146. Kühne and Miyazawa, 1979, pp.7-12,24-42. National Police Agency, 1987b, pp.4-7 and 1989a, pp.36-40. Archambeault and Fenwick, 1985, p.2. Kasai, 1973. Fenwick, 1982. Smith, 1983, pp.124-25. Parker, 1984, pp.17-18,197]. Except for traffic violations fewer crimes were committed in 1980 than in 1950 [Bayley, 1984, p.177]. Furthermore the clearance rate for major crimes lies consistently above those of other advanced industrial states [Miyazawa, 1990. National Police Agency, 1987b, pp.4-7 and 1989b, pp.33-37. Bayley, 1984, p.180. Ames, 1981, pp.62-65. Citizens Crime Commission, 1975, pp.8-10. Kühne and Miyazawa, 1979, pp.112-13]. While the precise figures reported in different studies vary slightly, compared to the average Japanese the average American has 4 1/2 times more of a chance of being burglarized, more than 6 times of being murdered, 25 times of being raped, and 142 times of being personally robbed [Keizai Koho Center, 1990, p.92. Citizens Crime Commission, 1975, pp.7-8. Bayley, 1976, p.56. Advanced Course, 1989, p.135. Miyazawa, 1990]. Compared to West Germany, a relatively crime-free

7

and orderly society by international standards, Japanese crime rates are lower by a factor of three (murder), four (burglary), six (rape) and thirty-one (robbery) [Keizai Koho Center, 1990, p.92. National Police Agency, 1987b, pp.4-7 and 1989a, pp.36-40. Takeyasu, 1986, p.22. Advanced Course, 1989, p.135. Miyazawa, 1990]. David Bayley, a leading student of Japan's police system, concludes that "Japan's low crime rate is unique among modern, industrialized countries not only because it has declined since the Second World War, but because it is often orders of magnitude less than others" [Bayley, 1984, p.177].

To some extent these low crime rates are the result of non-comparable crime statistics [Kühne and Miyazawa, 1979, pp.17-23. Dörmann, 1984. Takeyasu, 1986, pp.22-23]. Criminal law in Japan, for example, distinguishes between robbery and extortion: robbery is defined as seizing another's property under threat of violence; extortion is the relinquishing of property under the threat of violence. Adding both figures, Japan's rate is still only one-twentieth of the corresponding American figure [Bayley, 1984, p.179]. And German data on robbery include incidents that would be included under "extortion" and "larceny" in Japan. As a result one study concludes that the difference between German and Japanese robbery data "is not overwhelmingly large" even though it reports that difference as 1:23 per ten thousand of population [Takeyasu, 1986, pp.22-23]. And there is no evidence that Japanese figures are less reliable than those collected by other states. The magnitude of error in victimization rates reported by American and Japanese surveys is about the same. Indeed some evidence suggests that the underreporting of crime may in fact be much greater in the United States and in West Germany than in Japan, which makes the Japanese figures even more impressive [Bayley, 1978, pp.7-9 and 1984, p.179. Citizens Crime Commission, 1975, p.8. Kühne and Miyazawa, 1979, pp.76-90. Parker, 1984 p.100].

It would be wrong, however, to assume that Japan is free from political crime. Its samurai tradition is one of violence. Political assassinations have figured prominently both before and after 1945. The 1930s in particular was a decade of rightist terrorism. Before 1945 right-wing radicals instigated 47 terrorist incidents, committed 14 assassination attempts and planned 2 coups d'etat [Mainichi, 1986]. After 1945, particularly in the years 1948-52, the Japan Communist Party (JCP) and the North Korean League engaged in radical protest against the policy of incomplete democratization and the growth of anti-Communism. Between 1948 and 1952 in the ten largest riots 800 policemen were injured; and in a much larger number of demonstrations thousands of citizens were arrested [Keisatsucho, 1977b]. But these figures pale in comparison to the demonstrations in 1959-60 and 1967-70 [Bayley, 1976, pp.60-61]. In all of the demonstrations that occurred in 1959-60 a total of about 4.7 million demonstrators confronted a total mobilized police force of about 900,000; corresponding figures for 1967-70 were 18.7 million and 6.7 million [Asahi Nenkan, 1971, p. 314]. Since then the activities of extremist groups have changed in character, but they have not disappeared. As shown later in Table 2 and in the Appendix, more than two hundred bombing incidents were reported between 1969 and 1989. "Guerrilla" attacks such as the throwing of Molotov cocktails and arson occurred more frequently. Five hundred and seventy attacks were reported between 1978 and 1989. And in 1990 alone more than 120 attacks were recorded [Mainichi, 26 November, 1990, evening]. The best cross-national data set measuring the incidence of terrorism and violent social protest in Japan shows that, in comparison to West Germany, Japanese incidents are less frequent -- between mid-1983 and mid-1989 the figures were 144 for Japan and 315 for West Germany -- and less serious -- the number of deaths and injuries resulting from terrorist acts were only one-fourth of the West German figure (See Appendix). Despite Japan's astonishingly low crime statistics, terrorism and violence-prone social movements present a continuing problem [Advanced Course, 1989, pp.421-39. Bayley, 1978, pp.171-72,182. Ames, 1981, p.87. Parker, 1984, p.192. Clifford, 1976, pp.22-27. Apter and Sawa, 1984, pp.157-58,179-80. Kühne and Miyazawa, 1979, pp.72-75. Citizens Crime Commission, 1975, pp.48-49. Rinalduccie, 1972, pp.xl-xliii].

1A. Historical Overview

Although traditional right-wing extremists, activists of the JCP, and members of the North Korean group are still subject to police surveillance in the 1970s and 1980s, they have not been the major source of terrorism and violent social protest since the 1960s. Radical groups since the late 1960s have mobilized particularly on the Left [Interview no. 15, Tokyo, May 17, 1990]. Table 1 summarizes some data for the three most important periods of mass radicalization in post-war Japan.

The first mass protests were suppressed in 1948-52. The main legal instruments included provisions in the penal code punishing riots (Articles 106, 107) which the government invoked six times between 1948 and 1952; the Association Regulation ordinance to dissolve the Northern Korean League in 1949; and other administrative and executive powers of the American occupation authorities.

With the end of the so-called "Molotov cocktail struggle" (1951-1955) the second period of mass protest was initiated by a change in the JCP's military tactics at its sixth national convention in 1955. This caused the break-away of the first New Left factions from the JCP, including the Bund or Communist League and Kakukyodo or Revolutionary Communist League. During the second period social movements such as Ampo 1960 (a mass protest movement directed against the revision of the U.S.-Japan Security Act

Table 1: Three Periods of Mass Radical Movements (1948-70)

	Period	Mobilization	Arrests
1) North Korean League Offensive & JCP's Molotov Cocktail Tactics	April 1948-- July 1952 (55 mos.)	?	4,050
2) Ampo 1960	April 1959-- Oct. 1960 (19 mos.)	4,697,000	886
3) Ampo 1970	Oct. 1967-- June 1970 (33 mos.)	18,738,000	26,373

Injured Police	Largest Incidents
1) 860	Osaka Incident, April 23, 1948 (Crimes of Riot Law applied) 179 arrested, 63 police injured.
	Bloody May Day Incident, May 1, 1952 (Crimes of Riot Law applied) 1,219 arrested, 638 police injured.
2) 2,236	Hagerty incident, June 10, 1960.
	Rush into Diet Incident, June 15, 1960.
3) 14,685	Sinjuku Riot Incident, (Crimes of Riot Law applied), Oct. 21, 1968, 1,012 arrested, 1,157 police injured--Tokyo: 14,549 police.
	April 28, 1969 Okinawa Day Incident, 1,030 arrested, 481 police injured. Subversive Activity Prevention Law applied to Chukaku and Bund; 45,000 policemen mobilized.
	October 21, 1969 Incident, 1,504 arrested, 583 police injured, 97,115 police mobilized.

Source: Keisatsucho, 1977b.

in 1959-60) or Zengakuren (the National Student Unions Federation led by the Bund) achieved substantial roles and became independent political organizations.

The evolution in the organization of radical sects after the collapse of the Ampo 1960 movement was a complicated pattern of converging and diverging tendencies leading eventually, in 1966, to the establishment of a coalition of three factions in the Sanpa-Zengakuren (1966-68) or the National Student Union Federation -- Three Allied Factions; Bund, Chukaku or The Revolutionary Communist League The Core Faction; and Shaseido Kaiho-ha or the Youth Socialist League-Liberation Faction [Apter and Sawa, 1984, pp. 118-22. Farrell, 1990, pp. 31-79, Takazawa et al., 1981, pp.62-67]. After Sanpa-Zengakuren, a new type of student movement emerged in 1968-70 that aimed at direct democracy, Zenkyoto or All University Joint Struggle Council movement. It mobilized millions of students and surpassed the mass rallies organized by the established left-wing parties and groups, including the labor unions [Tozuka, 1973, p. 93. Asahi Nenkan, 1970, pp.306-10. 1971, pp.314-16. Takazawa et al., 1981, pp.84-102, 110-25. Takagi, 1988, pp.55-93].

The mass demonstrations staged in 1960 became the most important turning point in the postwar history of the radical Left as well as of Japan's major political parties. A broadly-based coalition of opposition parties, left-wing radicals and intellectuals succeeded in a strategy of mass mobilization that far exceeded even the worst fears of the government and the police [Takagi, 1988, pp.44-51. Takazawa et al., 1981, pp.40-50]. The outbreak of mass protest in 1959-60 occasioned an important rethinking of government policy especially by the National Police Agency (NPA). NPA officials viewed these protests as pointing to serious police failures [Interview no. 17, Tokyo, May 17, 1990]. In preparing for the anticipated 1970 Ampo mass demonstrations the police adopted, therefore, a set of new police strategies and tactics.

During the third period between 1967-70 Chukaku and the Bund often joined forces to organize mass demonstrations. However, their subsequent political failures prompted political activists to move underground to wage a violent and deadly struggle against the Japanese state [Takagi, 1988. Takazawa, Takagi, Kurata, 1981. Keisatsucho, 1988a. Keisatsucho, 1988b].

In the late 1960s, a large number of different groups emerged among the New Left which constituted the core of terrorist activities and violent social movement politics during the next twenty years. First, the most militant groups consisted of several new revolutionary groupings such as Kyosando (Bund) Sekigun-ha (the Bund Red Army Faction), Nihon Kyosanto Kakumei Saha Kanagawa-ken Iinkai (the JCP Revolutionary Left Kanagawa Prefecture Committee), and later the Bund RG faction. Secondly, the Zenkyoto armed mass-movement groups included most of the New Left factions such as

Figure 1: Factions and Sects of New Leftist Radicals (1955–90)

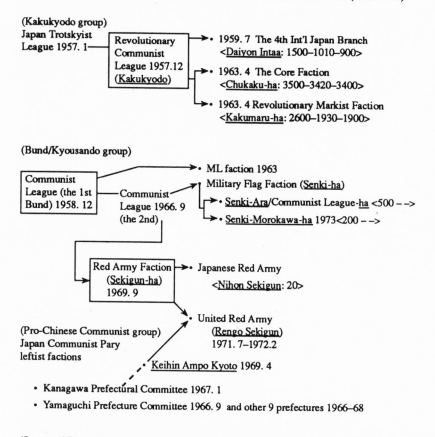

(Kakukyodo group)
Japan Trotskyist
League 1957. 1

Revolutionary
Communist
League 1957.12
(Kakukyodo)

• 1959. 7 The 4th Int'l Japan Branch
  <Daiyon Intaa: 1500–1010–900>

• 1963. 4 The Core Faction
  <Chukaku-ha: 3500–3420–3400>

• 1963. 4 Revolutionary Markist Faction
  <Kakumaru-ha: 2600–1930–1900>

(Bund/Kyousando group)

Communist
League (the 1st
Bund) 1958. 12 — Communist
League 1966. 9
(the 2nd)

• ML faction 1963
Military Flag Faction (Senki-ha)
  • Senki-Ara/Communist League-ha <500 – –>
  • Senki-Morokawa-ha 1973<200 – –>

Red Army Faction
(Sekigun-ha)
1969. 9

• Japanese Red Army
  <Nihon Sekigun: 20>

(Pro-Chinese Communist group)
Japan Communist Pary
leftist factions

• United Red Army
  (Rengo Sekigun)
  1971. 7–1972.2

• Keihin Ampo Kyoto 1969. 4

• Kanagawa Prefectural Committee 1967. 1

• Yamaguchi Prefecture Committee 1966. 9 and other 9 prefectures 1966–68

(Structutal Reformist group)

Socialist →
Innovation
Movement 1962. 3
(Shakakushin)

• Communist Workers Party→
  (Kyoro-to) 1967. 2

• CWP National Council
  <Kyoro-to: 73. 4.: 400 – –>
  • <Furonto: 70. 12.: 200 – –>

(Figure 1. continued)

(Socialist Youth Leagure group)

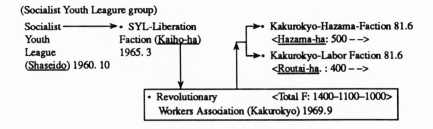

Socialist ————————▶• SYL-Liberation   ┌▶• Kakurokyo-Hazama-Faction 81.6
Youth   Faction (Kaiho-ha)   │   <Hazama-ha: 500 – –>
League   1965. 3   └▶• Kakurokyo-Labor Faction 81.6
(Shaseido) 1960. 10   <Routai-ha. : 400 – –>

                         ┌───┐
                         │ • Revolutionary   <Total F: 1400–1100–1000> │
                         │   Workers Association (Kakurokyo) 1969.9   │
                         └───┘

[Student Movement]

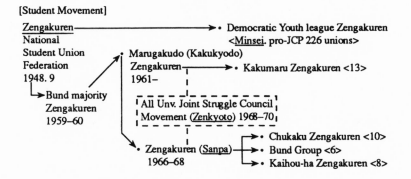

Zengakuren————————————————————▶• Democratic Youth league Zengakuren
National   <Minsei. pro-JCP 226 unions>
Student Union   • Marugakudo (Kakukyodo)
Federation   Zengakuren————————▶• Kakumaru Zengakuren <13>
1948. 9   1961–
   └▶Bund majority   ┌─────────────────────────────┐
     Zengakuren   ¦ All Unv. Joint Struggle Council ¦
     1959–60   ¦ Movement (Zenkyoto) 1968–70 ¦
                          └─────────────────────────────┘
                                 ┌▶• Chukaku Zengakuren <10>
                          • Zengakuren (Sanpa)—┼▶• Bund Group <6>
                            1966–68   └▶• Kaihou-ha Zengakuren <8>

Source and Note: < >: estimated force of the group sequentially ordered according to
Tashiro, 1985, Takagi, 1988 and 1990. See also Tozuka 1973, NPA 1988.
As for student movement, see Takagi, 1990.

14

Chukaku, Kakurokyo, (Revolutionary Workers Association), ML, the Fourth International Japan Branch, and several factions of the Bund. During the struggles of the 1970s, they split further into groups willing to wage armed struggle (among others Chukaku, Kakurokyo-Hazama, Senki) and mass movement groups (such as the Fourth International, Kakurokyo-Rotai, and Rodoto). Finally, the last group Kakumaru (Revolutionary Communist League-Revolutionary Marxist Faction), focused on organizing labor unions and student associations [Takazawa et al., 1981, pp.138-9. Takagi, 1988, p.22]. Several of these groups, including Chukaku, the Bund Red Army faction, the JCP Revolutionary Left (Kanagawa), and the Bund RG first began planting bombs as a means of instigating mass demonstrations. But bombing attacks soon became also a means of attacking the police and other state institutions. Here is the starting point of the terrorism and guerilla attacks that have characterized the Japanese Left during the last two decades. In the spring of 1971, mainly based on the Bund Red Army, the Arab Red Army, later the Japan Red Army, was formed in the Mid-East. Figure 1 summarizes the evolution of Japan's radical political groupings.

1B. Four Phases of Left-Wing Political Mobilization, 1969-1990

The history of leftist terrorism and violent protest can be divided into four phases (see Tables 2 and 3). The first phase (fall 1969-spring 1972) overlaps partly with the final phase of mass protest. In the fall of 1969 a few leftist groups started throwing bombs as a means of intensified armed struggle in the streets. This change in tactics responded to a sharp decrease in the number of activists after the arrest and detention of almost 15,000 protesters in 1969 and a change in public support as illustrated by the defeat of the Japan Socialist Party (JSP) in the general election of December 1969. One hundred and seven bombing incidents occurred between October 1969 and February 1972. Thirty-two attacks were credited to revolutionary groups like the Bund RG, Bund Red Army, and Keihin-Ampo-Kyoto (the mass struggle organization of the JCP Revolutionary Left Kanagawa Committee). The latter two groups eventually formed an alliance in 1971, known as Rengo Sekigun. Anarchist groups and other unaffiliated radical groups, including the East Asia Anti-Japan Armed Front, caused an additional 20 bombing attacks [Keisatsucho, 1988b].

Although the size of mass demonstrations was beginning to decrease, the mass movement groups still succeeded in organizing several, very large protest rallies: Anti-War Day, October, 1969; a demonstration against Prime Minister Sato's visit of the United States, November 1969; Okinawa Day, April 1970; Ampo 70 Day, June 1970; a demonstration opposing the Okinawa Agreement, June 1971; Sanrizua, Anti-Narita Airport Construction, September 1971; and a demonstration against the ratification of the Okinawa Agreement Ratification, November 1971. Among the mass movement groups

Table 2: Four Phases of Leftist Terrorism in Japan (Domestic attacks only) (1969 - 1989)

Radical Groups / Period Year	Bombings I 69 70 71 72	II 73 74 75 76 77 78 79	III 80 81 82 83 84	IV 85 86 87 88 89	Total	Guerrilla Attacks*** II 78 79	III 80 81 82 83 84	IV 85 86 87	Total
Bund RA	8 2 4 3				17				
Rengo RA	1				1				
KeihinAmpo	6 5 3				14				
Bund RG	8	1			9				
Anarchist Groups	2 11 2	2 9 1 2 6 1 1			37				
East Asia Anti-Japan AF	1 3	5 6 1			16				
Chukaku	14	3		7 5 11 2 3	45	40 20	13 3 16 8 24	65 54 16	259
Kakurokyo				2 2	4	10 15	1 3 9 2 6	10 25 5	86
Senki-Ara					0	(9)*	2 6 11	7 8 15	49
Senki-Moro					0	(9)*	1	2	3
4th Int'l					0	5 (9)*	1		6
Kyoroto					0	1 7		2	10
Kakumaru					0	4			4
Other		1			4	4 1			5
Unknown	1 1 1	2 1 11 1 2		1	89	55 17		3 0 1	100
Total	21 5 34 11	4 15 22 3 7 1 4	0 0 0 0 0	7 5 11 5 5	236	128 60	23 11 31 17 48	87 89 37	531**

Source: Keisatucho 1988 abc, Hidaka, 1989

* Joint Attacks of Senki-Ara, 4th International and Kyoroto.

** In 1988 an additional 39 attacks were staged, 13 of which were planned by Chukaku.

*** Data is available only after 1978.

Table 3: Main Incidents Caused by Leftist Radicals and Government Response

Date	Incident	Characteristics of Radicals
1. Oct. 8, 1967	The First Haneda Incid.	Triggered off the 1970 Ampo struggle, using "armed mass demonstration"
2. Oct. 21, 1968	Shinjuku Riot	Arrested: 1,012 Police injured: 1,157
3. April 28, 1969	Okinawa Day	Arrested: 1,030 Police Injured: 481
4. Oct. 21, 1969	Int'l. Anti-War Day	"Iron pipe bombs" used by RA (start of bomb tactics)
5. Nov. 5, 1969	Daibosatsu-toge	Military preparation for the November struggle by RA
6. March 31, 1970	JAL "Yodo" Hijacking	The first hijacking by Bund RA
7. Feb. 17, 1971	Maoka Gunshop Robbery	Preparation of Military Struggle by Keihin Ampo Kyoto
8. June 17, 1971	Meiji Park Bombing	Bombs were first used for killing by Bund RA
9. Aug. 22, 1971	Asaka Base Murder	A Self-Defense Officer killed
10. Dec. 18, 1971	Tsuchida Letter Bombing	The first actual personal terrorism
11. Feb. 19, 1972	Asama Villa Siege	The first shooting battle with police by Rengo Sekigun Deaths: 2; Injures: 23
12. May 30, 1972	Tel Aviv Airport	The first int'l terrorism by JRA
13. Jan. 30, 1974	Singapore Oil Refinery Attack	Followed by an attack of the Japanese embassy in Kuwait by another guerrilla group
14. Aug. 30, 1974	Mitsubishi Juko	The largest number of victims (8 killed, 376 injured), triggering sequential bombings of large corporate headquarters

Characteristics of Government Response

1. First application of the Penal Code (Article 208-2), "Crime of Unlawful Assembly with Dangerous Weapons" to political demonstrations

2. Application of the Penal Code (Articles 106, 107), "Crimes of Riot Law" after sixteen years (1952: JC's: Molotov cocktail incidents)

3. Application of the "Subversive Activity Prevention Law" (Article 40), to Chukaku and Bund 5 leaders

4.

5. Preventive mass arrest of Bund RA (53)

6. Two Senior Officials acted as substitutes for passengers

7.

8.

9. A new left leader was a fugitive and had not been arrested for 11 years

10. Apartment Roller Operation started immediately after the incident

11. Ten days duration: very patient encirclement and arrest operation

12. Later, Special Ambassador Fukunaga was sent to Israel

13. NPA and MPD bureaucrats were sent to Singapore

14.

Table 3: Main Incidents Caused by Leftist Radicals
and Government Response, continued

Date	Incident	Characteristics of Radicals
15. Aug. 4, 1975	Kuala Lumpur	After capturing the U.S. Embassy, JRA demanded the release of 7 of their comrades
16. March 2, 1976	Hokkaido Prefecture Office bombing	Two killed, 85 injured by EAAJA
17. Sept. 28, 1977	JAL Hijacking over Bombay (Dacca incid.)	JRA demanded the release of six prisoners and $6 million
18. March 26, 1978	New Tokyo Narita Airport Control Tower Attack	Forced to postpone the opening of the airport
19. Sept. 19, 1984	Fire bombing of the LDP head-quarter building	Renewed big scale querrilla activity by Chukaku
20. Jan. 1, 1985	U.S. Consul General Rocket Attack	Renewed bombing tactics with more advanced technology
21. Oct. 20, 1985	Narita Anti-2nd Extension Incident	(Chukaku)
22. Nov. 29, 1985	Anti-NR privatization	Chukaku; cut cables in 33 places
23. March 25 & March 31, 1986	Rocket Attacks on the Imperial House Palace Complex	Senki-Ara and Kakurokyo Hazama
24. May 4, 1986	Tokyo summit rocket attack	3.5 km range
25. Nov. 1, 1990	Bombing protesting the enthronement of the Emperor	MPD dormitories bombed by Kakurokyo-Hazama

Characteristics of Government Response

15. In exchange for hostages, Japanese government released
    and transferred five convicted terrorists

16.

17. Japanese government released six comrades and gave $6 million

18. Fourteen thousand police mobilized

19.

20.

21. Two hundred forty-one arrests (largest number since the opening
    of the airport)

22.

23.

24.

25. The Chair of the National Safety Commission required application of the
    organization control Articles of the Subversive Activity Prevention Law

Source: Mainichi, 1986; Keisatsucho, 1988a, 1988b, 1988c.

the apparent decline in popular support prompted a switch in tactics. Chukaku, for example, planted 14 bombs in 1969 alone. The preferred targets for bombing attacks included policemen or police stations, railway stations, military bases, airport facilities, and other public buildings.

But the armed street struggle waged by the active groups such as the Chukaku was undermined greatly by the discovery in March 1972 of the bodies of 12 former members of a radical leftist sect, the Rengo-Sekigun (the United Army 1971-72, a joint military organization of some members of the Bund Red Army Faction and Keihin-Ampo-Kyoto), victims of a grisly process of group violence [Steinhoff, n.d. Farrell, 1990, pp. 1-19. Takazawa et al., 1981, pp. 182-87]. Subsequently bloody inter-factional strife, particularly between Kakumaru and Chaukaku or Kakurokyo, intensified. Bloody feuds between different leftist groups had started in the late 1960s inside the Zenkyoto movement. However, violence escalated further after the murder of Toshio Ebihara, an activist of Kakumaru by Chukaku members in August 1970 and the murder of Daizaburo Kawaguchi, a symbathizer of Chukaku, by Kakumaru members in November 1972. In 1975 the Secretary General of Chukaku, Nobuyoshi Honda, was killed. Between 1968 and 1988 85 people died from inter-factional conflicts, and more than 5,000 leftist activists were wounded in outbursts of factional violence [Keisatucho, 1973-89. Takagi 1988 p. 139]. This violence delegitimated the New Left and, for all intents and purposes, by 1972 had terminated the armed struggle in the streets by organizations committed to military-style operations, strategies of armed insurrection and tactics of violence. As shown in chapter 5, during the last phase of this period, December 1971 to April 1972, the police attempted to eradicate the basis for political radicalism by searching apartments on a massive scale.

The second phase in the recent history of terrorism and violent social protest lasted from 1972 to 1979. It was marked by a further organizational differentiation and geographic dispersion of radical groups. Japan's Red Army Faction (Bund-Sekigun-ha) had split off from one of Japan's major left-wing national student organizations in May 1969. It spawned three different organizations. Operating in Japan, the remnants of the Red Army Faction merged with another radical group in December 1971 and continued to function under the name of United Red Army (Rengo Sekigun) until totally defeated in March 1972. Secondly, the Pyongyang Hijacking Group hijacked a plane to North Korea in March 1970 and has been in exile ever since. Finally, since 1971 the Japan Red Army (Nihon Sekigun) has had an operational arm in Lebanon which, under the leadership of Takeshi Okudaira and Fusako Shigenobu, broke with the United Red Army in 1972 [Steinhoff, n.d. Steinhoff, 1989a, pp.724-25. Farrell, 1990, pp. 85-125. Apter and Sawa, 1984, pp.122-23. Rinalducci, 1972, pp.xl-xlv. Takazawa et al., 1981, pp. 186-89, 197-98].

The reasons for this organizational differentiation and geographic dispersion were complex. The theory of "world-wide revolutionary war" which informed the political activities of these groups included plans to build up international bases of support (the international bases strategy). And the arrest of about 50 activists from the Red Army Faction in the police operation Daibosatu-Toge of November 1969 made it attractive for the Red Army Faction, from which the Japanese Red Army split off, to move their operations abroad. Between May 1972 and September 1977 Japanese terrorists organized a series of spectacular and grisly international terrorist attacks. Most notorious among these were, as Tables 3 and 4 indicate, the attacks at Lod Airport, Dubai, Singapore, Hague, Kuala Lumpur, and Dacca [Farrell, 1990]. Members of the Red Army "robbed banks and hijacked planes the same way Sony researches and markets new products" [Steinhoff, 1989a, p.733]. In their internal decision making processes these radicals, like organized crime and corporate management, relied on a characteristically Japanese style that acknowledged the importance of both political consensus and social rank and included among others work-group autonomy, vertical structures and consensual decisionmaking, attention to detail, careful planning, and a remarkable ability to learn from mistakes [Steinhoff, 1989a, pp.730-33,738. Smith, 1989, p.717. Kaplan and Dubro, 1986, pp. 145-46. The Economist, 1990].

But social protest often bordering on extreme political violence continued even after the police had rendered totally ineffective the Red Army Faction and its successors inside Japan [Steinhoff, 1989b]. While the Red Army groups remained part of Japan's political "superstructures", radical social movements sought to mobilize public opinion in the hope of becoming "populist rather than revolutionary . . . in what is probably the most mediating society in the world" [Apter and Sawa, 1984, p.240]. Smaller anarchist and unaffiliated groups continued their bombing tactics, targeting big Japanese corporations, and political symbols connected to the oppression of minority groups. Between 1972 and 1979 34 of a total of 56 bombings were committed by these small groups, prominently among them the East Asian Anti-Japan Armed Front (EAAJA). The Mitsubishi-Juko attack of August 30, 1974, left 8 people dead and injured another 376; and the Hokkaido-cho bombing of March 2, 1976, killed 2 and produced another 85 casualties. But Chukaku announced that it would be abandoning bombing after several activists died in 1975 while experimenting with explosives [Hidaka, 1989, p.47]. Despite the gains that the political opposition scored in Japanese politics in the 1970s, social movements did not succeed in recovering their power to mobilize the masses. Compared to 1968 the total number of Japanese who could be politically mobilized by these movements had fallen by half a decade later [Keisatsucho, 1973-90. Asahi Nenkan 1971, p.314. Takagi, 1988, pp.16-19].

Table 4: Main Incidents Caused by the Japan Red Army

Incident	Date/Place	Brief Description
Tel Aviv Lod Airport Incident	May 30, 1972 Lod Airport, Tel Aviv, Israel	Takeshi Okudaira, Yasuyuki Yasuda and Kozo Okamoto fired automatic rifles and tossed hand grenades at random objects at the airport, killing and injuring 96 passengers and others (24 deaths). Okudaira and Yasuda died by self-blasting, while Okamoto was arrested on the spot.
Hijacking of JAL plane over Amsterdam (Dubai Incident)	July 20, 1973 Over Amsterdam, the Netherlands	Osamu Maruoka and 4 Palestine guerrillas hijacked a JAL plane and forced it to land at Dubai Airport, capital of the United Arab Emirates and then at Benghazi Airport, Libya. After releasing the passengers and crewmen, they exploded the plane and surrendered to Libya.
Singapore Shell Oil Refinery Blasting Incident	January 31, 1974 Singapore and Kuwait	Haruo Wako, Yoshiaki Yamada and two Palestinian guerrillas blew up a Shell oil refinery plant and hijacked a ferry-boat with passengers. In the negotiation process, PFLP guerrillas captured the Japanese Embassy in Kuwait. In exchange for hostages, including the Japanese Ambassador, they forced the transfer of the Wako group to Kuwait and surrendered to Southern Yemen.
Capture of the French Embassy in the Hague (Hague Incident)	September 13, 1974 The Hague, the Netherlands	Junzo Okudaira, Haruo Wako and Jun Nishikawa, armed with hand grenades and handguns, captured the French Embassy in the Hague. They forced the release of their comrade who had been detained by the French authorities for the Paris Incident and obtained $300,000 in cash from the Netherlands and an airplane from France. They surrendered in Syria.
Capture of the U.S. Embassy in Malaysia (Kuala Lumpur Incident)	August 4, 1975 Kuala Lumpur, Malaysia	Junzo Okudaira, Toshihiko Hidaka, Haruo Wako, and two others captured the American Embassy in Kuala Lumpur, armed with hand grenades and handguns. In exchange for hostages, they caused the authorities to release and transfer their 5 comrades, including Jun Nishikawa, Kazuo Tohira, Kunio Bando, and Norio Sasaki, who had served their term or had been under detention in Japan. They surrendered to Libya.

Table 4: Main Incidents Caused by the Japan Red Army

Incident	Date/Place	Brief Description
Hijacking of JAL plane over Bombay, India (Dacca Incident)	September 28, 1977 Over Bombay, India	Five activists, including Osamu Maruoka, Jun Nishikawa, Kunio Bando, and Norio Sasaki, hijacked a JAL plane, forcing it to land at Dacca Airport, Bangladesh. They made the authorities transfer to Dacca Junzo Okudaira, Tsutomu Shirosaki, Ayako Daidoji, Yukiko Ekita, Hiroshi Sensui, and Akira Nihei, who had been in prison or detained in Japan and $6 million in cash. They used the plane to fly to Algeria, to which they surrendered.
Jakarta Incident	May 14, 1986 Jakarta, Indonesia	Some projectiles were launched from a nearby hotel at the U.S. Embassy and the Japanese Embassy. And also in the parking lot of the building in which the Canadian Embassy is located, a bomb set in a vehicle went off and 5 vehicles were burned out. Tsutomu Shirosaki's fingerprints were lifted from a room in the hotel from which some of the projectiles had been launched.
Rome Incident	June 9, 1987 Rome, Italy	Some projectiles were launched from a nearby hotel at the British Embassy and the U.S. Embassy. And also on a side road by the U.S. Embassy, some explosives, which had been planted in a vehicle, went off. In the incident the Italian police confirmed Junzo Okudaira and Tsutomu Shirosaki as the offenders and instituted an international search for them.
Naples Incident	April 14, 1988 Naples, Italy	An incident occurred in which explosives set in a vehicle went off on the road in front of a U.S. Army club, causing the death of 5 persons and the injury of 15 persons. In the incident, the Italian police confirmed Junzo Okudaira and the Japanese Red Army's leader Fusako Shingenobu as the criminals and instituted an international search for them. On the other hand, the Japanese Red Army repeatedly made such statements as, "The Italian police cooked up the story that our comrades have joined the operation in Naples," and, "We never played a part in the incident." But some fingerprints of Okudaira were detected on the lease contract papers for the rental car which had been blown up.

Source: NPA 1988, 1989a, Takagi 1986, Sakai 1987.

There was one exception to this growing inefficacy of the mass movement organizations that had moved underground in the early 1970s. Since 1966 protest against the airport construction at Narita outside Tokyo succeeded in attracting the support of a large number of radicals by shunning, for the most part, outright violence and relying instead on more moderate guerrilla tactics. The Sanrizuka movement, a coalition of farmers and radical student sects that organized in 1968, in its strong opposition to Narita Airport confronted the issue of violence. The farmers were inherently conservative, willing to protest and, if necessary, protest violently and even die. But they were unwilling to declare war on their own society. It was clear for them that "actual terrorism would not only have violated the law; it would also have destroyed the main emphases of the movement itself, the nurture of people as well as the soil, and the handmade quality of power" [Apter and Sawa, 1984, p.239]. Even so, the distance between advocating the overthrow of Japan's capitalist state through armed struggle as opposed to acts of terrorism was a thin one. The personal secretary of the leader of the Sanrizuka movement was a young militant relatively close to the United Red Army. Eventually this leader, Tomura, came to accept the necessity of violence to defeat militarism [Apter and Sawa, 1984, pp.156,238].

In their book Against the State David Apter and Nagayo Sawa draw a richly detailed and evocative picture of the Sanrizuka protest movement [1984]. Over a period of close to twenty years the movement articulated an enraged, alternative vision of politics fundamentally at odds with the technocratic and administrative logic of Japan's politicians and high-handed bureaucrats. Narita airport was the largest construction project the Japanese government had ever undertaken. During the first phase of construction which lasted until 1978 direct investment costs were 160 billion yen and indirect costs were about 800 billion yen. "The human costs include four policemen and two militants dead, thousands injured, and innumerable lives affected by court cases, legal proceedings, and other disruptions" [Apter and Sawa, 1984, p.202,and pp.104-05,112-14]. The low number of casualties, writes Robert Smith, offers "eloquent testimony that those who wield authority in postwar Japan have no sense it is the right of the state to take the lives of its citizens, however violent the form of their protest against its policies" [Smith, 1983, p.131]. The number of deaths pales in comparison with the number of those killed in the factional struggles among radical sects [Apter and Sawa, 1984, p.121]. The protest caused not only significant delays but also a permanent scaling back of the plans for the airport's expansion. While the movement did not "win", it galvanized protest politics in the 1970s and 1980s the way the Security Treaty demonstrations had done in 1960 and 1970.

The third phase of terrorism and violent social protest lasted from 1980 until the fall of 1984. In the early 1980s Japan's political climate had changed with the increasing power of conservatism, illustrated by the great election victory of the LDP in 1980 which reversed the defeat of 1979. In these years there were no bombing attacks and no more than about 10-30 guerrilla incidents per year. In this period of quiescence several groups such as Chukaku and Kakurokyo appear to have prepared their military forces while also attempting to gain a foothold in several social movements such as the anti-nuclear movement. The number of people which could be mobilized by new left groups approached 300,000 in the first half of the 1980s, a 50 percent increase over the level of the late 1970s [Keisatsucho, 1973-1990].

The fourth phase of left-wing protest started in the fall of 1984 and has lasted until this time of writing, spring 1991. Since the fall of 1984 Chukaku, Kakurokyo, and Senki have reinstated their "high technology guerrilla" attacks. The Japan Red Army also started up once more international terrorist activities from its bases in the Middle East (Table 3 and Table 4) [Farrell, 1990]. Domestic groups succeeded in developing new home-made weapons, including flame-throwing devices, automatically-driven, flame-throwing vehicles, and sophisticated time-delayed bombs. They also trained their military troops operating in the underground. The targets of renewed guerrilla attacks, bombings, and acts of terrorism became more diversified and included now the Imperial Household, police stations, military bases, railways and airports as well as private citizens and public officials, including those in charge of the construction at Narita [Interview no.16, May 17, Tokyo, 1990]. In addition group tactics became more sophisticated, for example, in the use of stolen vehicles, exchange of license plates and registrations, and physical alterations of suspects [Keisatsucho, 1988a and 1988b, p.72. Takagi, 1988, pp.175-187].

1C. Left-Wing Terrorist Organizations and Violent Groups

Because of its internal splits, the organization of leftist groups has become much more complex during the last 20 years (see Figure 1). There exist five major groups: Bund (Kyosando, Communist League), Kakukyodo (Revolutionary Communist League), Kakurokyo (Revolutionary Labor Association), Koukaku (Structural Reformist), and Nihon Kyosan-to Saha (Pro-Chinese Communist). These groups have a total of about 20 to 30 sects, excluding anarchists and unaffiliated (non-sect) movements. But not all of the five major groups are engaged in violent protest or terrorism. At present only JRA, Chukaku, Kakurokyo (Hazama faction), Kyosando (Senki-Ara and Senki-Morokawa) and potentially the Fourth International and many small Bund factions should be included as the core of the violence-prone groups in Japan. In all less than ten radical sects are involved in terrorist attacks. The NPA surveys these groups as does the Public Security Investigation Agency (PSIA) in its annual reports [Keisatsucho, 1988a, 1988b. Koan Chosa-cho, 1990].

Kakukyodo was organized in 1957 in opposition to the JCP's new policy of 1955 which had abandoned the policy of armed struggle. This Trotskyist group became also the first major anti-imperialist and anti-Stalinist grouping on the Japanese Left. It eventually split into three major factions: the Fourth International (1957), Chukaku (1963), and Kakumaru (1963). For the same reason as Kakukyodo, but based on splits within Zengakuren, the National Student Unions' Federation, the Bund organized itself in 1958. This faction was originally Leninist but was also influenced by Trotsky. Since the defeat of Ampo 1960 and Ampo 1970, it has fragmented into many smaller sects, among others Sekigun-ha or Bund-RA, the former main body of the Japan Red Army, Senki-ha (Ara and Morokawa), and Bund RG. In addition, many activists in the Bund have shifted to Chukaku and Kakurokyo. Kakurokyo had once been a faction of Shaseido (Youth Socialist League) founded by the JSP in 1960. Activists who orginally belonged to the Bund started Kaiho-ha in 1965, a group which developed into Kakurokyo in 1969. Because of their extreme radicalism these activists were expelled from Shaseido in 1971 [Takagi 1988, pp.20-28. Keisatucho, 1988a, 1988b. Tashiro, 1985].

Influenced by different currents in Italian Marxism, including Gramsci and Triatti, "structural reformism" was born in the early 1960s. Through the 1970 Ampo struggle, some structural reformists embraced an increasingly extreme radicalism. The Pro-Chinese Communist groups emerged in 1966 when the JCP formally broke relations with the Chinese Communist party after the divisive controversies surrounding the collapse of the Indonesian Communist Party in 1965 and the cultural revolution in China. Keihin-Ampo-kyoto, one of the extreme radical groups, merged with some of Bund RA in 1971 to constitute Rengo Sekigun. Anarchists and other unaffiated groupings have a long history. As active radicals they spread in the late 1960s throughout the student movement, Zenkyoto. During the mid-1970s 4,000 members were counted in the movement's 300-400 groups [Takagi, 1988, p.23. Asahi Nenkan, 1978, p.280].

The size of the entire new leftist political spectrum has been estimated at about 35,000 members since 1974. The PSIA and Masayuki Takagi have given lower estimates of the size of left-wing groups than has the police. Although their estimates of 50,000 left-wing radicals were virtually identical in 1970, since 1975 the NAP has consistently estimated the number of radicals to be twice as large as the PSIA [Koan Chosa-cho, 1990, pp.7-8]. In 1989 the PSIA counted 18,300 left-wing activists. One possible explanation for the substantial difference lies in the fact that the NPA estimate includes not only activists but also individuals who have dropped out of the radical movement altogether or are mere sympathizers [Takagi, 1988, p.16. Asahi Nenkan, 1983, 1984, 1985]. Based on police records, Takagi estimated in July 1987 that the 14,400 activists, and 19,900 mobilized persons, and other sympathizers would add up to the 35,000 estimate of the NPA. Takagi also reports that the peak number of radical activists was 20,000-30,000 in the early 1970s; but by 1990 the number had dropped to no more than 13,600. [Takagi, 1990, p.645]. Considering the variety of informal police methods used, the number of left-wing activists has been surprisingly steady. This is also true for the ability of these groups to mobilize between 200,000 and 300,000 annually for mass meetings and demonstrations in the 1970s and 1980s [Keisatsucho 1973-1990].

Although left-wing radical groups emerged from the student movement in the 1960s, by 1987 the percentage of students belonging to these groups had slipped to below 20 percent down from 70-80 percent for 1970, 40 percent for 1978 and 30 percent for 1980 [Koan Chosa-cho, 1990, p.7. Takagi, 1988, pp.16-19. Keisatsucho 1988a, pp.31,37]. Among the left-wing groups the Red Army Faction and Chukaku have become the most notorious since the late 1960s. In its early phase the Red Army Faction operating in Japan could count on about 500 to 1,000 members and a far-flung network of supporters and sympathizers. But by mid-1971 "only a small underground group remained active, with a support group of perhaps a few hundred" [Steinhoff, 1989a, p.733. Clifford, 1976, p.25]. Apter and Sawa estimate that the Red Army counted about one hundred members in Japan in the 1980s [Apter and Sawa, 1984, p.123]. Police estimates put the numbers of the Red Army at 30 core cadres abroad and at about 500 sympathizers and 13 organizations at home [Interview no.1, Tokyo, December 6, 1988]. By way of contrast the JRA operating in Lebanon fared much better. It began with two members "and grew to an estimated thirty to fifty, again with a much larger group of supporters and sympathizers" [Steinhoff, 1989a, p.733]. An official Japanese source estimates the membership at "a little more than 20 members" [Advanced Course, 1989, p.428].

Chukaku operates only in Japan and thus controls a much larger and more active organization. Its membership is estimated at about 3,400, and it can mobilize about 5,000 people [Takagi, 1990 p.649 and 1988, p.20. Advanced Course, 1989, p.421. Clifford, 1976, p.26. Tashiro, 1985, pp.104-08]. It is estimated to have about 500 professional activists who do not hold steady jobs [Apter and Sawa, 1984, p.131]. In the 1980s Chukaku accounted for a total of 259 guerrilla attacks and bombing incidents. In fact 49 percent of the total number of guerrilla attacks and 85 percent of the total number of bombings were committed by this group alone [Keisatucho, 1988a, 1988b, 1988c]. Before any of the other leftist groups Chukaku rallied to the cause of the opposition movement against the construction of Narita airport in February 1968 and to demonstrations against the Emperor system in September 1971 [Takagi, 1988, pp.64-66, 214-15]. And after the Subversive Activity Prevention Law was invoked against the organization's leader, Nobuyoshi

Honda, in April 1969, Chukaku created a secret military organization, the Peoples' Revolutionary Army, in the early 1970s [Mikoshiba, 1989 pp.31-32].

Members of the militant core of Chukaku (estimated at about 400 [Mainichi, November 4, 1990] and at about 200 [Takagi, 1988, p.176]) and of two of the other radical sects, according to one informed assessment, operate in isolation from each other.

"These members are mostly the hard-core activists who were involved in the 'Struggles of 1970.' Many of them have a record of arrest or are on the list of those wanted by the police. These military organizations give top priority to the security of their organizations. No lateral relation among their members are established, and vertical relations are also minimal. The entire system can not be disclosed even if several members are arrested. These organizations adopt thus thorough defensive measures. No member of a cell knows of or recognizes the members of any other cell. Even within the same cell, members use false names with one another to protect their identity" [NPA, 1988 p.9].

The police has estimated Chukaku's budget at 1 billion yen in 1986 [Asahi, April 12, 1986]. Membership fees are an important source of revenues for the organization. "Members contribute several percent of their monthly salary and 100 percent of their bonus income to the organization" [Asahi, August 29, 1985]. At a cost estimated at 500 million yen, Chukaku has built two headquarters in Tokyo and Osaka in 1981 [Asahi Nenkan, 1984, p.119. Suzuki, 1978, pp.253-59]. Besides generating the income of a medium-sized firm, Chukaku and several other radical groups, including Kakurokyo, the Fourth International, and the Japan Labor Party, fielded candidates in local elections and have won about 30-40 seats, including Chukaku's 1989 success in the elections to the Tokyo Metropolitan Assembly [Koan Chosa-cho, 1990, p.8; Takagi, 1988, pp.210-211].

But since the fall of 1984 Chukaku has resumed the bombing and terrorist attacks which it had engaged in already in the 1970s. The group has enlarged the range of its targets which now includes not only opposition to airport construction at Narita and facilities that relate to the Emperor, but also support of a discriminated minority group (Buraku), peace and anti-nuclear movements. In the process Chukaku has increased the secrecy of operation not only of its military corps but of the entire organization [Keisatucho, 1988a, pp.38-46. Interview no. 8, Tokyo, May 15, 1990 and no. 12, Tokyo, May 16, 1990].

After Chukaku Kakumaru is the second largest radical group. It has 1,900 members and can mobilize about 4,000 supporters [Takagi, 1990, p.650. Advanced Course, 1989, p.421. Clifford, 1976, p.26. Tashiro, 1985, p.108]. In 1983 the organization constructed its own headquarters at an estimated cost of 280 million yen [Asahi Nenkan, 1984, p.119]. It has a Special Action Corps which is mainly used for inter-factional conflicts with Chukaku and Kakurokyo [Tachibana, 1975, pp.150-52]. It enjoys some influence in the labor movement, especially among railway workers and among students. In 1987 it reportedly had affiliations with 23 student unions. During the last two decades it is the only one of Japan's major radical groups that has not involved itself in the struggle against Narita airport [Takagi, 1990, p.650].

Besides Chukaku and Kakumaru there exist several other radical groups that deserve to be mentioned. The 2,500 members of Kakurokyo are now divided into two militant sects: the Hazama faction (about 500 activists) and the Labor faction (about 400 activists) [Advanced Course, 1989, p.421. Clifford, 1976, p.26. Takagi, 1988, pp.20,26,27. Tashiro, 1985, pp.135-53]. Its Proletarian United Front Combat Forces counts on the activities of about 100 militants, supported by 1,000 activists who can mobilize an additional 2,500 persons [Takagi 1988 p.120, 1990 p.650]. A more militant faction, Hazama, began its bombing campaign in March 1988. Based on the Youth Branch Buraku-kaiho-domei (Buraku Liberation League), Hazama has stepped up its struggle against the Emperor System and, to that end, completed in January 1989 an evaluation of the military tactics the Sekigun employed in the 1970s [Hidaka, 1989, p.65].

The Bund group and its about 20 sects has about 1,700 activists including Senki-Ara with 500 members and Senki-Morokawa with 200 members [Tashiro, 1985, pp.116-35]. Senki-Ara's military corps, "Guerrilla Partisan Corps", committed about 9 percent, or 49, of the total number of guerrilla attacks in the 1980s [Keisatucho, 1988a, 1988b]. In 1988 Senki-Morokawa formed an alliance with two other radical groups, Kakurokyo-Hazama and Chukaku [Hidaka, 1989, p.65].

The Fourth International Japan Branch has 900 members and can mobilize 2,000 people. With the exception of the Japan Red Army it is the only domestic group which has built up an international network. It spearheaded the famous attack on the control tower at Narita airport in March 1978. But generally speaking its political methods are more moderate and emphasize mass organizing among the New Left [Takagi, 1988, pp.20,27. 1990, p.650. Tashiro, 1985, pp.110-16].

1D. Right-Wing Terrorist Organizations and Violent Groups

Right-wing extremism is also strong in contemporary Japan. Under the guise of anti-Communism these right-wing movements can now count on a combined membership of about 120,000 belonging to about 840 different associations [Advanced Course, 1989, p.426]. Although this number has not changed since the early 1970's, it is substantially larger than in 1960 [Emmerson and Humphreys, 1973, p.93]. Right-wing groups are becoming increasingly radical and tend toward "terrorism and guerilla activities" [Advanced Course, 1989, p.426. Keisatsucho, 1989b]. The police reportedly keep a watch on about 50 groups with 22,000 members [Lehner and Graven, 1990]. Furthermore right-wing extremism has intimate links with organized crime [Terzani, 1990a, 1990b]. The powerful Yakuza has a total of 350 associations with about 6,000 members among the rightist groups [Takagi, 1990, p.648]. Other sources estimate that one-third of the associations and one-fourth of the members are affiliated with yakuza [Iishiba, 1990, p.125]. And its share has increased in recent years, after the 1982 revision of the commercial law against sokaiya, an important gangster manipulating stockholder meetings [Takagi, 1990, p.648]. Its associations with organized crime has given the associational life of right-wing groups a greater degree of stability than that of left-wing groups [Interview no. 14, Tokyo, May 16, 1990].

Right-wing extremism has a long history in Japan. In the initial years after 1945 the collapse of the pre-war organizations was quickly followed by a rebuilding along the lines of anti-Communism and professed support for the new democratic Constitution. But in the 1950s pre-war organizations reconstituted themselves and organized in the 1960s around the concept of a strong Japan. Since 1970 right-wing organizations are increasingly seeking their inspiration from the National Renovation Movement of pre-war Japan [Hori, 1983, pp.86-95,219-45]. Since 1945 right-wing groups have accounted for about 30 major attacks, including one ill-prepared coup d'etat in 1961. But compared to left-wing groups, the political impact of right-wing extremists has been quite small, particularly on questions of internal security. This is no doubt due to the status quo orientation of these groups. They favor the Imperial Household and often support the LDP and business. And they lack mass support. In the early 1960s, for example, the hard-core among the right-wing groups could mobilize no more than 15,000 supporters [Hori, 1983, p.35]. Table 5 summarizes a few data on the evolution of the extreme Right in Japan.

For an analysis of Japan's internal security and right wing groups we can distinguish between three periods since 1945. During the first period, the late 1950s to the mid-1960s, the relationship between right-wing groups and the government was one of mutual support. This was very evident in the enlistment of organized crime at the height of the 1960 demonstrations against the U.S. Security Treaty. When it looked like the police was going to be badly outnumbered by the demonstrators during the planned visit of President Eisenhower, the LDP leadership approached Kodama Yoshio, a right-wing boss with extensive ties to organized crime. In less than two weeks about 28,000 gangsters, 4,000 members of right-wing radical organizations and

Table 5: Right-Wing Extremist Associations

A. Number of Associations and Memberships

	Associations	Members
1939:	1,733	702,942
1943:	610	182,192
1963:	400[1]	115,000
1978:	600	120,000
1988:	840[2]	125,000

Notes: 1. This number contains 20 well-organized associations,
         with 15,000 members.

        2. This number contains 50 well-organized associations,
         with 22,000 members.

Source: NPA, 1968 cited in Hori, 1983, p.189; NPA, 1979; Takagi, 1990.

B. Number of Incidents and Arrests (5 years total, 1960-1989)

	Incidents	Arrests
1960-64	514	930
1965-69	320	562
1970-74	853	1,664
1975-79	1,185	2,281
1980-84	1,925	2,753
1985-89	1,216	1,816

Source: Hori, 1983 p. 143, Keisatsucho 1973-90.

several thousand men affiliated with other organizations were mobilized, and plans for their deployment were drawn up for the Eisenhower visit which, however, in the end was cancelled [Hori, 1983, pp.35-36. Kaplan and Dubro, 1986, pp.85-86. Ames, 1981, pp.122-24]. Because of their excessive confidence in the political support of mainstream conservatives, right-wing extremists committed a growing number of politically motivated murders in the early 1960s. These included not only the assassination of a socialist leader, Inejro Asanuma, in October 1960 and the attack on the house of Shimanaka in February 1960 but also the attack on Prime Minister Kishi, the leader of the Liberal Democratic Party (LDP) in July 1960, and on other prominent politicians like Ikeda (LDP) and Nozaka (JCP) in November 1963.

Eventually these attacks caused a crack-down from both the police and politicians, thus initiating a second period which lasted from the mid-1960s to the mid-1970s. In March 1964 a new Headquarters for the Investigation of Organized Crimes began its first sustained operation. And the Law on the Punishment of Violent Actions was passed in June 1964. Both moves also aimed at constraining the activities of violent right-wing groups [Hori, 1983, p.58].

Alienated from the LDP government and disappointed in the government's cautious approach to the issue of a Constitutional amendment, splits within the right developed during the second period. Nichigakudo (Japan Student League) established in November 1966, Tatenokai founded by Yukio Mishima in September 1968, and Zenkokugakukyo (National Student Study Groups Council) founded by an extremist right Shintoist group, Seichono Ie, in May 1969 eventually constituted an emerging new Right. Because they shared in a visceral hostility against Japan's post-war political system, all three groups differentiate themselves from the old Right. These groups resent what they sometimes called the Yalta-Potsdam Establishment -- Japan's new constitution, the U.S.-Japan Mutual Security Treaty, and U.S.-Soviet hegemony [Hori, 1983, pp. 67-77].

A famous novelist and the leader of Tatenokai, Mishima, killed himself on November 25, 1970, after locking up a general of the Self Defense Forces and appealing to young military cadets to participate in a coup d'etat. In his last appeal, standing on a balcony, he emphasized that all chances for passing a constitutional amendment had been lost on October 21, 1969. On that day the largest mass demonstration of the late 1960s did not lead, as Mishima had hoped, to a mobilization of the Self Defense Forces and a coup d'etat. Instead the demonstration was contained successfully by the police. Mishima declared also that he had waited four years (since 1965) for the Self Defense Forces to legitimate their political standing through a coup d'etat [Hori, 1983, pp.98-103].

The third period has lasted since the mid-1970s to the time of writing in the spring of 1991. The new right-wing groups and Mishima's actions re-energized right-wing extremist groups. Between 1972 and 1978 400-500 right-wing activists were arrested annually, and the number climbed to 500-700 for the years 1981-1985. In fact, in the years 1981-84 the number of arrests due to crimes committed by members of right-wing groups exceeded corresponding figures for radical left-wing groups [Keisatsucho, 1973-1990. Table 5]. New right-wing groups attacked the Kodama residence in March 1976, Keidanren in March 1977, Prime Minister Ohira in December 1978, LDP leader Miyazawa in March 1984, Sumitomo Fudosan, a big real estate company in January 1988, the Prime Minister's Residence in March 1989, and the largest newspaper, Asahi Shimbun, since January 1987 (May 1987, September 1987, March 1988). In fact, members of these groups were now telling the public "we won't hesitate to use bombs", and they admonished their activists, "hide and don't get caught." More and more, these groups were emphasizing guerrilla activities, especially after the Diet had passed the Law Against Street Progaganda in December 1988. Between 1985 and 1989, rightist groups committed 51 terrorist and guerrilla attacks. [Takagi, 1990, p.648. Keisatsucho, 1989b. 1990, p.273].

II.
THE JAPANESE POLICE BEFORE 1945

2A. Historical Overview

"The modern Japanese police system that was created in the Meiji period owed little to the police structures and patterns that existed in the Tokugawa period." The Tokugawa police can be characterized as feudal in the sense that it was marked by a "differentiation of jurisdiction by status and by region"; it was managed by a "small number of specialized policing officials." Even in Edo, with a population of more than a million in the first half of the 19th century, only 290 officials were attached to the city magistrates [Westney, 1987, pp.35-36]. But this changed dramatically with the Meiji restoration. Like other Japanese bureaucracies the police was modelled after foreign experiences, specifically, for a brief period the English system, then the police system of Paris, with some subsequent modifications adopted from the German police. The continental police system that was imported was subsequently adapted to some of Japan's historical legacies as well as specific needs.

In the new police system introduced in the second half of the 19th century internal security issues ranked very high [Westney, 1987. Bayley, 1978, pp.164,185-6 and 1985, pp.33,48,65,198. Ames, 1981, pp.9-12,23-25. Clifford, 1976, pp.73-76. Murayama, 1980, pp.8-14,89. Parker, 1984, pp.32-41,187-191. Kaneko, 1975, pp.28-34. Ogawa, 1976. Archambeault and Fenwick, 1983, pp.4-7]. In the short-term the Japanese government sought to reclaim full sovereignty over its internal affairs through a revision of the unequal treaties and through the eradication of potential sources of violent opposition from within and from without [Westney, 1987, pp.89-90]. Over the long-term government policy aimed at catching up with the Western powers. The creation of a prosperous country through a strong army and police (fukoku-kyohei) was an overriding principle of a policy that promoted industrialization and the adoption of Western ideas including those about the police [Kyogoku, 1982, p.24].

In fact the police was established at the same time as the military, immediately after the Meiji Restoration, in February 1871. Satsuma han was ordered to supply 2,000 policemen the day after an order to raise a military force of 10,000 had been issued to the three major hans [Obinata, 1987, p.6. Taikakakai, 1970, vol. 2, pp.563,571]. At the time, these were very substantial figures, considering the fact that in the 1850s and 1860s Tokyo's total police force consisted of only 350 officers, 60 of whom were dealing exclusively with members of the samurai class. "For the commoners of this great city of over a million people there were no police at all" [Smith, 1983, p.39]. The first Japanese policemen were initially deployed in Tokyo in 1871 as a guard for the new capital. The supervision of this guard soon ended up in the hands of the Justice Ministry in 1872. Finally, in 1874 the police was incorporated in the newly established Naimusho, Ministry of the Interior (MOI). Under the leadership of Okubo, the first Minister of the MOI, the Police Affairs Bureau (PAB) in the MOI and the Metropolitan Police Department in Tokyo (MPD), an imitation of the French police system, were created at the same time. Japan's police force numbered 26,640 men in 1877, a number which by 1945 had increased to 93,913 [Taikakai, 1970, pp.625-626]. Before 1945 there were two periods that recorded relatively large increases: 1916-1921 and 1935-1940. The first expansion was a reaction to emerging social oppositions that led, among others, to the Rice Riot (Kome-Sodo) of 1918. The second increase was due to a general mobilization for war.

Between 1874 and 1881 the police acted in many ways like a military. As a guardian of the Meiji Revolutionary Government one of its major tasks was to suppress traditional elites who in the revolution had lost power, status, wealth and income. After numerous disturbances and several riots, the final armed battle occurred in the Seinan War in 1877. The MPD was armed with 7,000 guns, borrowed from the Army, and deployed 81 security corps with close to 6,000 policemen. Because they had to fight uprisings all over the country in 1877, these police units were temporarily put under the command of the PAB [Obinata, 1987, pp.46-56].

After the end of the armed uprising of 1877 the police system was reorganized. The difference between police and army became more sharply marked. A military police (kempei) was established in 1881, and the PAB and the MPD were again clearly separated. The government adopted soon thereafter a constitution modelled after Prussia which made all but impossible a further introduction of French or British police institutions or practices. With this consolidation of Prussian influence, the task of constructing a modern Japanese police system was virtually completed by the end of the Russo-Japanese War (1904-1905).

In the face of a growing wave of democratization, the government issued many security ordinances. Eventually these were incorporated in 1900 into the Public Peace Police Law (Chian Keisatsu Ho) and the Administrative Execution Law (Gyosei Shikko Ho). The security or political police was streamlined to focus henceforth on supressing political opposition movements.

At the same time, during the build-up of Japan's military in 1886-88, the police turned to a more decentralized system. The number of police boxes which had numbered only 3,938 in 1888, increased by 7,103, reaching a total of 11,041 in 1889 [Obinata, 1987, pp.87-88].

After 1904-05 the police had to adjust to the new conditions of Taisho democracy. The police remained wedded to the task of suppressing anti-government opposition movements or parties. Using some suspected radical activity in 1911 as a pretext (Taigyaku-jiken), the MOI strengthened the Higher Police (to counter democratic parties), and it set up the Special Advanced Police (to suppress socialist tendencies and to create the beginnings of a thought-control police). In 1910 Japan's military police began to rule Korea like a colony [Obinata, 1987, pp.134,137]. But growing police power was challenged by a democratic party politics. In the process, the MPD confronted, in 1898 and again in 1906, specific political proposals for its abolishment. In response the MPD softened its stance and henceforth persecuted not all political parties but only the opposition parties. But the police was also the target of general public opposition. It was attacked in numerous riots such as the Hibiya uprising of 1906 when 211 police stations and 264 police boxes were destroyed. The situation was similar in the Kenseiyogo Riot of 1912, and the Rice Riot of 1918 [Obinata, 1987, p.118. Taikakai, 1970, vol.2, p.825]. In response the police, and in particular the MPD, began to stress also public relations activities, such as providing counselling services and offering numerous forms of small assistance to citizens. It also began to organize residents in keisatsu-koen-kai (police cooperation associations), jikei-dan (vigilante squads), and hoan-kumiai (community-based security organizations) [Obinata, 1987, pp. 141-150].

This ambivalence between tendencies toward democratization on the one hand and growing police powers on the other was even more pronounced in the late 1920s. At the very time at which the universal suffrage bill was passed in 1925, the Peace Preservation Law (Chian Iji Ho) became a counterweight with which conservative forces sought to buttress the Emperor system and a capitalist economy. For the next two decades the political police and the military police expanded their powers dramatically over all sectors of Japanese society and created a climate of opinion that permitted the institutionalization of "thought-control", administered, since 1928, by the political police (Special Higher Police) [Mitchell, 1976. Tipton, 1990. Steinhoff, 1991]. In addition the police created a new force controlling amusement districts and entertainment businesses; and it supervised social life closely in the factories and communities throughout Japan.

2B. Police Organization

The first Superintendent General of the MPD, Toshiyoshi Kawaji, known as the "father" of the Japanese police, modelled the prewar police along British and French lines. Yokohama's police force, organized in the foreign residential area, was organized by an Englishman in 1867 [Taikakai, 1970, vol. 2, p.57]; it was emulated by the first police force organized in Tokyo. In particular the institutionalization of a patrol police (Rasotsu) was an imitation of the walking Bobby. The French influence on the MPD was visible in a centralized system of financing, a formal regulatory structure under the direct supervision of the central government, a police chief serving as a political appointee at the discretion of the head of government, and in an allocation of a broad range of administrative functions to the police, including public health, licensing of prostitutes, supervising a wide range of businesses, enforcing the laws regulating newspapers, and enforcing public morality. In addition, the French influence was also very evident in the police authority to administer punishments for certain types of offenses, the size of about 6,000 officers, the administrative separation between the judicial and the administrative branches of the police, and, finally, in the specialization of the administrative divisions of the police bureau under the MOI [Westney, 1987, pp.44-63. Steiner, 1965, pp.44-45]. And with the important exceptions of the local, political and the military police "the German influence had little impact on the formal structure" [Westney, 1987, pp.77-78].

But the Japanese system also exhibited a number of notable departures from the French and other European systems. Because a divided jurisdiction between national and local police forces appeared unduly complex, Japan did not copy France's police system at the local level [Westney, 1987, pp.64,72. Taikakai, 1970 vol.2 pp.564-84]. The system of local police boxes was introduced at the suggestion of Heinrich Höhn, a captain of the Berlin police who served as an advisor to the MOI between 1885 and 1891 [Obinata, 1977. Ames, 1981, p.23]. Rather than concentrating police officers into a few locations, as had been traditional Japanese practice before the end of the 19th century, the new system distributed the police rather evenly throughout Japan. However, generally speaking, the Japanese police developed a higher degree of standardization and centralization than did its French counterpart [Westney, 1987, pp. 90-91. Taikakai, 1971, vol.4, pp. 279-276]. In addition, the Japanese police kept several traditional features of the samurai bureaucracy. In fact, in 1890 83 percent of the senior officials of the MPD were former samurai [Obinata, 1987, pp.98-99]. More important for the long-term evolution of the Japanese police, however, were two practices initiated in the 1880s: the spatial dispersion of the police in local police boxes (koban), and direct recruitment of qualified applicants for upper-level career positions from the law faculties of the major universities [Westney, 1987, pp.52-63].

It is difficult to overemphasize the importance of the MOI. It had jurisdiction over policy issues which, broadly speaking, since 1945 have been divided among four ministries and one agency; a precise listing of all the policy issues once covered by the MOI shows that its power has been dispersed among eleven ministries and nine agencies. Within the MOI the Police Affair Bureau was placed at the very core, together with the Local Bureau. In 1942 the Police Affair Bureau employed 357 officials, or about one-fifth of the Ministry's central staff numbering 1,601. Because of his political importance, the minister in charge of the MOI often held the position of Vice Prime Minister in the Cabinet, as was true, for example, of Toshimichi Okubo, Aritomo Yamagata, Takashi Hara, and Reijiro Wakatsuki among others. The Director General of the Police Affair Bureau, a political appointee, was in charge of national police affairs, particularly the political police outside Tokyo [Taikakai, 1971, Vol.7, pp.571-581,600. Taikakai 1970, Vol.2, pp.586-91,612-13. Taikakai, 1971, vol.4, pp.183,257-60].

The MPD was the successor to the guard for the new capital (Rasotsu), the first modern police organization in Japan. It kept strong traces of its military origin, especially in the 1870s and 1880s. The MPD was a national police placed directly under the government both in terms of organization and finance. Until 1906 it was directed by the Prime Minister as well as the Minister of the Interior. The Superintendent Generals of the MPD attended the cabinet meetings [Momose, 1990, p.125]. Before 1914 all the Superintendent Generals of the MPD were recruited from Satsuma one of the four major han (traditional district), but subsequently they were recruited also from other areas. During the second decade of the 20th century, the MPD's staff was larger than that of the Tokyo prefectural government. Its status was so high in the 1880s that chiefs of police stations in the MPD enjoyed a standing that equalled or surpassed that of the chiefs of the prefectural police. The Superintendent General's salary was higher than that of the Governor of Tokyo or of the Director of the PAB. The strong position of the MPD made it a prominent symbol for attacks from both left-wing and right-wing radicals [Taikakai, 1970, vol.2, pp.592-98,614-16. Momose, 1990, p.124].

In 1886 the MOI created a special section for the political police (Higher Police) charged with the surveillance of political activists. The system was developed further after the 1890s when the first general election was held in Japan. Although the political police was strongest in the major urban centers, informally it extended its influence throughout Japan. Local policing within prefectures was formally entrusted to governors appointed by the MOI. But until 1886 the Chief Directors reported directly to the Minister of the Interior. Even after the law was changed this practice continued.

After 1906, the major function of the political police changed from surveillance of all political parties to harassing and arresting prominent members of the major opposition parties. With the aim of increasing the suppression of the moderate and radical social movements, the Special Higher Police Division (Tokko) was set up inside the MPD in 1911. With the reorganization of all prefectures and a substantial increase in the staff size of the MOI in 1928, its operations were systematized and greatly enlarged. In

1932 the MPD added a special department which contained various divisions dealing with foreign affairs, labor, Koreans residing in Japan, censorship, industrial mediation, and the investigation of radicals. The last division in turn was divided into two subdivisions dealing with right-wing and left-wing extremist groups. All organizational and personnel affairs were placed under centralized control, as was illustrated by the annual Special Higher Police Division Directors meeting that convened immediately after the National Chief Directors meeting [Taikakai, 1970, vol.2, pp.749-52].

Together with the military police, the Special Higher Police created between the late 1920s and the end of World War II what historians often call a "Reign of Terror" or "Police State." The Peace Preservation Law of 1925 (subsequently revised in 1928) gave the police an overwhelming advantage over any social movements or oppositional group. After the mass arrest of left-wing activists on March 15, 1928, the police subsequently arrested and tortured numerous individuals suspected of Communist or Socialist leanings coupled with systematic attempts to cure them of their "misguided" political beliefs and to make them again firm supporters of the Emperor system [Okudaira, 1977, pp.134-55. Mitchell, 1976, pp.127-47. Tipton, 1990. Van Wolferen, 1989, p.184. Shiso no Kagaku Kenkyukai, ed. 1959. Steinhoff, 1988b.]. While leftist leaders were increasingly converting to other ideologies between 1928 and 1935, the organization of the JCP was destroyed by the police [Steinhoff, 1991. Obinata, 1987, pp.188-98]. Since the adoption of the Industrial Conflict Mediation Law of 1926, the Special Higher Police also played a mediating role in industrial conflicts and in disputes between tenant farmers and land owners. And it helped found the Patriotic Industrial Association (Sanpo) and other organizations favoring the war effort [Obinata, 1987, pp.206-09,236-39].

With the exception of the 1870s, the MPD was relatively slow to introduce a riot police. Until 1925 it had no emergency plans like those adopted by the national police after the Kanto earthquake of 1923. And only after the attempted coup d'etat of May 1932 did the MPD establish its own riot police. It was as late as 1944, that such a riot police was also organized in thirteen prefectures. The MPD's security police had only 312 men as compared to about 4,000 of the post-war MPD riot police force. Because the MPD police could rely on strong backing from the military police and, at worst, the army, its major emphasis continued to be surveillance and crime prevention through the Special Higher Police and the system of local police boxes [Taikakai, 1970, vol.2, pp.609-11,730-32. Obinata, 1987, pp.217-21].

Japan's military police (kempei) was established when the 1881 reform removed all military functions from the MPD. The reasons for a separate military police included concerns about potential leaks of classified military information, an insistence on enforcing military discipline, preparation for possible uprisings, and the organization of reserves for the civilian police.

However, the reform also ameliorated latent conflicts between the military and the police, and it constrained somewhat the vast powers of the MPD. Based on Elanor Westney's estimates the size of the military police was initially much smaller than that of the French [Westney, 1987, p.73]. The French gendarmerie had about 20,000 men in 1881 compared to 1,600 for the Japanese military police. While the military police in Japan remained very small for many decades, and increased sharply only in the last years of World War II, 22,000 military policemen were stationed in Korea, Taiwan, and other areas of Asia [Momose, 1990, p.313]. Japan's military police was stationed largely in urban areas. It was involved heavily in regular police work, and after 1932, when its Special Higher Division was set up, its behavior became indistinguishable from that of the Special Higher Police [Momose, 1990, p.312]. Moreover, the military police was a tool of Prime Minister Tojo in some of the most notorious incidents of Japan's war-time regime, such as the murder of Nakano Seigo (the leader of an extreme right-wing movement) by the military police in 1943 [Taikaki, 1970, vol.2, pp.602-604].

Although the police traditionally had considered any reliance on the the army, as Kawaji put it, as a needless disgrace, it had to depend on the military in times of crisis [Westney, 1987, p.47]. In the 20th century the Martial Law Ordinance was issued five times. Ten cases of the military's intervention in domestic politics--three labor strikes, five instances of wide-spread social unrest, and two political riots -- were based upon requests for assistsance by the MPD and the prefectural governors. In addition, in some relatively small disturbances the military police mobilized the army on its own accord [Taikakai, 1970, vol.2, pp.770-72. Momose, 1990, pp.278-79].

2C. The Normative Foundations of Police Power

As a result of Toshiyoshi Kawaji's efforts, Japan's prewar police became the "guardians of internal order and security, just as the army and navy were the guardians of external security" [Westney, 1987, p.47]. For Kawaji, the concept of guardian implied not only playing the role of a military guard, but also that of a teacher or parent [Obinata, 1987, pp.42-45]. In Eleanor Westney's words the police were "at one and the same time agents of change and guardians of tradition; they facilitated the expansion of certain organizations and restricted the growth of others, such as political parties and newspapers" [Westney, 1987, p.94]. Besides the army and the schools, the police was the third major institution "to foster a modern set of orientations toward the nation" [Bayley, 1985, p.198]. The first chief of Tokyo's metropolitan police put it succinctly when he argued that "the government should be seen as the parent, the people as the children and the policemen as the nurses of the children" [Van Wolferen, 1989, p.183]. In order to perform their complex role, the police was granted, through ordinances and laws, a broad and substantial role in society. While it is difficult to pinpoint the exact nature of the normative role that the police played in Japanese society, it would be a great mistake to neglect this role altogether, despite the highly visible, oppressive exercise of police power in defense of conservative, and sometimes reactionary, political forces.

The inculcation of norms through systematic police instruction was a matter of utmost political significance and one of the most important innovations adapted from the French [Westney, 1987, pp.82-89]. For senior police officials the MOI established a central police academy in three different periods: 1885-1889, 1899-1904, and 1918-1946. Moreover, a Police Association reinforced the professional esprit de corps of the police, supported by membership fees collected from all police officers. For the lower-level and local police, the MOI ordered the establishment of a police training school in 1886. When it opened, a training period of only a month or two was mandatory. This period was extended in 1923 to two or three months, and, finally, in 1928 to three or four months [Taikakai, 1970, vol.2, pp.639-51]. Due to its samurai origin and its strong political orientation the education of the police occurred in virtual isolation from the society at large [Westney, 1987, pp.88-89].

The police were tied very closely to the legal foundations of Meiji Japan. Some of the ordinances which prescribed the status of the Emperor had a direct bearing on the police and problems of internal security, including: the Emergency Ordinance (Constitution of the Great Empire of Japan: Article 8), the Ordinance for Administrative Implementation, Security and Welfare (Article 9), the Administrative Authority Ordinance (Article 10), and the Martial Law Ordinance (Article 14). "After the Restoration Settlement the vast array of imperial prerogative set down in the 1889 Constitution of the Great Empire of Japan gradually became institutionalized so that by the 1920s Japanese politics was characterized by a high degree of confused competition among the instutitions of imperial prerogative to monopolize the Imperial Will in politics -- that is, to make or control national policy making" [Titus, 1974, p.4].

With regard to the police, it should be noted that, as was true of the military, its organization was based on the Emperor's Authority over State Affairs (Ten'no Kokumu Taiken). Therefore, the police always regarded itself as morally superior to the public. Police authority, that is, was based not on laws, but on ordinances that were legitimized by the Emperor [Sugai, 1957, pp.4-8]. As was true of the military (1871), compulsory education (1872), and the draft (1873), the founding of the police (1871) preceded the Cabinet (1885), the Constitution (1889), and the Diet (1890). However, after the constitutional system was completed, the police remained under the Emperor's authority (Articles 9 and 10). On the basis of this constitutional provision not only the Emperor, but the MOI, MPD, and governors were able to issue numerous ordinances for police purposes [Sugai, 1957, p.3].

The police also held judicial and quasi-judicial powers, based on both ordinance and law. The Summary Procedure Ordinance for Police Offenses (Ikeizai Sokketsu Rei) of 1885, for example, stipulated that the chiefs of police stations had the discretionary power to deal with minor crimes, a police practice dating back to the early 1870s and integrated into the first Penal Law in 1880. The Administrative Execution Law of 1900 granted police officials the powers of the confiscation of weapons and preventive detention of persons as well as the power to conduct house searches without a court warrant [Sugai, 1957, p.3. Taikakai, 1970, vol.2, pp.708-14]. Compared to other security laws and ordinances, these were not very conspicuous; but they were very substantial nonetheless. Based on this authority, between 1932 and 1937 200,000 to 300,000 suspects were punished annually for minor police offenses [Homusho, 1990, pp.314-315]. In reflecting on the prewar police, a former Commissioner General of the NPA, Yutaka Arai, concluded that the major difference between the prewar and the postwar police was the reduction in police powers due to the abolishing of the Summary Procedure Ordinance of 1885 and the Administrative Execution Law of 1900 [Arai, 1979, p.20].

The enormous power of the prewar police also reflected the weakness of substantive notions of due process as articulated by Articles 23, 24, and 25 of the Constitution. Under the prewar system the lower courts had no jurisdiction in administrative cases, including those relating to the police. These cases were heard in administrative courts. However, because the jurisdiction of the administrative courts was very limited, those who suffered damage from illegal police actions possessed almost no legal means of recourse except for suing individual policemen [Sugai, 1957, p. 4].

Over the years many far-reaching security ordinances and laws were passed -- the Defamation Ordinance (1873), the Association Ordinance (1880), the Association and Party Law (1887), the Public Safety Ordinance (1887), the Preventive Control Ordinance (1892), the Publishing Business Ordinance and Law (1875, 1893), the Newspaper Ordinance and Law (1875, 1897), the Public Peace Police Law (1900), the Peace Preservation Law (1925), and many additional laws passed during the war. The MOI claimed all of them as falling within its jurisdiction and classified all of them as administrative police ordinances and law rather than judicial criminal laws. Even after the laws were passed, the Emperor's ordinances still played sometimes a very large part. The revision of the Peace Preservation Law in 1928, for example, typified the enormous authority of the Emperor when, despite the Diet's negative vote on the revised legislation, the new ordinance contained the very language that the Diet had rejected [Taikakai, 1970, vol.2, p.717. Okudaira, 1977, pp.97-105]. The weakness of substantive notions of due process was evident also in the application of particular laws. Under the Peace Preservation Law, for example, the MOI arrested 64,070 people between 1928 and 1946 while clearing only 6,061. However, the JCP estimates that hundreds of thousands of people were arrested while 75,681 were cleared. The JCP also claims that 179 people were murdered under torture and 1,503 died in prison [Taikakai, 1970, vol.2, p.874. Okudaira, 1977, pp.114-17. Akahata, March 12, 1976]. In view of the openly acknowledged anti-Communism of the police, and especially of its leadership, these figures cannot simply be dismissed.

2D. Police Practices

As part of the organization of a modern police, the Japanese government institutionalized a system of patrol police (1874), household police surveys (1876), and local police stations (1877). These organizational features were serving a new police strategy of relative decentralization, adopted by the Police Affair Bureau, then advised by Heinrich Friedrich Wilhelm Hoehn, a German police officer and lecturer at the first Police Academy (1885-1889). As a result of this reform, the patrol police was stationed in each of Japan's lowest administrative units. In the cities there was one policeman for every 500-1,500 residents; in the countryside that ratio amounted to about one policeman for every 1,500-3,000 residents. The new administrative units were created by merging original villages from the same district. At its peak in 1930, the Japanese police system consisted of 1,207 police stations, 4,847 police boxes, and 14,324 residential police boxes [Taikakai, 1970, vol.2, pp.604-09. Westney, 1987, pp.78-82. Obinata, 1987, pp.37-9,86-90].

The most important police function, the household survey, was instituted in 1876 when the patrol police and the police boxes began to compile information on the residents in their areas. This information included, among others, names, addresses, land or home titles, former status group, occupation, and family membership. According to the 1882 rules residents were classified in three categories. The kou category included officials, lords, and common folk who owned property and had fixed occupations. They were surveyed every six months. The otsu category contained potentially suspicious people, the poor, and people living in lodging houses. They were checked up on every month. Finally, the hei category included suspicious people who were under surveillance, for example, ex-convicts, people owning no property, and those not holding a steady job. They were visited by the police three times each month. The household survey was very important for the variegated tasks of the administrative police and for the exercise of police discretion in dealing with minor offenses [Obinata, 1987, pp.37-9,195-96].

Besides penetrating every nook and cranny of society the Japanese police was also slowly drawn into the larger world outside Japan. After World War I foreign affairs divisions were created in the MOI, the MPD, and the Osaka as well as some of the other prefectural police forces. At the same time, police officers were assigned to Japanese embassies or consulates in Vladivostok, Harbin, Shanghai (1921), London, Berlin (1925), Beijing,

Guangdong (1926), Rome (1938), and San Francisco (1941). Their principal duty was to gather police intelligence on Communism, often including incidents of espionage and terrorism [Taikakai, 1970, vol.2, pp.752-54]. Compared to the army the police had a minimal presence abroad. The Japanese army sent military attachés to all embassies. In addition it also set up 30 intelligence bureaus abroad, mainly in China, Manchuria, and the Soviet Union [Momose, 1990, pp.291-94].

The police in prewar Japan was very powerful, certainly in comparison with the police that emerged in the early 1950s. Embedded in the dominant MOI, the police enjoyed great proximity to the centers of decision making and considerable prestige. Police power rested not only on a substantial number of security laws and ordinances but also on the broad quasi-judicial and administrative powers it was granted. Furthermore, the ultimate source of police power was an ordinance of the Emperor, not law. In focusing its work on crime prevention the police spent a significant part of its manpower on intelligence and security investigations and relied, in times of need, on the military to contain popular protest or uprisings. In addition, the police was politically well connected. Several top positions of the police were filled by political nominees, and the political police inevitably build close links with party politicians.

On the other hand, in two respects, the prewar police was perhaps not as strong as its successor after 1945. First, its control over the police budget was less total, and, over the years, the site of the police budget thus varied significantly. The general rule was that the central government was expected to provide 60 percent of the MPD's budget and 30 percent of the police expenses in other prefectures. But since the central government's contribution was based on the financial accounts provided by the prefectural governments, true exercise of central financial control was fraught with difficulties [Taikakai, 1970, vol.2, pp.664-68. Keisatsuseido Kenkyukai, 1985, pp.474,478-79]. Furthermore, governors were appointed by the MOI and together with the prefectual assemblies they had a substantial degree of influence over the police budget [Momose, 1990, p.123]. Secondly, the prewar prosecutor exercised more control over the prewar police than after 1945. In particular, the police had no more than an auxiliary role in conducting criminal investigations and was clearly subordinated to the public prosecutor. Finally, the prewar police had to act under the shadow of a very powerful and much larger army. While the Self Defense Forces outnumber Japan's postwar police by only a factor of 1.5, before World War II that ratio was, at a minimum, 4.0 and at a maximum 86 (Table 10). But the dominance of the army was not just a matter of size. In times of crisis the army was entitled to act under the Martial Law Ordinance. And it controlled the military police, which gave it an organizational base for intervening in domestic politics.

The politics of prewar Japan reflected a delicate and unstable balance of seemingly contradictory and ambivalent elements. The modernization of society was enforced by a strong bureaucracy which was an integral part of a state at the apex of which stood a god-like Emperor bestowing legitimacy to an oligarchical elite of conservative military leaders and political bosses striving to implement a strategy of conservative modernization. Contradictions and ambivalences were embodied in the Meiji Constitution. It tried to be constitutionalist while also seeking to preserve the authority of the Emperor through which the Meiji oligarchs hoped to control the process of social change that they in turn sought to accelerate. The police stood at the intersection of these contradictions and ambivalences. As they were resolved, at least for some time, in catastrophic military defeat, the position of the postwar police was to become simpler and less powerful.

III.

THE STRUCTURE OF THE JAPANESE POLICE
AND INTELLIGENCE SERVICES

Japan's police is part of a network of relations that are both organizational and political. Bayley, for example, describes Japan as having a multiple, coordinated police system which delegates central enforcement to subordinate levels of government [Bayley, 1985, pp.58-59]. Political and organizational relations link different government bureaucracies; they establish connections between government bureaucracies and a variety of societal institutions and actors; and they join government bureaucracies with a variety of transnational structures and actors. Japan's internal security policy is shaped in part by the constraints that these structures impose as well as the opportunities that they provide for the exercise of power.

During the past three decades the total number of policemen has almost doubled from 118,700 in 1955 to 220,900 in 1988. The total police budget has increased by a factor of 40 between 1955 and 1988 from 61,393 million to 2,443,970 million yen [Keisatsucho, 1977b, pp. 492-506, 551-556, 1989a, pp. 331, 336]. In 1961 Japan spent 0.53 percent of its GNP on policing. Since then the percentage gradually grew and it reached 0.74 percent in 1981, a high point during the three decades [Table 11. Nihon Seisansei Honbu, 1989, p.31]. Setsuo Miyazawa offers corroborating evidence for these figures. His comparative estimates suggest that the Japanese police has a much lighter workload than the American police. "The Japanese police forces are more than twice as large as the United States forces relative to the need for criminal investigation" [Miyazawa, 1991b, p.255]. And the territorial density of the Japanese police is such that "the country has been saturated by a larger number of officers than many other countries" [Miyazawa, 1991b, p.5]. A major reason for this saturation lies in the particularly heavy concentration of the police in Japan's capital. "A large number of police officers must be assigned to functions which are unique to Tokyo," the protection, in other words, of Japan's internal security (Table 8.) [Miyazawa, 1990, p.37]. In the mind of one retired senior NPA official this poses the very real question why the need exists "to investigate 100,000 people to catch a criminal" [Novick, 1989].

Japan's police is characterized by a combination of organizational stability and a great flexibility in the practical work of the police. The MPD illustrates this well. As one of the most important security police departments, between 1969 and 1989 the MPD has increased its budget by a factor of seven [Tokyo-to, 1969-89]. Despite these enormous changes in the allocation of resources, no formal organizational changes occurred between 1969 and 1988 in either the Security Bureau or the Guard Bureau. It was only in July 1988 that the MPD finally created a special division dealing with the activities of the JRA. The lack of organizational change does not seem to have impaired the police work of the MPD dealing with political extremists. On the contrary, the MPD accomplished many tasks. But it operated largely in secrecy. Nobody outside the MPD, including journalists regularly covering the police, for example, knows precisely how many people work in the different divisions of the MPD, and how much money is allocated to each division [Interview nos. 1,11,12, Tokyo, May 14, 15, and 16, 1990. Interview no.7, Tokyo, January 16, 1991].

Stability, flexibility and secrecy are defining characteristics of the political arrangements that typify post-war Japan. A brief historical description of these arrangements is an essential introduction to a description of the institutional structures in which Japan's internal security policy is formulated.

These political arrangements have been defined by the postwar Constitution of May 1947 that reflected the strong leadership of the General Headquarter (GHQ) of the Supreme Commander for the Allied Powers (SCAP). The Constitution embodies the concepts of demilitarization, liberalization, and democratization that were the object of the early American occupation policy. That policy sought to punish war criminals and purge from public office the militarists and their collaborators. Traditionalist and reactionary politicians thus suffered a loss of power and identity in a Japan bereft of the political leadership and symbol of the Emperor and the institutions of a strong state. Prominent casualties included Ichiro Hatoyama and Nobusuke Kishi [Tominomori, 1977. Goto et al., 1982].

The outbreak of the Korean War decisively forced the change in occupation policy that had begun with the American prohibition of the general strike called for February 1, 1947. Those who had been purged suddenly found themselves back in politics, organized several new political factions, and favored overwhelmingly a revision of the 1947 Constitution. This "revisionist" movement led by Ichiro Hatoyama, Ichiro Kono, Nobusuke Kishi, and Mamoru Shigemitsu appealed to many politicians critical of the Yoshida policy of economic reconstruction and political compliance. These factions finally took over the established parties and united into one dominant conservative party in 1955, the Liberal DemocrKokuatic Party (LDP). The party's platform demanded a revision of the 1947 Constitution. For several years during the

1950s the revisionists controlled not only the LDP but were also in charge of the Japanese government as a whole. They strengthened in these years what came to be known as a policy of the "reverse course", which originally had started in the late phases of the Yoshida era. [Tominomori, 1977, pp. 53, 62-66, 83-88.]

Shigeru Yoshida had been Prime Minister for more than six years under the authority of the American occupation. During this period he helped lay the foundations for the power of many prominent postwar politicans, including Eisaku Sato, Hayato Ikeda, Shigeru Hori, Kiichi Aichi, and Kakuei Tanaka. The policy line adhered to by the Yoshida school, since the Sato government of the late 1960s, has been referred to as Hoshu-honryu (Conservative Mainstream). It consists of serveral elements: cautious constitutionalism (loyalty to the Constitution of 1947), a foreign policy centered around U.S.-Japan relations (the Peace Treaty and the U.S.-Japan Mutual Security Treaty), and emphasis of economic growth [Hori, 1975. Tominomori, 1977, pp. 29-46, 143-147].

In contrast to the "revisionist" and "cautious" constitutionalism marking the LDP, the opposition parties, particularly the JSP has been a whole-hearted supporter of the 1947 Constitution. Although the JSP was dominated by the Shakaishugi Kyokai (Socialism Association) faction until the mid 1970s, and although the party's official platform adopted in 1964 and revised in 1966 ("The Road to Socialism in Japan") under the influence of the Kyokai faction explicitly denied the future status of the 1947 Constitution as the basic law, the behavior of the JSP and of its supporters have been fully supportive of the Constitution. In fact in the immediate postwar period the JSP participated twice in the government, and it embraced virtually all provisions of the Constitution. In contrast to the LDP it was throughout the postwar period a basically constitutionalist party, as is illustrated by the career of its present leader Takako Doi, a former professor of constitutional law.

While the confrontation between the revisionists in the LDP and the JSP had all the hallmarks of an openly partisan politics, the relationship between the revisionists and constitutionalists inside the LDP has been very complex. The two sides have sometimes engaged in serious infighting within the party; at other times they have clashed on principles of policy. At times this split was noticeable even in the political attitudes of important politicians like former Prime Minister Eisaku Sato [Tominomori, 1977, pp.143-47]. This on-going battle was exemplified during the process of revising the LDP's platform in 1985 [Asahi Nenkan, 1986, pp.106-07]. Although it is concealed from public eye, this fission in the LDP is one of the most important keys to comprehend the dynamics of Japanese politics. Otake has seen an abiding conflict between social democracy, economic liberalism, and traditional authoritarianism. The LDP's "liberal democratic" name sometimes disguises a "traditional authoritarian" substance [Otake, 1983, 1987]. Emphasizing

Figure 2: Structure of Internal Security Organizations in Japan (1988)

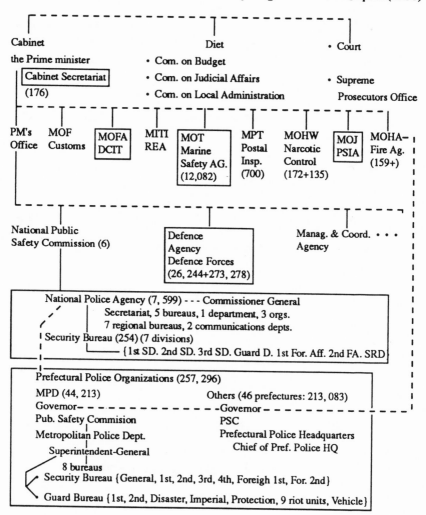

(Figure 2: continued)

Ministry of Justice (50, 046)

  ┌ Criminal Bureau   Public Safety Dept.

         (40)   International Dept.

  └ Imigration Bureau (165)+regional office: 18 (1,443)

Public Security Commission (10)

Public Security Investigation Agency (1,810)

  8 regional bureaus, 43 district offices

  Public Prosecutors Offices (11, 238)

┌ Supreme 1   Security Depts.

├ High   8

└ District 50

• M. of Foreign Affairs (4, 148)

  • Dept. of Counter

    International

    Terrorism

Cabinet

Prime Minister— — — — — — — — — — — — — — — — — National Security Council

  PM's Secretaries (5)

  ┌ Chief Cabinet Secretary   State ministers   Ministers

    (State Minister)

    CCS's Secretaries (3)

  ┌ Deputy CCS (parliamentary) DCCS (administ.) - - - The Committee for
                                                      Information Exchange
    Cabinet Secretariat (176)

  ┌• Cabinet Counselors' Office (5)

  ├• Cabinet Councillors' Office on External Affairs (19)

  ├• Cabinet Councillors' Office on Internal Affairs (46)

  ├• Cabinet Security Affairs Office (24)

  ├• Cabinet Public Relations Office (47)

  └• Cabinet Information Research Office (84)

Prime Minister's Office

  • Central Disaster Council

Source: Made by the authors based on Somucho 1988

similar dynamics, Muramatsu and Krauss have identified a "patterned pluralism" [1987].

The institutional structure in which Japan's internal security policy is made reflects these political cleavages between JSP and LDP and, more importantly, within the LDP. First, as argued above, all the important security organizations -- the National Police Agency (NPA), the MPD, the PSIA and the Defence Agency -- were either established or reformed under the influence of the Cold War in the 1950s. And in the second half of the 1950s, the effect of the Cold War continued to be felt in the policy reforms of the "reverse course". They encompassed ideologically conservative reforms in education, labor, and anti-monopoly regulation; the creation of the "Constitutional Research Council" in 1957 to prepare for a revision of the Constitution; the institutionalization of the Cabinet Research Office in 1957; and the unsuccessful attempt to revise the Police Duties Exercise Law in 1958.

Furthermore, all security organizations have been suffering from a lack of consensus on security issues due to the intense conflict of the early postwar years and before the 1980s also from a lack of legitimacy. With the exception of the MPD, which also acts as a prefectural police, all organizations involved in the area of internal security thus have tried to avoid public scrutiny in the Diet.

3A. Organizational Structures and Internal Security

Japan's organizations dealing with questions of internal security are not easily analyzed [Kühne and Miyazawa, 1979, pp.114-125. Clifford, 1982, pp.76-79. Parker, 1984, pp.41-43, 193-96. Murayama, 1980, pp.11-14,35-44,72-74. Bayley, 1978, pp.55,68-70,72,96,98,173-79,187-94. Bayley, 1985, pp.162,167,171,182-83. Ames, 1981, pp.12-14,87-88,142-48,151-79,180-226. Vogel, 1979, pp.208,210,219-20. Hoffman, 1982. Archambeault and Fenwick, 1985. Schembri, 1985. Rinalducci, 1972, pp.xvii-xxi,xliii. Fukushima, 1972, pp.4-8]. Besides the hardly exceptional preference of Japan's various security organizations not to be the subject of academic analysis, these institutions have some distinctive features that impair systematic research. One of the major obstacles lies in the de facto rather than de jure flexibility of Japanese police organizations, in the gap, that is, between the apparent absence of formal, organizational change on the one hand and the pervasiveness of informal change in police practice on the other. It is thus very important to understand fully the political dynamics that have made possible the very substantial informal changes in police practices that have occurred within existing organizations.

The Korean war for all intents and purposes stopped the American policy of demilitarization and prompted American and Japanese policy makers to begin the process of reestablishing Japanese security forces. In the early

1950s many municipal police forces were absorbed by the local branches of the national police. This prepared the ground for the eventual reorganization of the national police system in 1954. An embryonic military force, the National Police Reserve, was set up in August 1950 and was enlarged to the Safety Force in 1952 and finally, in July 1954, was renamed the Self Defence Forces (SDF). In addition, the Special Investigation Bureau in charge of investigating organizations hostile to the occupation authorites was formed within the Ministry of Justice (MOJ) in February 1948. This Bureau became in July 1952 the PSIA, under the authority provided by the Subversive Activity Prevention Law.

With the revision of the Police Law in 1954, the NPA was formally established and Tokyo's MPD was reorganized in the same year. Also in 1954 the Defense Agency became the successor to a reorganized Safety Agency (1952-54), and the National Defence Council was set up in the same year. The Maritime Safety Agency was formed as early as 1948. Finally, by transferring the staff of the Prime Minister's Office in 1957, the Cabinet Research Office was transformed into the Cabinet Secretariat. Despite the social upheavals which mass protest and terrorist violence caused in the 1960s, 1970s and 1980s no major organizational changes have occurred in the police field since the years 1954-57.

At the end of World War II the Allies insisted on a thorough democratization and decentralization of the Japanese police. Allied preferences compelled Japanese authorities to "depolice" many aspects of public life, thus sharply reducing the importance of the police [Hoshino, 1974. Hironaka, 1973. Taikakai, vol.2, 1970. Sugai, 1957. Steiner, 1965, pp.90-94]. In following the recommendations of two reports issued by American authorities, the Valentine and Hollander reports, the role of the administrative police was reduced sharply. Administrative functions such as the licensing of businesses and social clubs, the regulation of factories, the issuing of building permits, the oversight of insurance, health and sanitation regulations, the organization of disaster relief operations, and the organization of fire control, all of these duties were transferred from the police to other government agencies.

In addition the police system of censorship was abolished [Hoshino, 1974]. All political police forces, including the Special Higher Police, were abolished. More generally the police was put under democratic control. Before 1945 the organization of the police as well as its principles of operation were based on the Emperor's authority and not on that of the Diet. After 1945, by way of contrast, reform legislation affecting the police was passed only by the Diet.

With General Dougals MacArthur's permission Prime Minister Katayama issued the necessary orders and a new police system was established with the passing of the Police Law of 1947 and of the Police Duties Execution

Law of 1948. Like the dissolution of the zaibatsu and the creation of the anti-monopoly law, the reform of the Japanese police was at the heart of the American reform policies designed to democratize Japan, as evidenced by the disproportionate initiative the American authorities took in the development of the new police legislation [Iokibe, 1990, pp.114-117].

The new system had the following characteristics. First, the police was deprived of its traditional cabinet status. By the end of 1947, the once powerful MOI, the home of the pre-war police, was abolished. It was the only ministry which went out of business altogether after 1945. Secondly, the reforms created a decentralized system of municipal police forces for all communities with more than 5,000 residents, including Tokyo, as well as a system of public safety committees charged to oversee these local police forces. Of a total police force of 125,000, 95,000 were allocated to the local police. Thirdly, the role of the national government was restricted to exercising administrative authority over a relatively small (30,000) local police force and the establishment of a National Public Safety Committee [Sugai 1957, pp.5-6. Hoshino, 1974].

Under the pressures of the Cold War, however, without concurring Diet legislation, American authorities issued in April 1949 an Ordinance for the Regulation of Associations, directed against groups opposing the Occupation. The 1947 Police Law was partially revised in 1951 and 1952 thus granting local governments the right to voluntarily abolish their local police forces, and it gave the national government some power over Tokyo's MPD. Finally, in 1954 the political climate had changed sufficiently that a number of important legislative changes were made. Two new defense laws and two new education laws were passed and the issue of the revision of the Constitution suddenly moved to the top of the political agenda [Hoshino, 1974, p.305. Sugai, 1957, pp.7-9].

It was also in 1954 that the Police Law was totally rewritten in line with a more conservative political climate and the policy of the "reverse course". The 1954 law instituted a police system organized along the following lines [Hironaka, 1973, pp.147-148. Hoshino, 1974, pp.346-347. Sugai, 1957, pp.11-12. Rinalducci, 1972, pp.1-17. Steiner, 1965, pp.255-58]:

(1) A single system of a prefectural police replaced the dual system of local police forces under the authority of the municipal and the national government.

(2) A national Public Safety Commision was put under the jurisdiction of the Prime Minister, and it was chaired by a minister with cabinet rank. The Commission has the authority to nominate officials for many of the top positions of the police: the Commissioner General of the NPA, the Superintendent-General of the MPD, the chiefs of the

prefectural police headquarters, and other individuals whose rank is above the level of senior superintendent. Personnel matters such as the appointment of the chief officers of the NPA or the MPD involve the Prime Minister as well.

(3) The Commissioner Gernal of the NPA has the authority to direct and supervise the prefectural police on fourteen specified issues, including the security police, emergency planning, police education, communication, and weapons. Seven regional bureaus of the NPA are also authorized to review the prefectural police on ten of the fourteen issues.

(4) In times of emergency the Prime Minister can temporarily take control of all police matters.

(5) In contrast to the 1947 law the power of the Public Safety Commission was restricted solely to controlling, rather than partly managing, police affairs.

(6) Only prefectural police officers with a rank above superintendent   are national rather than local public servants. The size of the local police force in each prefecture is decided by the national government.

(7) That part of the police budget over which the NPA has jurisdiction -- such as the salary of senior officers, the security police, education, communication, weapons -- is provided by the NPA.   All other expenses are funded by the prefectural governments.

In short, as a result of the 1954 reform of the Police Law, the national government has taken control over questions of internal security through its control of the security police, personnel affairs, and budgets. However, although they lost a lot of authority, prefectural goverments continue to pay most of the police budget. In this sense, "centralization is much more conspicuous than in the prewar system" [Sugai, 1957, p.12. Arai 1979, p.21]. In the words of Tamaki Uemura, a member of the Public Safety Commission between 1948-1954, the Public Safety Commission exercises no more than nominal control and in the new atmosphere soon became a mere "agent for transmitting government policy" [Asahi, October 30, 1958, cited in Hatakeyama 1984, p.97.].

In 1954 the NPA had four bureaus and a secretariat; in 1988 it had five bureaus, one department, and a secretariat. It employs about 1,000-1,100 police officials, 900 members of the Imperial Guard, as well as 5,000-6,000 civilians. In 1988 two-thirds of the NPA officials were serving in seven Regional Police Bureaus, and two Communication Divisions. Over 15 percent of the personnel are assigned to three affiliated organizations: the Imperial

56

Guard Headquarters, the National Research Institute of Police Science, and the National Police Academy. Of the 1,304 officials working in the NPA's inner bureaus, 254 are placed in the Security Bureau, second largest after the Criminal Investigation Bureau [Somucho, 1988].

Compared to the total police force of Japan, the NPA has decreased from 0.76 percent in 1962 to 0.54 percent in 1988; corresponding budget figures are 18.2 percent in 1955 and 7.4 percent in 1988. In 1988 more than 99 percent of the total police force and more than 93 percent of the total police budget was supplied by the prefectural governments. And the contribution of the prefectural police is increasing. The load the prefectures carry now is much heavier than before the war. In 1932 only 34 percent of the police budget was paid by the prefectures [Momose, 1990, p.123]. Evidently, the burden of an increasingly expensive police system is falling more heavily on the prefectures than on the national government [Keisatsucho, 1977b, 1989a].

The dual system of police introduced in 1954 has given the national police a convenient way for evading budgetary accountability at the national and prefectural level. The NPA has succeeded in evading close budgetary oversight. The prefectural headquarters also have succeeded in keeping out of trouble because they can always point to the NPA's control of national police matters. Legally governors, prefectural assemblies and the Ministry of Home Affairs (MOHA) have some control over the prefectural police budget. But in reality that budget has been treated like a "holy ground" [Nagamatsu, 1987, pp.92-93]. Former NPA Commissioner General Yutaka Arai has argued that:

". . . the Police Law is working pretty well; after all officials both in the NPA and in the MOHA were colleagues in the MOI before 1947. Communications among them are very smooth. This police system is very advantageous to the police. The term 'advantageous' might be criticized. Because under this system, the police can decide on the size of the authorized police force and make what it regards as necessary changes without itself having to pay for the additional personnel expenses that are covered by the budgets of the prefectural governments. There exists the danger that we, the police, will be considered to be too egoistic. After all we are owing everything to the MOHA's generosity that we so deeply appreciate" [Hoshino, 1974, p.348].

The NPA is not merely an executive office but possesses an independence which permits it to conduct its affairs independently within broadly defined legal limits. It normally facilitates the coordination and communication between different prefectures and operates primarily through the prefectural police, especially the MPD. However, for matters involving the security police, the emergency police, highway and traffic regulations, and the security of the Imperial Palace, it has the power to act directly [Saito, n.d., p.67]. Despite these responsibilities, the NPA lacks control over a police force of its own. Instead there is the Imperial Guard with 900 members and, under the jurisdiction of seven regional bureaus, the NPA maintains the Regional Bureau Riot Police, staffed since 1969 by 4,210 prefectural police officers.

Although the NPA rarely investigates crimes, it has taken measures to counter the threat by political extremists especially since the mid-1960s. In 1965 a division to counter right-wing extremism was spun off from NPA's domestic division and in 1972 an independent division for dealing with left-wing extremism (the Third Security Division) was established. Since 1978 the NPA has taken special measures against the JRA, and a special anti-terrorist division (the Second Foreign Affairs Division) was set up in 1988. It seeks to integrate the scattered work on international terrorism and the JRA done in different divisions of the NPA. Its specific purpose is to stop the return or immigration of international terrorists, to locate and arrest terrorists living in Japan, and to eradicate organizations supportive of the JRA. But this recent division does not investigate terrorists who have their basis exclusively inside Japan like, for example, the Chukaku [Kokusai Tero Mondai Kenkyukai, 1989, p. 56].

Although only a few major changes were made in the structure of the NPA's Security Bureau less visible changes have occurred since the late 1970s. A number of new subdivisions were added for natural catastrophies (May 1976), for the Imperial Household Guard (April 1977), for protection against the Red Army (April 1978), for security planning (April 1979), for foreign affairs research (April 1981), and for the communication and liaison with foreign security organizations (April 1984); a new office for the protection of VIPs was created in April 1986 [Keisatsucho, 1973-1989].

Within the structure of the NPA the security police plays ani important role. It has been noted that the security police has dominated the criminal police since the late 1960s. With the exception of the present Commissioner Akio Kanazawa (1988-) after Yutaka Arai (1965-1969) the next seven NPA Commissioner Generals have served on their way to the top also as Directors of the Security Bureau. The appointment of Kanazawa was considered as a slap in the face of the security police which had been embarrassed in 1986 by the JCP wiretapping case [Asahi Nenkan, 1989, p.129. Miyazawa, 1989]. Alternatively this may have been a symbolic gesture to placate criminal police officials so long excluded from the NPA's top position [Tahara, 1986a, pp.96-97. Tahara, 1990, p.315].

The strength of the security police in the NPA is illustrated also by the career path and ranking of senior police bureaucrats (Table 6). The proportion of important posts in the security police occupied by high ranking officials is

Table 6: Hierarchy within the Police:
Ranking within the Police Bureaucrats (1990)

Year of Entering the NPA	NPA Line	NPA Other	MPD	Other Prefectural Police	Other Ministry/Agency	Other [Amakudari]
1954 (1)[1]	•Commissioner General					2[2] [16][3]
1955 (1)			•Superintendent General			1 [27]
1956 (1)	•Deputy CG					3 [13]
1957 (2)	•Dir. of Police Affairs Bureau		•Osaka HQ Chief		•Ambassador Sri Lanka	[12]
1958 (3)	•Dir. of Security Bureau				•Defense Deputy DG •PSIA Dir. of Kyushu Bureau	[13]
1959 (8)	•Dir. of Criminal Bureau	•Pres. Police Academy •Kinki Reg. Bur. Dir. •Imperial Guard HQC •Kanto Reg. Bur. Dir.	•Deputy SG		•Cabinet PR Chief •Cabinet Info. Res. Chief	[7]
1960 (10)	•Chief Secretary •Security Councillor	•Vice-pre Pol. Academy •Chubu Reg. Bur. Dir. •Tohoku Reg. Bur. Dir. •Shikoku Reg. Bur. Dir.	•Dir. of General Affair	•Hokkaido HQC. •Kanagawa HQC •Niigata HQC.		[5]
1961 (11)	•Dir. of Safety Bureau •Dir. of Traffic Bureau	•Kyushu Reg. Bur. Dir. •Chugoku Reg. Bur. Dir.		•Aichi HQC. •Ibaraki HQC. •Hyogo HQC. •Shizuoka HQC.		1 [2]

Table 6: Hierarchy within the Police:
Ranking within the Police Bureaucrats (1989)

Year of Entering the NPA	NPA Line	NPA Other	MPD	Other Prefectural Police	Other Ministry Agency	Other [Amakudari]
1961				•Saitama HQC. •Nagano HQC. •Fukuoka HQC.		
1962 (8)	•Chief Inspector •Safety Councillor	•Kanto Reg. Bur. Dir. of General Aff. •Dir. of Special Inv. Center	•Dir. of Traffic	•Chiba HQC. •Kyoto HQC. •Hiroshima HQC. •Osaka Pol. Aff.		1 [2]
1963 (9)	•Criminal Councillor •Councillor •Kinki Reg. Bur. Dir. of Poli. Aff.	•Kanto Reg. Bur. Dir. of Security •Imperial Guard Police Aff. Dir.	•Dir. of Security	•Nagasaki HQC	•Cab. Inf. Researcher •Manag. Cood. Ag. Traffic Office Chief	[1]
1964 (9)	•Traffic Councillor	•Edu. Dir. of Pol. Acad. •Kanto Reg. presid. of Pol. Acad. •Kyushu Reg. Dir. of Gen. Aff.	•Dir. of Guard	•Miyagi HQC •Fukushima HQC	•Cab. Inf. R. Researcher •Imperial House Ag. C. Secretary	

Source: Chihozaimu Kyokai 1990.

Notes: [1] Number of career police bureaucrats within the regular promotion system.
[2] Number of career police bureaucrats outside the regular promotion system.
[3] Number of retired career police bureaucrats.

greater than in any other police department. And the security police is spending a substantial part of the NPA's budget. Because the operational expenses incurred by the security police in the prefectures are financed by the NPA, the security police budget may run as high as 60 percent of the total [Hironaka, 1973, p. 161. Interview, no.12, Tokyo, May 16, 1990].

The MPD is Japan's second major police organization. As an actual policing organization, the MPD is the largest and the most powerful police force in Japan. The MPD is proud of "being the only organization that can provide protection against terrorist attacks" [Interview no.16, Tokyo, May 17, 1990]. Through the rotation of personnel MPD and NPA are closely linked and it appears that over time the traditional independence of the MPD from the NPA has become weaker [Interview no. 3, Tokyo, May 14, 1990]. While the MPD is legally and financially one of the prefectural police forces, organizationally it resembles the NPA and in particular its security section [Kubo, 1984, pp.93-102].

With respect to the organizational development of the security police, the MPD has been a driving force. Although the 1947 Police Law separated the MPD from the national police, it has behaved like a national security police. This is clearly shown in the development of the riot police. In 1948 it created the first two units of the riot police, then called the reserve corps, with 1,800 men. (At that time, the next largest riot police unit in Osaka had only 70 men). Increased to four units in 1949 and seven in 1952 (with 2,350 men), police brutality against demonstrators around the Sunagawa base led to much public criticism and a subsequent reduction to five units with 1,800 men [Hironaka, 1973, pp.185-87. Interview no.17, Tokyo, May 17, 1990]. In 1969 massive popular demonstrations caused a doubling in the number of riot police units in the MPD with a total of 5,100 men. Since then the organizational structure of the riot police inside the MDP has remained unchanged, with the manpower fluctuating between 3,000 and 5,000; the maximum of 5,200 was reached in 1971 [Farrell, 1990, p.181. Hironaka, 1973, p.309. Asahi, June 29, 1978. Yomiuri, 1986, p.208. Hosaka, 1986, p.189. Mizutani, 1987, p.117].

The riot police has developed its own special equipment. In addition to helmets with a plexiglass shield and duralumin shields, vests and leg guards are added, thus creating the appearance of the riot policeman as a knight-in-armor. One of the units in the MPD riot police is the special vehicle unit which disposes over many reinforced personnell carriers that hold up to 37 riot policemen, barricade cars, water cannon trucks and other special equipment [Farrell, 1990, pp.182-83]. This police force is serving also as part of other units such as the special anti-guerilla forces. While the riot police is part of the prefectural police, all of its costs except salary is funded by the NPA. Table 7 gives an overview of the development of the riot police.

Table 7: History and Size of the Riot Police (1948-80)

January 1948	Osaka, 70 only	
May 1948	MPD-Local Gov't Police only, 1,792	
January 1952	Nationally funded local police 2,300 (45 corps)	
July 1954	Uniform Riot Police Program established	
April 1957	MPD Riot Police 1,800 (5 corps) (reduced from 2,350, 7 corps)	
October 1962	Revision of the Riot Police Program	
October 1969	Pref. MPD (10 corps)	5,127
	Osaka (2 corps)	882
	Kanagawa	520
	Saitama	342
	Chiba	342
	Fukuoka	342
	Other	2,665
	Pref. Total	9,700
	Pref. Special	15,000[1]
	NPA Regional	4,000
Around 1980	Pref. Riot Police	9,700
	Pref. Special (stand-by Riot Police)	15,700
	NPA Regional	4,210

Note: [1]In addition, a Public Security Investigation Corps of 17,650 men was standing by to assist in the arrest of radicals as did 50,000 police reserves.

Source: Hironaka, 1973, pp. 77, 132, 165, 249, 309, 324. Asahi Nenkan, 1970, p. 304, Tahara 1986b, p.160, Farrell, 1990, p. 181.

The organizational structure of the MPD is more complex than that of the other prefectural polices forces and of the NPA. Two bureaus among seven, the Guard Bureau (Keibi-bu) and the Security Bureau (Kouan-bu), are in charge of security policing. Both bureaus can be traced back to 1952 just after the passage of the Subversive Activity Prevention Law. The Guard Bureau has grown from two divisions in 1952 to five today. Its primary responsibility is to provide physical security and to manage the riot police. Its duties include the escorting of VIPs. A Secret Service in the American sense was set up in 1975 after an attack of right-wing radicals on Prime Minister Miki [Keisatsuseido Kenkyukai, 1985, p.244. Suzuki, 1980, pp.114-24]. In 1989 at the Emperor's funeral ceremony the unit escorting VIPs, including secret service officers, reached a size of 1,600 men [Asahi, Feb.24 evening, 1990]. In addition, starting with 104 members, a Women Guard Corps has existed since 1972 [Asahi, 1973, p.284].

The Security Bureau supervises the surveillance, investigation, and arrest of political radicals. It has become progressively more complex. It began with three divisions (in charge of Communist, Labor, and Foreign Affairs) and added a new division (for filing and research) in 1957. In 1962 it divided its Foreign Affairs division into two (for international espionage on the USSR and on Asian countries), and in 1969 it created a new division investigating left-wing extremism as well as the Special Investigation Corps specializing in the arrest of left-wing radicals [Hironaka, 1973, pp.186,238,311. Takigawa, 1973, p.4].

Since 1969 the work of the Security Bureau of the MPD has become more and more secret. Within the existing organization sharp increases in manpower occurred. In 1960 its manpower was divided among the following sections: general affairs (32), Communists (123), New Left (41), labor (70), right extremism (35), foreign affairs (298), and filing (84). The total work force in the Security Bureau was 709 [Asahi Nenkan, 1961, p. 245]. In December 1971 the MPD set up a Headquarters for the Regulation of Violent Crimes by Ultra-Leftist Groups consisting of 800 police officers. The Security Bureau supplied 600 officers, nearly half of its force [Takigawa, 1973, pp.119-20]. After the terrorist attacks at the time of the 1986 Tokyo Summit, the MPD decided to double its force against the New Left from 250 to 450 according to one source [Yomiuri, June 19, 1986] and from 290 to 600 according to another [Mainichi, June 19, 1986. The Japan Times, June 17, 1986]. The additional personnel was repeatedly transferred from other sections rather than newly hired. Chukaku is a specific target of this enlarged police force. [Interviews, no. 8, May 15, 1990 and no. 12, May 16, 1990]. By way of contrast only 70 members of the security police are covering right-wing extremists, and their number is declining [Interview no.7, Tokyo, January 16, 1991].

The Security Bureau is organized along the following lines: the General Affairs Security Division (general affairs, the JCP); the First Security Division (the JRA and new leftist, radical groups); the Second Security Division (labor unions and mass movements); the Third Security Division (rightist groups); the Fourth Security Division (filing and apartment roller operations); the First Foreign Affairs Division (USA, Europe, Socialist countries); and the Second Foreign Affairs Division (Asia) [Interview, no.19, Tokyo, May 18, 1990. Takeda, 1980, pp.148-53. Takigawa 1973, p.4. Maruoka, 1990, pp.58,64].

Compared to the normal bureaucratic units (ka) the size of the divisions of the MPD is very large. In 1989 the MPD had 44,282 employees (41,381 policemen/women and 2,901 civilians). Its organization was divided into two basic parts: (1) headquarters (including 8 bureaus with 49 divisions and 32 other units; 9 district headquarters; and the MP academy with 4 units); and (2) 98 local police stations with 1,248 police boxes [MPD, 1989, pp.1-6]. Unfortunately we have data on the deployment of personnel between these two parts only for the period 1948-57 [Miyauchi, 1960, pp.222-23]. In the 1950s, about one fourth of the total MPD force was assigned to the headquarters. If the proportions were not to have changed since then, excepting the riot police, the average number of officers in each unit would be about 100. General affairs divisions are probably smaller, and investigation and field work divisions somewhat larger. One newspaper reports the size of one security police division dealing with new leftist groups around 300 (before 1986) and around 600 (after 1986) [Mainichi, June 20, 1986]. Other divisions in the security police are estimated to run around 100 to 200 staff members. Compared to the average size of bureaucratic units of about 20, divisions with 100 or 600 staff members are enormous. The MPD's practical police work is not done by these units but by informal subunits which are called tanto (charge) and han (group) [Kobayashi, 1986, p.108. Maruoka, 1990, p.64]. But since only the large divisions are under the formal supervision of the Tokyo Metropolitan Assembly, the delegation of practical police work to smaller units insulates the MPD from potential outside interference and thus helps to strengthen its penchant for flexible operations.

Since information about the police forces and operations assigned to intelligence and work against radicals are classified as top secret, such estimates must be taken with a grain of salt. We do know, however, that the Special Investigation Corps in the Security Police Division is used to investigate incidents covered by the Subversive Activity Prevention and Crime of Riot Article in the Penal Code. According to two reports, since the early 1970's several anti-terrorist emergency squads have been set up at the prefectural level. The existence of one or several combat teams with a total of 105 men was reported in 1976, trained and maintained at a high state of readiness to swing into action at times of crisis [Asahi, May 29, 1976 and June 28, 1978. Nishio, 1984, p.26]. According to a second source special anti-guerilla squads, armed with automatic rifles and belonging to the Sixth Riot Corps of the MPD, were established in Tokyo and Osaka on January 10, 1978 [Maiinichi, May 11, 1982]. These units were set up because of a NPA order to the MPD and the Osaka prefectural police in response to an international agreement Prime Minister Fukuda reached at the Bonn Summit in 1977. The members of this unit are selected and trained secretly as ordinary riot police [Mainichi, May 11, 1982. Nishio, 1984, p. 26].

In addition, the nine units of the MPD's riot police form a special unit of 700 men. The MPD also is involved in field investigations in other prefectures outside of its jurisdiction. In December 1987-January 1988, after an arrest of JRA leader Osamu Maruoka in November 1987, for example, the MPD's Security Bureau was reported to have searched about 160 houses all over Japan [Yomiuri, December 28, 1987. Asahi, January 13, 1988. Mainichi, January 29, 1988].

Political supervision of the MPD and the other prefectural police forces by the Tokyo Metropolitan Government and other prefectural governments is almost non-existent. During the 1970s when progressive political parties controlled many municipal governments, such as the Minobe Tokyo government between 1967 and 1979, political frictions between the government and the MPD was always possible, particularly over the growth in the number of the police. For a number of years, such as 1969, 1973, 1976, and 1978, the size of the Tokyo police force became a major political issue. In 1973, for example, the MPD's request for an additional 1,450 men was cut back to 900 [Asahi, January 20, 1973]. The attempt of the MPD to persuade the Clean Government Party in the Tokyo Prefectural Assembly to use its political influence on Governor Minobe was, at that time, of little avail. But after the election victory of the LDP in the local elections of 1979, mainly because of a success of coalition making with the Clean Government Party and the Democratic Socialist Party, the MPD no longer was concerned about serious budgetary constraints [Suzuki, 1980, pp.191-93].

Like the NPA the MPD has always been strongly opposed to being held accountable under the terms of the Public Information Ordinance (Jyoho Kokai Jorei). The MPD insists on its special status in part because it receives information from other prefectural police forces and in part because it enjoys very close working relations with the NPA [Yomiuri, 1986, pp.192-93]. In fact, the MPD sees itself at the center of Japan's internal security policy and does not want that position put at risk either by political interference, as in the 1970s, from elected government officials or by unwanted public attention and information. In contrast to many of the other prefectural police forces which operate at the periphery of Japanese politics and are less intimately tied to the NPA, the MPD offers its security police a powerful base for operation [Kubo, 1984].

The police is very secretive and not easily held accountable. Policemen are not organized in any union or other forms of organization giving voice to a possible division within the organization. Heihachi Yamazaki is a notable exception as he became a witness for a defendant in one criminal case. And Tadamitu Matsuhashi was one of the few career officers who has actually published a book containing criticisms of the behavior of the security police [Matsuhashi, et al., 1986, p.259].

This penchant for secrecy makes it difficult to give reliable data about the total size of Japan's security police, including the riot police, security police, police guards, and the secret service. But the best estimates available put the size of the security police at about 10,000 in the mid-1960s. This figure includes 5,700 members of the Riot Police, 1,800 to 2,500 of whom were thought to be serving in the Metropolitan Riot Police, as well as 1,200 investigation police officers (with 700 serving in the Metropolitan Security Police) [Tsuji 1966, p.319. Asahi Nenkan, 1961, p.245. Miyauchi, et al., 1960, p.222. Hironaka 1973, pp.223-24, 308-11]. In the early 1960s the total security police was about 7-8 percent of Japan's estimated total police manpower. By 1988 estimates for the size of the security police had increased threefold to 30,000-40,000 men, including 3,000-5,000 members of the Metropolitan Riot Police, 1,500 riot policemen permanently stationed at Narita Airport, 5,000 other riot policemen, 4,800 members of the regional riot police, 15,000 members of a stand-by riot police force and about 2,000 Metropolitan investigation security police officers and probably the same number of police guard officers. By 1988 the share of the security police had risen to approximately 13-18 percent of the total police force [Asahi, June 29, 1978. Mizutani, 1987, p.117. Jiyuhosodan, 1986, p.203]. Other sources provide similar estimates. One such estimate for the year 1972, for example, reports that the police force was divided between the security police (10.9%), the riot police (5.4%), the criminal police (16.8%), the traffic police (14.0%), the crime prevention and safety police (5.6%), the patrol police (39.6%), and other types of police (7.7%) [Asahi Nenkan 1973, p. 284]. Since 1971 the government has never published any data on the size of the security police. The most closely guarded secret is the size of police force in charge of security investigation and intelligence [Asahi, August 4, 1987].

Another rough estimate of the size of Japan's security police force can be gained by calculating the relative "excess" in the MPD compared to the forces in other prefectures. Table 8 indicates that based on the average police density in all other prefectures, Tokyo was "overpoliced" by 14,900 in 1961, 19,700 in 1972 and 21,500 in 1980. Even compared to Osaka, the second largest prefectural police force in Japan, Tokyo was overpoliced by 7,300, 13,000, and 16,000 in each of the three years. On the other hand, crime rates in prefectures show relatively small variation. Tokyo's rates in each year were almost the same level or recently even lower than those of Osaka, although

Table 8: The MPD's Police Force in Comparison to Other Prefectures: 1961, 1972, 1980

	1961	1972	1980
A. MPD # of police force	27,051	37,490	40,125
B. Osaka # of police force	11,220	16,260	17,630
C. Total prefectural police force	131,930	181,350	210,100
D. Hypothetical Tokyo Police Force size[1]	12,130	17,780	18,720
E. Hypothetical Tokyo Police Force size[2]	19,740	24,350	24,180
F. Degree of over-policing (A-D)[1]	14,920	19,710	21,495
G. Degree of over-policing (A-E)[2]	7,310	13,140	16,035
H. Police Density in Tokyo (population/policemen)	358	304	289
I. Police Density in Osaka (population/policemen)	491	469	481
J. National Average Police Density (population/policemen)[3]	798	642	621

Notes: [1] The figure assumes that the national average of the population/policemen ratio as reported in Row J existed in Tokyo.

[2] The figure assumes that the Osaka average as reported in Row I existed in Tokyo.

[3] The figure is calculated based on all prefectures except Tokyo.

Source: JSP Kokumin Seijinenkan 1962, p.251, Keisatsucho 1973, 1981.

around 50 percent higher than the average rate of all other prefectures [Keisatsucho, 1973-90]. Tokyo is overpoliced because it must deal with political crimes. For example between 1966 and 1980 the MPD arrested 22,400 persons suspected of having violated the law dealing with Crimes of Obstruction of Public Duties -- more than half of the total arrests for this crime nationwide and ten times the figure for Osaka. In short compared to the police/population ratio in other prefectures the MPD had probably 20,000 policemen dealing with security affairs.

All estimates, however, are very tentative and probably much too conservative. In times of crisis the NPA and MPD can redeploy most of their personnel freely and assign an extraordinarily large percentage of their total manpower to the protection of Japan's internal security [Interview, nos. 1 and 11, Kobe and Tokyo, January 14 and 18, 1991].

A discussion of the position of the security police in the NPA, the MPD and the other prefectural police forces conceals the defacto integration of these different branches of the security police. The security police in Japan apparently works like one organization [Interview no. 16, Tokyo, May 17, 1990. Yomiuri, 1986, pp.192-93]. Apart from the regular round of meetings before, during or after important incidents touching on Japan's internal security, national meetings of directors or director generals in charge of security and police guard affairs in the prefectural police forces are held on an ad hoc basis. Such meetings, for example, have reportedly been held on January 9, 1987, April 4, 1986, as well as earlier on March 28, 1978, and July 17, 1963 [Sankei, January 9, 1987. Nikkei, April 4, 1986. Nikkei, March 29, 1978. Asahi, July 17, 1963]. The coordination of the work of different intelligence and security organizations dates back to the late 1960s and accelerated with the series of terrorist attacks in the 1970s. As part of the reform of the Cabinet Secretariat in 1987 coordination was institutionalized in the form of the Joint Information Exchange Meeting.

This de facto integration on a national basis offers a sharp contrast to the criminal police where competition between different prefectural police forces is often quite intense. Furthermore, the criminal investigation divisions and public security divisions of the police apparently do not cooperate closely. This was illustrated by how the police handled a series of bombing cases in 1974 and 1975 (Table 2) and several hostage cases in the 1980s [Interview no. 10, Tokyo, May 15, 1990. Takigawa, 1973, p.145. Tahara, 1990, pp.304-14].

The informal integration of the security police throughout Japan is one instance of a more general feature of Japanses politics. The sectionalism and bureaucratic pluralism of Japanese bureaucracies has often been noted [Inoguchi, 1983. Campbell, 1984. Yamaguchi, 1989]. It is partly overcome by the exchanges, loans, and transfers of personnel between different bureaucratic organizations. This practice had been given formal cabinet approval as early as July 19, 1955; and it was reinforced by another cabinet agreement and new cabinet guidelines in January-February 1965. The guidelines spelled out that all career officials be required to have at least two years' work experience at another ministry or agency with transfers to be arranged on an exchange basis [Keisatsucho, 1977b, pp.572-73].

The rotation of NPA personnel shows a distinctive pattern. The NPA sends about 70-90 officials to other ministries and agencies while receiving only about 20 officials from other ministries, most of them at the prefectural police offices. Furthermore, very few officials from other agencies reach senior office positions inside the NPA. In 1980, for example, there was only one senior official from the Ministry of Home Affairs (MOHA) working at the NPA. In 1984 four "exceptional" positions of chief of prefectural police headquarters were held by officials from the Ministry of Foreign Affairs (MOFA), Ministry of Construction, Defence Agency, and National Railway [Mainichi, June 29, 1984]. In contrast, police bureaucrats whose work focuses on internal security have been very successful in reaching senior positions in the Cabinet Secretariat. In 1986 the NPA placed 14 officials in the Cabinet Secretariat, three in the Defence Agency, and two in the Imperial Household Agency. And the NPA sends many of its promising junior officers to the major ministries. Twenty-six junior NPA officials worked for the Cabinet Secretariat in 1989, 16 for the Ministry of Foreign Affairs (MOFA), 6 for the Defense Agency, 5 for the Administrative Management and Coordination Agency, 4 for Justice, and 3 for the Imperial Household Agency.

Table 9 illustrates that compared to other ministries and agencies, the NPA is less open to officers from other ministries, and its senior positions are staffed almost exclusively by insiders. In this it resembles other important autonomous and exclusive ministries such as the Ministry of Finance (MOF), the Ministry of International Trade and Industry (MITI) and the Ministry of Agriculture, Fishery, and Forestry (MAFF). Former NPA officials, mainly drawn from the security police, have gained senior positions in the Defence Agency, the Defence Facility Agency, and the Imperial Household Agency. It thus appears that the security police has succeeded in carving out for itself a powerful position not only within the police but also within the security-related government ministries and agencies. After Masaharu Gotoda became the Deputy Secretary General in the Tanaka Cabinet in 1972, several former NPA bureaucrats became politicians in the 1970s and 1980s: Akira Hatano, Shizuka Kamei, Masaharu Gotoda, Kokichi Shimoinaba, Tsuruzo Kaieda, and Teibin Suzuki, among others, are prominent names that illustrate this trend [Jiyuhosodan, 1986, pp.232-53. Tahara, 1986b, Appendix].

This is a marked contrast to the 1950s and 1960s when the police remained relatively independent from politics. Since it has always been pragmatic in its approach and realistic in its expectations in dealing with other

Table 9: Personnel Transfer by Government Organization

A. Proportion of the Senior Bureaucrats in each ministry/agency who transferred from other ministries/agencies

100% - 67%		67% - 20%		20% - 5%		5% - 0%	
Land. Ag.	100	Imp. House Ag.	53	M. Health Welf.	17	MITI	3.3
Pub. Pollut. Com	100	AntiMon. Com	53	M. Home Aff.	14	M. of Constr.	3.1
Environ Ag.	97	Eco. Plan. Ag.	46	Defen. Ag.	12	M. of Transpt.	2.8
Manag. Ag.	77	Tax Ag.	33	MOFA	10	M. of Post. Telec.	2.3
PM's Off.	76	Hokkaido Ag.	28	Board of Audit	9	Police Ag.	1.7
Cabinet Secr.	72	Personnel/Auth.	22	MOJ	8	M.Ag.For.Fish	0.7
Fire Ag.	72	Prosecutors Off.	20	Def. Fac. Ag.	7	M. of Educ.	0.5
Okinawa Ag.	70			Supr. Court	6	Min. of Fin.	0.3
Science & Tech. Ag.	68			M. of Labor	5		

B. By type of organization

	100% - 67%	67% - 20%	20% - 5%	5% - 0%
PM's Agency	7	4	2	1
Ministry's Agency	1	2	0	0
Cabinet & Indpdt.	1	1	1	0
Ministry	0	0	5	7
Other	0	0	1	0

Source: Toyokeizai Shinposha 1985.

government agencies, the police does not make unnecessary enemies. This characteristic of the police dates in fact back to the prewar bureaucrats in the MOI [Inoguchi, 1989, p.109. Tahara, 1986b, pp.116-17]. In the words of Yutaka Arai "a <u>Naimukanryo</u> (bureaucrat in MOI) is always extremely pragmatic and flexible and has realistic expectations of how to achieve his stated objective whatever existing authorities and laws may stipulate. An outstanding example of these traits is Masaharu Gotoda, former Commissioner General of the NPA" [Tahara, 1986b, p.92].

In their relations with politicians the police also attempt to stress a role that appears to be apolitical at least on the surface. Two former Commissioners General of the NPA, for example, Kashimura (1958-1963) and Arai (1965-1969) took no strong stance towards a bill reviewing the Police Duties Execution Law that was initiated by Prime Minister Kishi in 1958. And for lack of manpower they could not take responsibility for maintaining law and order during the large-scale demonstrations against the revision of the US-Japan Security Treaty. In 1961 Kashimura refused to resign when politicians forced him to take the blame for several political assassinations [Suzuki, 1978, pp.105-19. Hogaku Semina, 1987, p. 340. Asahi, December 4, 1985]. But during the last two decades the police has lost its political distance to the core of the government. The increase in its political status is also a measure of an increasing police involvement in politics. However, Tahara quotes Gotoda who did so much to enhance the political standing of the police as arguing that "in comparison to the old [pre-war] police which was controlled by the central government, the police is now independent from politics." And in response to a question probing the strategic long-term thinking of former police bureaucrats about Japan's future, Gotoda argued, "if such strategic thinking exists at all among former high-ranking police officials, it certainly is a mistake . . . The police should adopt reactive tactics to achieve its purposes. Police tactics must be very different from military tactics; countermeasures are always the best option for the police" [Tahara, 1986b, p.28].

Besides the police there exist other institutions that deal with questions of internal security. They include the MOJ, Prosecutors Offices, the PSIA, and less importantly the Defence Agency and the Self Defense Forces. In addition, legally speaking, many other organizations listed in Figure 2 such as the Narcotics Control Division, the Marine Safety Agency and the Fire Agency also are involved peripherally with questions of internal security.

Compared to the situation in prewar Japan, the MOJ has lost most of its influence on questions of internal security. Questions of judicial administration are now handled by the judiciary branch and, with the exception of a few cases like political scandals, the investigation of crimes is now a police matter. The Special Investigation Division of the MOJ in Tokyo has a staff of only 32, and in Osaka of less than 10 [Asahi, Jan.14, 1988, evening]. But the Ministry's Criminal Affairs Bureau supervises and controls the work of the public prosecutors offices, and it operates the Ministry's Public Security Division as well as the International Division which was first created as a section in April 1978 and developed further in 1989.

The Public Prosecutors Offices investigate criminal cases. It has 8 High Offices, 50 District Offices, and 452 Local Offices all operating under the authority of the Supreme Public Prosecutor's Office. Each office has a unit dealing with internal security, employing a total of about 300 prosecutors and an additional staff of about 100 [Interview no.18, Tokyo, 1990]. The relationship between the Prosecutor's Office and the MOJ on the one hand and the NPA has not been a close one in the best of times and openly hostile in times of crisis. This was clearly evident in some of the most spectacular scandals of the postwar era such as the Shoden scandal in 1948 and the Lockheed scandal in 1976 [Tahara, 1979, pp. 263-282]. Since both the prosecutors and the police suspected the other one of leaking information to politicians, they tried as much as possible to conduct their investigations independently from one another. At other times, however, prosecutors and police have made quite effective deals, as for example, during the wiretapping scandal of the JCP in 1986-87 [Ogata, 1987. Asahi Journal, 1987a. Asahi Nenkan, 1989, p.125].

The wiretap was discovered in November 1986. In clear violation of the law some security policemen in Kanagawa prefecture had wiretapped the executive of the JCP. Although the Special Investigation Division in the Tokyo Prosecutors' Office accepted the evidence and examined it for eight months, it decided not to prosecute the policemen. Even after the Prosecution Examination Committee recommended prosecution at two separate occasions, the Prosecutors' Office continued to adhere to its position. Miyazawa's analysis of this case points to problems in the internal control over police operations as well as problems in the external supervision of the police by the public prosecutors and the courts. Shigeki Itoh, Prosecutor General at the time, said shortly before his death that in principle he shared the police perspective on the need for a vigorous policy of internal security, including the necessity for occasional wiretaps. His decision not to press charges in this case was influenced by a letter of top-level police officials promising not to engage in wiretapping in the future. Itoh was apparently very worried over the Prosecutor's Office ability to prevail over the police in this conflict. Furthermore, even if it did, how great would be the damage to the relations between the two organizations dealing with Japan's internal security [Miyazawa, 1989, pp.21-24]?

The PSIA is an external branch of the MOJ. It specializes in the investigation and surveillance of subversive organizations. It is the successor to the Special Investigation Bureau of the MOJ which was set up in 1949 to follow up on the GHQ Ordinance of the Regulation for Associations. Under direct supervision of the American occupation, this bureau investigated militarists and communists in an attempt to purge them from public office. Today the PSIA engages in counterespionage work and domestic surveillance. Since the establishment of the PSIA through the Subversive Activities Prevention Law public criticism of its anti-constitutional character has not ceased. The operation of the PSIA is rigidly constrained both by law and by a system of Public Security Commissions. The Law of Subversive Activity Prevention in 1952 has been applied in only eight cases; and only peripheral articles (Articles 38,39,40) were used. The central feature of the law, the prohibition of specific organizations and the regulation of their activities (Articles 5-9) has never been invoked. In 1952 it was used in four separate instances against JCP activists, all of whom had been acquitted by 1967. A group of right-wing activists were arrested in 1961 and some of them were convicted in 1970, although not based on crimes committed against this law. And between 1969 and 1971 the law was used to arrest several left-wing radicals. After prolonged court proceedings three members of Chukaku were finally convicted by the Supreme Court twenty years later in 1990 [Mainichi, September 29, 1990].

These legal restraints have apparently been sufficiently effective to restrict the PSIA exclusively to surveillance and research work. The organizations that are the subject of the PSIA's attention include among others on the Left the JCP, the General Federation of Korean Residents in Japan (Chosen Soren), Chukaku, JRA, and, less prominently and apparently for reasons of political balance, a number of organizations on the Right [Asahi, 1978, p.264]. The emphasis of the PSIA surveillance can perhaps be inferred from its own publications. In the 1989 annual report the JCP was discussed in five chapters, the Federation of Korean Residents in two, left-wing radicals in two, the JRA in one, and right-wing radicals in one. The USSR was referred to in four chapters, China in four, North Korea in two, Eastern Europe in one, and international terrorism in one [Koan Chosa Cho, 1990].

For historical reasons the PSIA lacks the authority to initiate investigations. In 1952 the police and some important politicians blocked the attempt to grant the PSIA the authority of initiating prosecutions under the provisions of the Subversive Activity Prevention Law [Ishimura, 1988, p.117]. Therefore the PISA seeks the cooperation of individuals it suspects by providing economic incentives designed to exploit the financial difficulties individuals may have [Asahi, 1978, pp.266-67; Richelson, 1988, pp.263-64]. Despite the change in political strategy which the JCP and Korean Federation adopted in 1955, and especially after 1964, the surveillance of these two organizations has remained unchanged. In some quarters this has raised questions about the raison d'etre of the PSIA. The Agency's attention appears to be frozen on questions of anti-Communism, both at home and abroad, which topped the agenda in the late 1940s and early 1950s when it first started operating but which appear to be rapidly less important in contemporary politics.

The agency began in 1952 with a relatively large budget of 480 million yen and a staff of 1,702 employees [Nihon Kingendai-shi Jiten, 1978, p.189]. It grew moderately until it reached its peak in 1973 with 2,019 employees and a budget of 5,374 million yen [Asahi, 1978, p.276. Ishimura, 1988, p.119]. Since then, the PSIA has actually shrunk after the government imposed in 1984 a ten percent reduction in the Agency's overall expenses and downgraded its local investigation bureaus at the prefectural level [Rinoho/GyokaKushin OB-Kai, 1987]. As a result, personnel was cut by 143 to 1,849 employees. In response the Agency organized a special lobbying effort in the LDP without any apparent result [Interview no. 14, Tokyo, May 17, 1990. JCP, 1988, p.132].

The PSIA shares with the NPA and the MPD in the surveillance of radicals. However, in contrast to the general pattern of effective information exchange on questions of internal security mentioned above, relations between the PSIA and the police do not appear to be close. The MOJ reached an agreement with the NPA in 1969 to enhance cooperation by providing three senior posts in the PSIA for members of the NPA [Yoshihara, 1976, p.93]. But the PSIA and the MOJ do not have posts in the NPA. This experiment has apparently not been successful [Interview no.14, Tokyo, May 17, 1990]. An exception was the Daibosatsutoge operation in 1969 when, based on information provided by the PSIA, the MPD was able to arrest at one time about 50 cadre members of the Red Army [Interview no.12, Tokyo, May 16, 1990]. But in the last two deacdes the PSIA has evidently lost a lot of ground. In the 1950s it still enjoyed some superiority over the MPD and other agencies working on internal security. But since the 1970s the police has pushed the PSIA to the political periphery. The MPD, in particular, clearly surpassed the PSIA by doubling its staff size working on internal security and new left radicals to a reported 450-600 in 1986, out of an estimated total staff of 2,000 investigation security police officers in Japan [Mainichi, June 19, 1986 Yomiuri, June 19, 1986].

The Defence Agency and the three armed forces are also to some extent involved in internal security issues [Mendel, 1975, p.157. Sigur, 1975, p.193. Endicott, 1975, pp.448,450]. The reason is historical. "The Japanese government has seen its defense policy and its armed forces as a means of countering both internal and external threats to national security" [Weinstein, 1975, p.57]. Prime Minister Yoshida's plan for the Japanese military was to make it strong enough to assure Japan's internal security against any potential threat of a Communist subversion or insurrection. The United States on the other hand was to assure Japan's external security. When the bulk of American forces stationed in Japan were moved to Korea in July 1950, at the outset of the Korean war, General MacArthur overcame his long-standing opposition to a Japanese military and authorized the Japanese government to establish the 75,000-man National Police Reserve which was subsequently expanded in the spring of 1952, when the Peace Treaty and the Security Treaty came into effect, into the National Safety Agency, composed of a force of more than 100,000 men.

Because of the prohibition of military force in Article 9 of the "Peace Constitution", until 1954 the Japanese Government had disguised its military as a kind of police force [Otake, 1988]. In 1954 Prime Minister Yoshida pushed the Diet to adopt the Defense Agency Establishment Law and the Self-Defense Forces Law. At that time the SDF numbered in excess of 140,000 men and were adequately armed to defend Japan's internal security throughout the 1950s and 1960s. As late as 1968 only four of the thirteen divisions of the Ground Self-Defense Forces were deployed in Hokkaido, the most likely point of a Soviet attack. The remaining nine divisions were all stationed close to major metropolitan areas and industrial districts on the heavily populated islands of Honshu and Kyushu, in easy striking distance to contain any possible internal threat. In the early 1970s a substantial minority of 20 percent of the Japanese public explicitly acknowledged this strategic mission of the Self Defense Forces in a number of opinion surveys [Weinstein, 1971, pp.106-09,117-121. Mendel, 1975, p.163].

Defense Law nos. 78,79 and 81 provide the legal basis for relying on the SDF for maintaining law and order. In the 1950s the Defense Agency and the National Safety Commission reached several practical agreements to prepare for that eventuality. However, even at the height of the demonstrations against the Security Treaty in May 1960, with Prime Minister Kishi pushing strongly for the use of the military, the opposition of the Director General of Defense, Akagi, chairperson of the National Safety Committee, Ishihara, and Commissioner General Kashimura of the NPA to the deployment of military force was too strong [Tominomori, 1977, pp. 106-107. Goto et al., 1982, p.183. Interview nos.15 and 17, Tokyo, May 17, 1990. Hori, 1983 p.37. Yomiuri, 1986, p.208]. The issue has remained sensitive to this day. As a carefully calculated show of strength at a time of mass political mobilization, the Self Defense Forces demonstrated in public some of their exercises for emergency interventions in domestic affairs in October 1969. But in normal times both the Defense Agency and the NPA are reluctant to train in public [Asahi, 1971, p.301. Interview no.15, Tokyo, May 17, 1990].

The Defense Agency as well as the three armed forces have research divisions responsible for intelligence affecting Japan's national defense. Among the relevant organizations, the Second Section's Annex Chamber of the Investigation Division in the Self-Defense Ground Forces (Chobetsu) in particular should be recognized for its relatively large size and strategic position in connecting the Cabinet Research Office with the NPA. Apart from the three divisions in the three armed forces specializing in military intelligence, the Self-Defence Ground Forces also collect and interpret military intelligence. They employ a staff of approximately 1,000, with 480 in Ground Forces, 190 in the Maritime Forces, 230 in the Air Force, as well as 50 civilians; all are recruited from the Defence Agency and the three armed forces. The Director, however, is drawn from the NPA even though he has the title of Cabinet Researcher. The Chobetsu is thus directly responsible to the Cabinet Information Research Office, whose directors also come from the NPA [Richelson, 1988, p.256. Deacon, 1982, pp.241-42. Asahi, 1978, p.269].

The Japanese military is no serious competitor for the police. In fact "many 'civilian' staff members of the National Self-Defence Agency, which has the same status as a ministry, are former policemen" [Van Wolferen, 1989, p.200]. Ex-police bureaucrats have often occupied the post of the Chief Secretary, the Director General of the Personnel Affairs Bureau, the Director of the Education Affairs Bureau, and the Director of the Research Division [Hirose, 1989, pp.83,87-90, Appendix pp.5-6]. And some of them like the incumbent, Tomoji Yoda, reached the highest bureaucratic post of the Agency, Deputy Director General.

The organizations dealing with the internal security of Japan have changed in their relative importance. This shift can be observed both quantatively and qualitatively. Table 10 shows that since 1955 the police force at the prefectual level has increased by a factor of 1.6 or 88,000 policemen. The Defence Forces increased by a factor of 1.4 or a gain of 69,000. The PSIA increased by the factor of 1.1, or 173 security officers.

Budgetary data (Table 11) reveal a similar trend. The total police budget combining the NPA and the prefectual police budget indicates a 3.9 increase during the last three decades (1955-88), larger than that of the Defence Forces (2.6) and the PSIA (1.6).

The relative size of police and military forces since 1945 has been very different from that of pre-war Japan. The police has clearly gained compared to the military. And the police has been successful in keeping other organizations away from internal security policy issues. The major resources of the security police have been concentrated in the MPD. And through its authority over staffing the NPA has controlled all prefectual police forces.

Over the years the changing importance of the issue of internal security has been reflected in the budget allocations which Japan's police has received. Three indicators can be used for such an analysis: the total police budget, the annual growth rates of the police budget, and, finally, the MPD's and the NPA's proportions of the budget (Table 12).

A comparison of annual growth rates of the police budget and the general account budget demonstrates that the police was favored in its budget

Table 10: Strength of Police and Military Force in Japan
1877–1988

	Police (A) National	(B) Tokyo (MPD)	Kempei (C) (Mil. Police)	Military (D) (Army/Navy)
1877	26,640			
1887	28,557			
1897	29,976		5,070	162,000
1907	38,640		2,094	263,000
1916	45,761	6,000	6,578	279,000
1926	58,796	12,000	2,837	255,000
1935	66,578		2,847	323,000
1940	85,580		–	1,463,000
1945	93,913		23,000	8,090,000

	(E) National (prefectural)[1]	(F) Tokyo (MPD)[4]	(G) PSIA	(H) Defense Forces[5]	(I) Cab Res Off[6]
1955	118,700	–	1,637	178,234	36
1960	131,930	27,050 [2]	1,643	205,894	69
1965	147,410	34,340 [3]	1,923	225,373	78
1970	175,350	37,490	1,979	235,803	81
1975	195,000	40,210	2,009	237,837	91
1980	210,600	41,012	1,982	241,874	95
1985	215,870	41,065	1,938	245,292	100
1988	219,679	41,312	1,810	247,131	84

Notes: [1]The numbers count only prefectural policemen. The total numbers including NPA and civilian officials in the prefectural police were in 1975=232,700; in 1980=248,400; in 1985=253,631; and in 1988=257,296.

[2]1961.

[3]1967.

[4]The total numbers including civilian officials were in 1967=37,410; in 1970=40,600; in 1975=43,357; in 1980=44,075; in 1985=43,966; and in 1988=44,213.

[5]Actual rather than authorized manpower.

[6]1955–85: Cabinet Research Office; 1988: Cabinet Information Research Office.

Source: (A) Taikakai, 1970 vol. 2 pp. 625–626. (B) Obinata, 1987, p. 153. (C) (D) Ishimura, 1988, p. 108. (E) Keisatsucho 1977b, Keisatsu Hakusho. (F) Toyko-to. (G) Ishimura, 1988, p. 108; Somucho, 1988. (H) Higuchi, n.d., p. 134. (I) Ishimura, 1988, p. 108; Somucho, 1988.

Table 11: Budget Size Comparison of Police, PSIA, Defense, and Cabinet (1955-1987)

	(A) Police		(B) PSIA		(C) Defense		A:B:C	(D) Cabinet	
	mill.	index	mill.	index	mill.	index		mill.	index
1955	61393	100	802	100	132765	100	100:1.2:216	382	100
1957	68779	112	1001	125	141165	106	100:1.5:205	785	205
1959	78930	129	1226	153	153318	115	100:1.6:194	962	252
1961	106453	173			180924	136	100: - :170	1261	330
1963	153763	250	1890	236	247550	186	100:1.2:161	1644	430
1965	198533	323	2490	310	301415	227	100:1.3:152	1861	487
1967	261560	426	2834	353	387045	292	100:1.1:148	2562	671
1969	352430	574	3333	416	494941	372	100:0.9:140	3062	802
1971	508594	828	4337	540	693511	522	100:0.9:136	3567	934
1973	753408	1227	5374	670	979047	737	100:0.7:130	5177	1355
1975	1056482	1721	8025	1000	1367425	1030	100:0.8:129	7065	1849
1977	1387221	2260	9325	1163	1699265	1280	100:0.7:122	8403	2200
1979	1649922	2687	10293	1283	2092616	1576	100:0.6:127	9418	2465
1981	1909387	3110	11232	1400	2429053	1830	100:0.6:127	10031	2626
1983	1996586	3252	11833	1475	2761039	2079	100:0.6:138	10370	2715
1985	2133425	3475	12401	1546	3169684	2387	100:0.6:149	11449	2977
1987	2372345	3864	13205	1646	3507832	2642	100:0.6:148	12076	3161

Notes & Sources: (A) The numbers are based on the revised budgets. Keisatsucho 1977b, Keisatsu Hakusho 1973-89. (B) Ishimura 1988, 1991. (C) (D) The numbers are based on final accounts. Okurasho 1989.

Table 12: Changes in Police Budget (1955-1988)							
	(A)	(B)	(C)	(D)	(E)	(F)	(G)
	Total Police Budget (NPA & Prefectural Police Forces) (adjusted) (mill. yen)	Index (1955 = 100)	Annual Growth Rate of (A) %	Annual Growth Rate of NG Account	Prop. of MPD in (A) %	Prop. of NPA in (A) %	Police Budget Costs per capita (Yen)
1955	61,393	100				18.2	696
'56	63,868	104	4.0	7.5		18.1	715
'57	68,779	112	7.7	9.0		17.7	763
'58	73,211	119	6.4	12.5		17.5	805
'59	78,930	129	7.8	13.4		17.3	860
'60	91,571	149	16.0	16.7		15.9	988
'61	106,453	173	16.3	19.4		14.6	1,140
'62	125,483	205	17.9	21.6		13.4	1,331
'63	153,763	250	22.5	19.3		13.5	1,615
'64	178,537	291	16.1	9.3		12.7	1,857
'65	198,533	323	11.2	12.1		12.5	2,043
'66	225,274	367	13.5	19.5		12.3	2,292
'67	261,560	426	16.1	16.2	18.2	12.1	2,641
'68	299,451	488	14.5	13.7	18.2	11.4	2,989
'69	352,430	574	17.7	17.1	17.9	11.1	3,498
'70	436,124	710	23.7	18.5	17.5	10.2	4,253
'71	508,594	828	16.6	17.6	17.8	10.0	4,904
'72	605,243	986	19.0	25.5	16.9	9.5	5,597
'73	753,408	1227	24.5	26.0	16.2	9.0	7,002
'74	1,000,156	1629	32.8	25.7	15.7	8.0	9,167
'75	1,056,482	1721	5.6	8.5	18.7	8.6	9,555
'76	1,246,947	2031	18.0	18.3	17.1	8.1	11,139
'77	1,387,221	2260	11.2	19.1	16.9	8.1	12,266
'78	1,503,561	2449	8.4	17.4	17.0	8.5	13,170
'79	1,649,922	2687	9.7	15.2	17.1	8.9	14,323
'80	1,789,267	2914	8.4	10.1	16.9	8.3	15,404
'81	1,909,387	3110	6.7	7.9	16.8	8.1	16,311
'82	1,956,046	3186	2.4	0.9	17.8	8.0	16,600
'83	1,996,586	3252	2.1	6.9	17.7	7.8	16,800
'84	2,058,620	3353	3.1	1.3	17.6	7.6	17,300
'85	2,133,425	3475	3.6	3.3	17.7	7.6	17,800
'86	2,247,014	3660	5.3	1.1	17.3	7.5	17,900
'87	2,372,345	3864	5.6	8.2	17.0	7.5	17,900
'88	2,443,970	3981	3.0	6.2	17.4	7.4	19,900

Source: Keisatsucho, 1973-89, 1977b; Okurasho 1989; Tokyo-to, 1968-89.

allocations in the early 1960s (1963-1965), the late 1960s (1967-1971), the mid-1970s (1974, 1976), and the mid-1980s (1982, 1984-1986). Concurrently during these years, the MPD's share of the total police budget exceeded its average share between 1967 and 1988. The share of the NPA which, because of the fixed number of positions at the NPA normally tends to decrease, increased in the mid-1970s and mid-1980s. Only in the years 1978-1979 did the MPD's and NPA's proportions both increase because of security measures undertaken to counter the Narita airport movement and left-wing radicals; for example, 1,500 members of the police guards deployed around Narita since 1978 are financed by the NPA as were police preparations for the first Tokyo summit in 1979.

The exceptional budget growth in the first period (1963-1965) is probably the only one that can be explained with factors other than those directly relating to internal security. At that time the modernization of the police made costly infrastructure reforms necessary: a new telephone system, new buildings, new computers, and new automobiles. Furthermore, the "civil police" was strengthened through additions to the transportation police (10,000 men in 1963-64), the criminal investigation police (5,000 men in 1964-65), and the patrol police (18,000 men in 1966-68) [Keisatsucho, 1977, pp. 501-503, 552-553].

The second period (1967-1971) of an expanding police budget coincided with mass demonstrations and widespread rioting by students and New Left radicals. While official figures record a tripling in the size of the riot police from 5,000 to 15,000, because other police forces were transferred to the riot police in times of crisis, the fully mobilized police force against mass demonstrations was widely reported to have approached 100,000 men. And substantial funds were spent on the facilities and activities of the riot police (See Table 7) [Keisatsucho, 1977b, p.553. Hironaka, 1973, p.310. Asahi Nenkan, 1970, p.304, Tahara, 1986b, p.160].

The third period (1974-76) brought, in the wake of the "oil shock" and various budget anomalies, a rise of police budgets to cope with the first big wave of major public events such as President Ford's visit in 1974, Queen Elizabeth II's visit in 1975, the Emperor's visit to the United States in 1975, and the Emperor's 50th anniversary in 1976. And an expansion and modernization of the computer system of the police also was very costly [Keisatucho, 1977b, pp.504-06, 1976, pp. 296-297].

Finally, despite the administrative reform movement and a policy of fiscal austerity, police budgets, especially those of the MPD, expanded in the mid-1980s. This was in anticipation of a series of major public events requiring special security precautions after 1984. New technological equipment was introduced, including a blimp, 5,000 hand-held radio-telegraphs, 50 video monitors, 1,000 patrol cars equipped with computers, a computerized police activity display system, and an automatic license plate reader. In addition to other normal budget items, additional reserve funds of the government were spent on security programs: in 1984 3,048 million yen (including 788 million yen for President Chun's visit), in 1985 7,031 million yen, and in 1986 6,739 million yen. By way of contrast, in 1979 only 423 million yen were spent on security measures taken during the summit meeting [Keisatsucho, 1985, 1986, 1987. Ashahi Nenkan, 1985, 1986, 1987, p.129; Japan Socialist Party 1985, 1986, 1987].

As these figures illustrate, over time the police has done very well in fighting for scarce resources within the bureaucracy, much better, for example, than the MOFA or the MOJ. The bureaucratic balance of power has changed, especially among the organizations dealing with internal security. The police has moved closer to the center of power in the government. The NPA, and possibly the MOHA have arguably increased their power, to some extent at the expense such important economic Ministries as the MOF and the MITI, and also in comparison to left-wing, progressive prefectural governments. Since the late 1970s many governors of major metropolitan areas have been defeated and have been replaced by office-holders many of whom had held important bureaucratic positions in the MOHA. Under Prime Minister Nakasone, himself originally an Inspector in the MPD, many former police bureaucrats who entered politics have been given important offices. From this vantage point the 1970s and 1980s appears to some as "the age of police bureaucrats or new Naimu (MOI) bureaucrats" [Tahara, 1986b]. Over time it has been the police rather than a revived MOHA that has created a link between the cabinet and politics. This key role of the police is evidence for a qualitative increase in police power.

The Cabinet in postwar Japan has no analogue to the powerful MOI which was in charge of police and other matters in prewar Japan. None of the government agencies dealing with questions of security have any direct representatives in the Cabinet. The chairperson of the National Public Safety Commission which supervises the NPA normally serves concurrently as Minister of Home Affairs and attends Cabinet meetings as a matter of course; but the head of the NPA does not. This practice was started in July 1960 when, what had formerly been an Agency for Home Affairs, was upgraded to a ministerial status. At the height of the mass protest in the late 1960s and early 1970s it was a sign of great political urgency that a minister was appointed (between November 30, 1968 and July 7, 1972) as chair of the National Public Safety Commission while holding no other office. The relative unimportance of the Chairmanship of the National Public Safety Commission on its own was reflected in the facetious remark of Takeo Kimura who observed in 1972 that since all Chairs had been considered as second-class politicians, he was given the post of Minister of Construction as a bribe [Asahi Nenkan, 1973, p.284. Suzuki, 1980, p.234]. The PSIA and the

Maritime Safety Agency are also represented only indirectly, respectively, by the Minister of Justice and the Minister of Transport. Those who hold the position of Director General of the Defence Agency can attend the Cabinet meetings but not in their capacity as Director General but only as a Minister of State. Like other agencies operating under the Prime Minister's office, the Prime Minister himself legally represents the Public Safety Commission as well as the Defence Agency.

In contrast to its relatively weak formal position the NPA has succeeded in gaining substantial power in the Cabinet Secretariat, normally the center of power of Japanese politics. After Prime Minister Ikeda was attacked in 1961 high-ranking police officers have held one of the Prime Minister's four secretary positions as well as one of the three secretaries of the Chief Cabinet Secretary (See Table 14) [Yomiuri, 1986, p.180. Nikkei, February 4, 1990. Nishio, 1984, p.164. Toyokeizai, 1986-1990]. In other words the police made up for its weak representation in the Cabinet through its direct presence at two of the most important centers of Japanese politics.

Before the reform of the Secretariat in July 1986, there had been four offices: the Cabinet Counsellors' Office with 5 officials, established in 1957; the Cabinet Councillors' Office with 46 officials charged with drafting position papers, also established in 1957; the Cabinet Research Office with 84 officials, established in 1957; and finally the Cabinet Public Relation Office with 48 officials, established in 1973 [Sentaku, 1986, p.127]. In the period before 1986 the NPA had held two chief positions in Research and Public Relations; in addition the NPA provided a significant amount of staff support to these offices. In 1971, for example, police officers held 27 positions which then represented more than one fourth of the total number of staff position of the Cabinet Secretariat [Matsuhashi, 1984, p.335]. Over time, as the number of police officers delegated to the Cabinet Secretariat increased, the political status of the police has also grown. In September 1984, for example, it was a high-ranking police official who was appointed as Chief of the Office for Crisis Management and Other Special Affairs [Nishio, 1984, p.163].

Rincho or the Provisional Committee on Administrative Reform (1981-83) and one of its main successor organizations, Gyokakushin or the Provisional Advisory Council for Promoting Administrative Reform (the 1st, 1983-86) implemented drastic administrative reforms, including substantial cuts in personnel and budgets. But the police has been exceptionally successful in avoiding being targeted. By contrast almost all other government bureaucracies suffered substantial cuts in their budgets. In the many reports issued by Rincho and Gyokakushin the police was mentioned only once -- three lines in the report on local administrative reform in July 1984 [Rincho/Gyokakushin OB-kai, 1987, pp.434-36]. In fact the police managed to strengthen its organization during this decade of administrative reform. In emphasizing the need for strengthening the cabinet's ability for comprehensive adjustment the report referred, among others, specifically to the increasing danger of terrorism and violent social protests; this became a weapon for the police in defending itself against the reform [Rincho/Gyokakushin OB-kai, 1987, p.514]. In addition it should be noted that two high-ranking former police bureaucrats -- Masaharu Gotoda (Chief Cabinet Secretary 1982-83 and 1985-87; Director-General of the Management and Coordination Agency 1983-85) and Hiromori Kawashima (Rincho: Counselor, Gyokakushin: the 1st Chief Examiner in three sub-committees) served in pivotal political positions [Rincho/Gyokakushin OB-kai, 1987, pp.838-43]. Eventually this report on the cabinet reform led in 1986 to the reorganization of the Cabinet Secretariat.

Among those following Japanese politics closely, the reorganization of the Cabinet Secretariat was widely interpreted as a sign of increasing police power and a check on the power of the MOF in the Cabinet [Sentaku, 1986. Tahara 1986b, pp.107-109]. The reorganization of the Cabinet Secretariat in July 1986 resulted in an increase of the original four offices to six. But the new organizational set-up includes not only the addition of two offices and the granting of greater autonomy to a third office, with the Cabinet Councillors' Office on External Affaris, the Cabinet Councillors' Office on Internal Affairs and the Cabinet Security Affairs Office, which previously had been part of the National Security Council, employing, respectively, 19, 46 and 24 new staff members. This reorganization further increased the political power of the NPA. In addition to retaining the power of staffing two of the most important positions in the Cabinet Secretariat, the NPA now also staffs the position of the Chief of the Security Office [Angel, 1990, pp.56-57. Sentaku, 1986. Toyokeizai 1986-1990].

The reorganization of the Cabinet Secretariat also established a new Standing Committee for Information Exchange at the level of the cabinet, particularly in periods of crisis management. The new committee holds private, monthly meetings involving the Deputy Chief Cabinet Secretary General (Chair), the Chief of the Cabinet Information Research Office, the Chief of the Cabinet Security Office, the Director of the Security Bureau of NPA, the Deputy of PSIA, and the Deputy Director of Information Research Bureau in the MOFA. The chair of this new committee was held by officials of the NPA or other successor Ministers of MOI. In a government in which agencies hoard information and guard it jealously, this is the only committee in which a substantial exchange of sensitive intelligence information appears to occur [Interview no.15, Tokyo, May 17, 1990]. But the effectiveness of the new committee, proven to many in the preparation for the possibility of terrorist attacks during the the Seoul Olympics in 1988 and the funeral of the Emperor in 1989, depends largely upon the leadership of the Chief Cabinet Secretary [Interview no.15, Tokyo, May 17, 1990].

It is the responsibility of the Cabinet Information Research Office, formerly the Research Office, to integrate different sources of information and to provide the government with a systematic analysis on strategic issues. In 1987 the Office was staffed by officials from a variety of ministries including MOFA, the Defense Agency, MOF, MITI, MOAFF, the Ministry of Labor (MOL), and MOJ. Around 1970 it had 100 staff members including about 30 "loaned" officials from other ministries, and in 1978 its staff had increased to 154 including 70 "loaned" officials. One 1987 estimate gave a figure of 94 staff members. The Office typically works with several other government-affiliated organizations. For example, in 1971 one third of the 200 persons loaned to the Cabinet Secretariat from six affiliated organizations was transferred temporarily to the Office [Richelson, 1988, p.254. Matsuashi, 1984, p.335. Asahi Nenkan, 1978, p.271]. Here, too, the NPA holds a prominent position. In 1987 15 of the 28 senior research officials of the Cabinet Information Research Office came from the NPA: eight from the Security Bureau, four from the Police Affairs Bureau, and three from other NPA bureaus [JCP, 1988, p.132].

The reorganization of 1986 extended also to the National Security Council. The Council was spun off from the National Defence Council, a relatively passive organization holding only an average of 2.3 sessions a year in the 1950s and 1960s which were restricted to the review of issues of external security [Hirose, 1989, p.56]. Because its authority was grounded in legislation establishing the Defence Agency, the National Defence Council was ineffective on questions of internal security over which it had no jurisdiction. The government tried to change the de facto operation of the National Defence Council in 1972 by including members such as the Chairperson of the Naional Safety Commission, the Minister of MITI, and the Secretary General of the Science and Technology Agency [Yomiuri, October 11, 1972. Hirose, 1989, p.54]. The new Council now has the authority to discuss questions of internal security. It thus further bolsters the political standing of the police. However, with few exceptions, such as the Seoul Olympics, it still appears to focus its work largely on questions of external security [Interview no.15, Tokyo, May 17, 1990].

The National Security Council and the Committee for Information Exchange are the only standing committees in the Cabinet that can review issues of internal security. Other committees hold meetings on an ad hoc basis, such as the Headquarters for the Prevention of Hijacking and Other Inhumane Violence. The Headquarters were first organized as a liaison committee in the Prime Minister's Office in August 1973. Its position was subsequently strengthened in October 1977 when it was charged to integrate relevant policy issues falling into the jurisdiction of different ministries and agencies. The Headquarters has eleven members: the Chief Cabinet Secretary, the Minister of Justice, the Minister for Foreign Affairs, the Minister of

Finance, the Minister of Transport, the Chair of the National Public Safety Commission, the Commissioner-General of the Cabinet Legislation Bureau, the Deputy Chief Cabinet Secretary (Parliamentary Affairs), the Deputy Chief Cabinet Secretary (Administrative Affairs), the Director-General of the NPA, and the Director-General of the Maritime Safety Agency. Below these top-level political representatives two groups (the Intergovernmental Group for Crisis Management, Director-General Level and the Intergovernmental Group for Crisis Management, Director Level) staffed from the same ministries and agencies, deals with specific, practical topics in greater detail. But the meetings of these groups and the Headquarters are ad hoc in coping with particular emergency situations [Interview nos. 12, 15, and 18, Tokyo, May 16, 17, and 18, 1990]. Moreover, many observers would still argue that despite the creation of new offices and standing committees in the Cabinet, in the words of one official, "there are no intelligence agencies in Japan" [Interview no.12, Tokyo, May 16, 1990].

This fact makes even more important the central positions that the NPA in particular has succeeded in habitually staffing in the Cabinet Secretariat. Although internal security questions do not figure importantly at the Cabinet level, the NPA has succeeded in the 1980s to increase its political power substantially in the Cabinet Secretariat. The ranking of different ministries and agencies among the graduates of the Law Faculty of Tokyo University, an annual contest of the status and power of organizations as well as of the abilities of individuals, confirms this assessment. The NPA was not able to recruit a career staff on its own until 1965. At that time it was ranked lowest among all ministries and agencies. But in the 1980s the NPA was able to hire about 20 of the new graduates, the same number that was attracted to the other major ministries. And together with the traditionally powerful MOF and MITI it was ranked among the top three ministries [Yomiuri, 1986, pp.83-90. Inoguchi, 1989, pp.108-109]. This is telling testimony of the growing political importance of the police in Japanese politics.

3B. Police and Society

Japan's relatively centralized system of police administration operates with a remarkable degree of openness towards Japanese society. In its relations with society the police has continuously emphasized its responsiveness to social needs through using key concepts such as the term for the good local governor in ancient China or people's shepherd (bokuminkan); winning the hearts of the people (zinshin-shoaku); and, in Akira Hatano's terminology, grass roots bureaucracy (kusano-ne Kanryo-shugi). Even in the 1980s the key word describing the recruitement and promotion of police personnel is zinshin-shoaku. For all members of the police contacts with individual citizens, civic associations, and reporters are very important [Taikakai, 1971, vol.1, pp.680-91; 1970, vol.2, pp.260-61,273-74. Tahara, 1986b, p.56. Inoguchi, 1989, pp.108-09. Kaneko, et. al 1987]. A 1984 public opinion survey revealed that almost one half of the respondents had been in direct contact with the police during the preceding year [Table 13,(2). Yomiuri, November 25, 1984]. Furthermore, the importance of police contacts with the public has probably increased over time [Sassa, 1984, vol. 1, pp.52-53].

The presence of the police in society is pervasive, unofficial and low-key [Bayley, 1978, pp.46-47]. "Police penetration of the community in Japan is more routine and personal than in the United States and it is more active in ways unrelated to law enforcement . . . In Japan private persons are mobilized in explicit ways to assist policemen in the performance of their duties, creating a cooperative relationship between police and public that is unknown, if not unthinkable, in the United States" [Bayley, 1978, p.91]. Indeed the vaunted effectiveness of the Japanese police system would probably be much smaller without the cooperation of some members of society (local businessmen and the old), often cultivated and organized under state auspices, and the acquiescence with which most citizens tolerate the extensive efforts of the police to gather as much information as possible through a variety of institutions and political practices [Clifford, 1976, pp.97-109]. The social service orientation that the police projects, and to some extent practices, is in fact a thinly disguised effort to create a favorable public climate in which continuous police surveillance is socially accepted and in which active cooperation with the police, in times of need, becomes a normal social practice. The police works hard to win the public's trust through constructing a reciprocal relationship.

The strength of communal bonds and traditions which Bayley stresses may account for some of the public's acquiescence in and support of the police information gathering practices. Equally significant though are the individual incentives which police discretion creates for individual cooperation, as Ames points out in his study. For example, the police use a lax effort of punishing traffic violations as an instrument to create such incentives and a favorable climate of opinion [Bayley, 1978. Ames, 1981. Interview, November 12, Tokyo, January 18, 1991]. Michael Hechter has come to a similar conclusion. The small-group structure of Japanese society as well as its homogeneity create a dependence of Japanese citizens on their social system, or what Hechter calls "control economies", that is greater than that found in other industrial societies [Hechter, 1987a, 1987b]. Furthermore, this convergence of solidaristic and individualistic incentives for the public's cooperation with the police occurs in a distinctive social setting. "A large part of the explanation for Japan's success in holding down the incidence of serious crime lies with that society's ability to maintain effective small-group interaction despite its population's predominantly urban concentration . . . In fact, each member of Japanese society is under a kind of group surveillance to make sure that he or she will measure up to required standards . . .

Literally, the individual in Japan is caught up in a web of expectations to conform and not to bring shame to his family, friends, and/or associates at work" [Shain, 1984, pp.226-27]. Walter Ames draws a similar conclusion. "The public is actively involved, because the demarcation between citizens and official police authority in law enforcement is not sharp . . . Japanese society, in effect, polices itself" [Ames, 1981, p.228. Mizoguchi, 1986].

The link between the police and Japanese society is the local police box which is called koban or hashutujo (if it has no residence attached to it) and chuzaisho (if it does) [Bayley, 1978, pp.13-32 and 1984. Ames, 1981, pp.17-55. Fukunaga, 1988, pp.43-46,68-69. Parker, 1984, pp.44-98. Clifford, 1976, pp.79-80. Kühne and Miyazawa, 1979, pp.125-131. Mizumachi, 1982. Inami, 1987b]. This system of policing has elicited different evaluations. In his sympathetic treatment David Bayley dubs the police as "the most pervasive government agency in society" [Bayley, 1978, p.87]. Karel van Wolferen in a more critical vein calls the koban system "the friendly neighborhood police state" [Van Wolferen, 1989, p.184].

Policemen stationed in police boxes account for 40 percent of the total police force and are involved in clearing up 70 percent of the total number of crimes committed each year. The area covered by patrol policemen ranges from less than one square kilometer to more than one hundred and thirty; the size of the ppopulation covered also varies from a few hundred to almost 20,000 [Fukunaga, 1988, pp.36,75]. With Japan's growing urbanization during the 20th century the number of rural police boxes has declined, from about 13,000 at the eve of World War I to about 10,000 in the early 1970s and 9,000 in 1987 [Ames, 1981, p.23. Bayley, 1978, p.13. National Police Agency, 1987b, p.26]. Rural police officers spend much of their time visiting with the people living in their jurisdiction and often socializing with them. They rely largely on their intimate personal knowledge rather than on the formal police records that they gather during their periodic house calls. "This extensive personal knowledge and the ability to elicit information from key village informants when necessary is the essence of the closeness to the community that is considered an ideal by the police" [Ames, 1981, p.27]. Typically rural police officers enjoy the respect of the general population and work closely with the social elites of the communities they serve.

In urban areas Japanese policemen also draw on information gathered through an extensive personal knowledge of their districts. Between 1913 and the early 1970s the number of koban more than doubled to about 5,800. By 1987 that figure had increased further to about 6,000 [Ames, 1981, p.23. Bayley, 1978, p.13. National Police Agency, 1987b, p.26]. The local police box is an adaptation of Japan's rural policing system to an urban setting. It "facilitates police closeness to the community by allowing a constant police presence at the neighborhood level" [Ames, 1981, p.34]. It is no accident that local police boxes, like elementary schools, are still frequently referred to by their old village names that have evolved into modern urban districts even though those names are no longer otherwise used today. "The significance is that the police rely on the long-established cooperation between households in the former villages for crime prevention and investigations. The local police box, like the elementary school, thus becomes a hub of traditional village solidarity and identity in a modern urban context" [Ames, 1981, pp.36-37].

The ubiquitous police box is a listening post for the police. "In order to function successfully as a koban patrolman, one ability above all others needs to be cultivated -- the art of patient listening . . . Listening is often an end in itself; it makes no contribution to further action on the part of the policeman or the private individual" [Bayley, 1978, p.21]. But it does breed a familiarity and trust between police and society that was largely lacking before 1945. And thus it creates an essential precondition for the effectiveness of the Japanese police. Opinion surveys in the 1980s revealed that more than 80 percent of the respondents knew the location of the police box in their neighborhood, and one third knew the policemen personally. In addition 80 percent of the respondents were ready to volunteer any information they might have about a crime (Table 13(1),(6)).

Since most streets are unnamed and houses are numbered in the order in which they were constructed, the most important function of the koban is to provide information to people about locations and addresses -- and thus to be able to informally survey the population on a continuing basis. In fact the koban is also an all-purpose source of help [Bayley, 1978, pp.15,27]. Bayley's rich description illustrates the range of personal help and social services it occasionally offers: providing an open ear, personal counsel or mediation services to individuals in distress involving, for example, marriage, money or a variety of practical problems; loaning money to people who overspend so that they can travel home (with a return rate of money lent reportedly as high as 70-80 percent); arranging for suitable hotel accommodations for strangers in the neighborhood; providing warm water for baby bottles and candy for youngsters; and generally looking not only over but often also after those at the bottom of Japanese society with whom the police has inevitably much contact [Bayley, 1978, pp.21,27,28-31. Ames, 1981, pp.74-76. National Police Agency, 1982, pp.40-43]. In this context, it is worth noting that the police has promoted a "police welfare plan", special measures for bed-ridden old people [Keisatsucho, 1986].

Masayuki Murayama's more recent research on the Tokyo patrol police has shown how closely information and service are related to surveillance and control. His research underlined the changes that have occurred in the work of the local patrol police since about 1970 [Murayama, 1980, 1989a, 1989b, 1990]. Some of Murayama's data point to the continuing social service role of the police. For example, between 1960 and 1985 emergency phone calls to the police increased six times, while the number of crimes committed

Table 13: Police and Residents: Opinion Polls 1981, 1984, 1990 (%)

(1) Police Box: Do you know the location of the police box in charge of your residential area? (1981:N=2520, 84:N=2407)

	1981	1984
Yes	86.5	86.7
No	13.5	13.3

If yes, is there any policeman whom you know in the police box? (1981:N=2179, 84:N=2086)

Yes	41.1	36.0
No	58.9	64.0

If yes, how do you feel toward them: friendly, neutral, or unfriendly? (1981:N=896, 84:N=751)

Friendly	37.9	37.5
Neutral	41.7	44.5
Unfriendly	8.0	10.8
DK	12.3	7.2

(2) Have you talked to policemen in the following situations? And, if yes, how was their attitude and politeness at that time?

Housecall	Yes	Good	Neutral	Can't Say	Bad	DK	N
1981	25.0	57.0	39.8	1.1	1.1	1.0	630
1984	21.1	55.5	40.7	2.2	0.2	1.4	508
Asking for Directions							
1981	7.7	53.3	40.5	1.0	4.6	0.5	195
1984	7.9	56.0	36.1	4.2	2.6	1.0	191
Investigation							
1981	4.9	44.4	50.0	0.8	4.0	0.8	124
1984	3.7	40.9	45.5	1.1	10.2	2.3	88
Not Talked							
1981	45.4						
1984	51.3						

(3) Housecall (a) Frequency: How many times have policemen visited your house in the previous year?

	More than 3 times	Twice	Once	No Visit	Forget/DK	N
1981	4.2	5.4	24.6	50.5	15.3	2520
1984	2.3	4.4	25.6	51.4	16.2	2407

Table 13: Police and Residents: Opinion Polls 1981, 1984, 1990 (%)

(4) Housecall (b) Ideal frequency: How many times, at a minimum, do you think policemen should visit in a year?

	More than 3 times	Twice	Once	No Need	DK	N
1981	16.2	24.0	33.6	13.8	12.4	2520

(5) How many times do you think policemen (or police cars) are patrolling around your residential area each day?

	More than 3 times	Twice	Once	Once in Few days	No	DK	N
1981	3.7	6.8	12.9	9.2	21.5	45.9	2520

(6) If you know something about an incident or suspects, will you report it to the police, voluntarily; only when asked by policemen; or won't you answer?

	Voluntarily	When Asked	Won't Answer	DK	N
1984	50.8	35.3	1.5	12.4	2520

(7) Do you have a good or a poor impression of policemen?

	Good	Rather Good	Rather Poor	Poor	DK	N
1990	14.8	50.7	18.2	2.2	14.2	2268

(8) How do you evaluate police crime investigations?

	Very Good	Pretty Good	Not Good	Bad	DK	N
1990	18.6	59.3	10.4	0.4	11.4	2268

Source: Public Opinion Poll on Police by Prime Minister's Secretariat, PR Office, Prime Minister's Office, 1981, 1984, 1990.

remained quite stable. The patrol police obviously serves as a primary contact point for citizens concerned about the maintaining of public order and in need of help. In fact little more than 10 percent of all calls concern crimes [Murayama, 1989a, pp.21-22].

But Murayama's data also provide persuasive data for the growing importance of law enforcement activities in local policing during the last two decades. Since the late 1960s field investigations rather than tips from the public have become the second most important factor in the success of the police to clear up crimes [Murayama, 1980, pp.42-44, 1989a, p.19 and 1989b, p.5a]. Furthermore, patrol officers value law enforcement activities more highly than other police work, in part because of the expectations of their superiors and the professional rewards which police organizations offer [Murayama, 1980, pp.55-56 and 1989b, pp.8-14]. Changes in the performance evaluation of the patrol police, introduced in the summer of 1989, aim at weakening this growing law enforcement orientation and upgrading once again other aspects of Japanese police work. It is too early to gauge the effects of this recent change in policy.

The police establishes its presence in the community also by regular house calls. In fact a substantial amount of a policeman's day is taken up by the semi-annual visits (junkai renraku) that each officer is expected to pay to each household and business in his area [Ames, 1981, pp.38-40. Bayley, 1978, pp.26-27,84-87. Fukunaga, 1988, pp.253-77. Parker, 1984, pp.55-58]. Opinion surveys in the 1980s showed that one-third of the respondents remembered a house call during the previous year and three-fourths thought more than one house call a year was desirable [Table 13,(3)]. In contrast to the prewar household survey, individuals do not have to provide the information which the police requests. But most do so willingly anyhow. "The police say that 'only Communists' refuse to answer" [Ames, 1981, p.38]. One national survey from the mid-1980s reports that less than 15 percent of the Japanese reject the official explanation for the necessity of regular house calls. While the ostensible purpose is that the police needs detailed information for providing public services such as giving directions, the real reason is to provide the police with information of potential use in criminal investigations [Miyazawa, 1990, p.40]. Its primary purpose is not to socialize with the public but to gather intelligence useful to the police [Interview no.4, Kyoto, January 14, 1991].

According to recent, first-hand observation the general information about each individual is noted on cards that stay in the koban. But the police pays particular attention to any special information (chui hokoku or watch report); it is noted on separate slips and sent from the koban to the police station and possibly on to higher echelons in the police hierarchy. Eliciting such special information is probably the real purpose for which the residential survey provides the general pretext. In their promotion police officers get heavily rewarded for providing such information [Interview no.12, Tokyo, January 18, 1991. Fukunaga, 1988, pp.240-41, 272]. During these visits the police officer enters into his record book official information such as names, places of origin, birthdays and occupation of family members, as well as emergency contact names and phone numbers. More importantly policemen pick up information and gossip about events in the neighborhood. The koban thus contains a wealth of additional information that is relevant for police investigations, including among others lists of: people working late at night, individuals normally cooperative with the police, persons owning weapons, rented houses and apartments that might serve as hide-away for fugitives, people with criminal records, the organizational structure and membership of local gangs, neighborhood associations as well as their leaders, all bars and restaurants, recent crimes committed in the neighborhood, and members of left- and right-wing political groups active in the area [Ames, 1981 pp.39-40].

While the police insists that this information is used only for public service, such as helping someone to locate an address, in fact the residential survey is designed "to produce data which could be utilized for other specialized police activities" [Murayama, 1989a, p.5]. Clearly articulated in an internal police directive in 1957, the residential survey's main purpose is to get information which the patrol police can make useful for the criminal and security police [Murayama, 1990, p.179]. Police detectives reportedly spend a great deal of time going over these police records [Ames, 1981, pp.38-39]. The security police is a major beneficiary of what can be viewed as a decentralized memory bank that it can access when needed [Murayama, 1989a, p.12. Bayley, 1978, p.85]. Actually, the apartment roller operation, started in 1971 to investigate suspects of bombing attacks, is considered by the police as a particular method of house call [Fukunaga, ed. 1988, p.261].

The police has tried to develop special techniques for dealing with the security threat posed by the large concentration of apartment complexes in urban areas. These include the creation of special "apartment sections' (apa-tai) staffed by older policemen who are more at ease in dealing with private citizens than are their younger colleagues [Interview no.12, Tokyo, January 18, 1991]. Actually, opinion surveys in the 1980s reveal that the police appears to have targeted less than half of the total houses, focusing much of its attention on apartment residents (Table 13,(2),(3)). Apartments are important because they are the preferred residences for radicals and, more recently, for foreign workers. A survey conducted by the police in 1989 has investigated the question of foreign labor focusing in particular on residents living in apartment houses [Keisatsucho, 1990, p.27]. While acknowledging the existence of multiple factors Murayama goes as far as to conclude on the basis of his data that "if the police have suppressed crime efficiently, it is because police have developed an efficient surveillance system based on residential survey [sic] and have emphasized law enforcement in their routine work" [Murayama, 1989b, p.2].

The extent to which this systematic gathering of information gives police officers a good knowledge of their neighborhoods remains, however, a matter of some dispute. Ames and Bayley report in their research that police officers assimilate much of this information and thus get to know their districts very well. Furthermore these records are apparently very helpful for policemen who are transferred to a koban. In the mid-1970s one study reported that police officers had to make about 130 routine visits a year [Citizen Crime Commission, 1975, p.27]. But in a subsequent study Parker reports that policemen do not know their neighborhoods as thoroughly as Ames and Bayley had concluded. And that at least in Tokyo each patrol officer was on average responsible for 450 routine visits a year. In areas with high turnover the basic information recorded during the semiannual routine visits is often sketchy and inaccurate [Parker, 1984, pp.55,68]. Another study in fact reports that in Tokyo a police officer may be responsible for as many as 1,200 homes, and that the residential areas for routine visits sometimes contain more than 1,000 households [Yomiuri, 1986, p.168]. We do know, however, that the patrol police does not like to conduct interviews with citizens. Increasingly this task is being delegated to residential survey specialists, typically older officers or those who cannot keep up with the demanding police work schedule for reasons of health. As mentioned above these specialists focus their attention on problem neighborhoods and large apartment complexes.

In fact in urban and rural areas alike policemen are beginning to report that community bonds are weakening, for example in large apartment complexes, and that the social distance between them and the citizens living in their districts is increasing in recent years, especially among the young [Parker, 1984, pp.65,94. DeVos, 1984, pp.238-39]. In the early 1970s the police started to consolidate small neighborhood koban into larger ones. But it was soon recognized that this would accelerate the loosening of the bonds between the police and the public [Ames, 1981, pp.54-55]. The police thus reversed the policy and again increased the number of koban. It also pulled back from a further motorization of its force [Hoshino, 1984, pp.212-14. Bayley, 1984, p.194]. Despite Japan's growing traffic density the police has resisted outright reliance on the motorization of police patrols. It is true that since the late 1970s the NPA has tried to strengthen its force of special purpose cars, as well as helicopters, to increase the mobility and flexibility of the police. But in Osaka, as in other metropolitan areas in the 1970s, still five-sixths of all policemen worked in the koban and only one-sixth in patrol cars [Bayley, 1978, p.14]. In the late 1980s nationwide the ratio was still four to one in favor of officers working in the traditional police boxes [Interview no.7, Tokyo, May 15, 1990]. The police thus recognizes "the enormous value of maintaining close contact with neighborhoods and not mechanizing the relationship between police and citizen" [Bayley, 1978, p.14].

Almost all functions touching on police-citizen relations are controlled or supervised by the Safety Police Department in the NPA and by similar departments in the police force of each prefectures. But the patrol police developed its own set of programs of "community relations" (CR) in the late 1960s to reinforce the gradually eroding bonds between police and citizens and thus to increase police effectiveness. Most of its content had been considered as a matter of course by the patrol police. But a new concept, CR, was introduced to revitalize the bonds between the patrol police and society [Fukunaga, 1988, pp.36-39]. The CR movement was a deliberate response at the grass-roots to the rise of radicalism in the late 1960s. It was adopted not only by the patrol but also by the crime prevention and guard police [Takigawa, 1973, pp.63-65]. The first reported example of the new policy was the "one area, one problem solution movement" (1970) which bore a striking similarity to the Quality Circle movement in manufacturing industries with its emphasis on a problem-solving approach by small groups. The CR movement spread rapidly at the prefectural level throughout Japan in the 1970s. It aimed at improving the public image of the police and strengthening Japan's system of crime prevention. Among other services that the patrol police has stressed more recently worth noting in this context is a counselling service for citizens that annually involves about 800,000 phone conversations and 200,000 personal visits [Keisatsucho, 1986]. In addition, the patrol police has institutionalized its own liaison councils with residents; in 1988 4,400 such councils existed throughout Japan [Keisatsucho, 1989a]. Because of the structure of Japan's police, the potential of the system for police surveillance of society is much greater than for social participation in police affairs [Miyazawa, 1990b, p.12].

The police gathers important information also through organizing an elaborate system of crime prevention associations. These associations are managed by the crime prevention divisions in each local police station. The system evolved spontaneously in the chaotic period at the end of World War II. The All Japan Crime Prevention Association was founded in April 1962 and a rapidly growing network of local crime prevention checkpoints was created in the following years. The national federation of crime prevention associations consists of 47 prefectural associations, 1260 regional associations (with each region corresponding roughly to the jurisdiction of a police station) and about 8,000 municipal associations [National Police Agency, 1987b, p.64. Advanced Course, 1989, p.260. Bayley, 1978, pp.89-91. All Japan Crime Prevention Association, n.d., p.20. Mizumachi, 1982 p.155]. These crime prevention associations are run substantially by local businessmen and older residents and cooperate closely with the police. Other residents, including women and children, are not directly represented, and neither are the Japanese workers and white-collar, salaried employees commuting each day long distances [Bestor, 1989]. Since most people are passive in their relationship with the police what matters apparently most for an active cooperation between the police and the community is a core of active neighborhood leaders. Where associations are active they offer an institutionalized mechanism for eliciting citizen support. The police typically rely on their personal relationships with the leaders of these associations for information and cooperation.

In essence these crime prevention associations are police-support groups. They parallel and to some extent overlap with local all-purpose associations called chonaikai in urban areas and burakukai in villages [Ames, 1981, pp.41-46. Parker, 1984, pp.37-39,67-68, 172-80. Kühne and Miyazawa, 1979, pp.110-111. Clifford, 1976, p. 101. Bestor, 1989]. These associations normally exclude people living in apartments. They have evolved from the basic, appointed unit of local government as it existed before World War II to an elected body with much less power after 1945. The associations still retain some semi-administrative functions or some social service functions, in part funded by a parallel level of government (village, town, city, prefecture, or nation) [Bayley, 1976, pp.66-67]. Many of these local associations have their own meeting halls built and maintained by a small monthly fee collected from each household. Although not all of them are active, by virtue of its location every household belongs to a local unit. "These voluntary institutions are directly integrated with police functions although staffed by volunteers. Participants are not paid, but they are reimbursed out of the national government budget for expenses incurred in connection with their activities" [De Vos, 1984, p.239. Interview no.5, Tokyo, May 1990].

The system of local crime prevention checkpoints (bohan renrakusho) expanded rapidly after 1962. In 1966-68 170,000 check points were established with individual households, thus increasing the total number to 410,000. By 1974 the number had reached 600,000. This development was largely unrelated to the increasing threat to Japan's internal security in the mid-1970s. In 1987 the crime prevention police renewed its drive to enlist more individual households and, with the help of the national organization, increased the total number of checkpoints from 680,000 to 790,000 within a year [Interview, no. 5, Tokyo, May 14, 1990. Keisatsucho, 1988a, pp. 816-17. Bayley, 1978, pp.93-94. Parker, 1984, p.173. Clifford, 1976, p.101]. In Tokyo in the 1970s and 1980s the figure has been constant, one checkpoint for every thirty households [Citizens Crime Commission, 1975. p.30. Metropolitan Police Department Tokyo, 1989, p.18]. But in his study of the police system in various regions of Japan Walter Ames reports that about one house in fifty is designated as a "crime prevention checkpoint" a figure which agrees with the national average in the late 1980s; the least favorable ratio for the police that Ames encountered in his research was one in ninety-six [Ames, 1981, pp.42,49. National Police Agency, 1982, p.44. Advanced Course, 1989, p.260]. The crime prevention checkpoints are the primary channels by which the police provides information to each neighborhood; and they are also an additional source of information and support.

Since the late 1970s the police has put a great amount of effort into organizing crime prevention associations at the workplaces. This is viewed as one of the most promising areas for the development of preventive crime control. By 1988 541 such associations had been established at the prefectural level, 1,781 at the city level, and about 10,000 at the level of the police station [Keisatsucho, 1978, 1989]. Furthermore, the police has also strengthened the associations at the prefectural level.

Legislation passed in February 1985 (Fueiho) deals with the regulation of the entertainment industry. It illustrates the incentives the police provides for the collective self-policing of bars on the issue of closing time. Self-policing is preferred to involving laws that are not easily enforced in Japan's entertainment districts. In addition, the legislation permits prefectural-level crime prevention associations, seeking to defend the moral standards of particular communities, to apply for funding from the government [Interview, no.5, Tokyo, May 14, 1990. Aichi-ken-boren, 1990, pp.5-6].

Crime prevention associations represent only the tip of an iceberg of an extensive network of cooperative institutions linking police with society. "In the urban jurisdictions of koban, officers of chonaikai and members of police-support groups form the core of the extensive network of police tipsters." Although the usefulness of traditional tipsters has declined quite sharply during the last three decades, the police continues to cultivate its contacts with local notables, local businessmen and individuals who "often belong to prominent and stable families, know most things that occur in their neighborhoods, and are usually willing to talk about them to the police" [Ames, 1981, pp.44,65-66]. And the police cultivates carefully also its relationship with the officials of the neighborhood associations, socializes with them, and occasionally may give them small gifts of appreciation for the help, small favors and information they provide. But the relationship is reciprocal. Local elites in turn will extend small favors to express their gratitude for the special esteem in which they are held by the police. In short, the entire system is a mixture of surveillance, control and public relations.

"Japanese society is honeycombed with committees made up of private citizens and officials that consult on matters of public safety . . . There are hundreds of private organizations representing almost any role a person can play in society that petition the police about matters affecting their members" [Bayley, 1978, pp.98-99]. Public involvement in law enforcement and the entire justice system is very pervasive in Japan [Bayley, 1978, pp.98-99.

Kühne and Miyazawa, 1979, p.111. Advanced Course, 1989, pp.261-62. Fenwick, 1982, p.68. Enomoto, 1984, p.233. Interview no.12, Tokyo, January 18, 1991]. This involvement spans the full spectrum from active cooperation in Japan's traditional communities which are rapidly vanishing, to a mixture of indifference and barely concealed hostility in the large apartment complexes in Japan's sprawling metropolitan areas. Probably most typical is social acquiescence in the police practice of gaining access to or information from a large variety of local networks that enmesh the lives of most Japanese. Volunteers are also involved in arbitration and conciliation. And the police maintains special offices in more than 90 percent of the schools (gakko keisatsu renraku kyogikai) and in a large number of firms (shokuba keisatsu renraku kyogikai) [Clifford, 1976, pp.101-02. Ames, 1981, pp.82-84. National Police Agency, 1989a, p.64]. These offices aim at a targeted and preventive approach to juvenile delinquency. Although in criminal investigations they lack any standing, they exert a strong, informal pressure on the young.

A further example of active cooperation between the police and society is a national organization, "Friends of the Police", formed in 1960 to foster morale among the police by showing public support at a time of mass riots against the U.S.-Japan Security Treaty. Membership which numbered about 10,000 in the mid-1970s is by invitation only. Financed by the contributions of large corporations the organization seeks endorsement of prominent individuals willing to lend their name for public support of the police. Selected from all over Japan, policemen are honored at semi-annual banquets in Tokyo, and members of the group give speeches at police schools bolstering the self-confidence of young recruits. In this instance as in most others, it remains true that the police is willing to cooperate with virtually any social group in order to defend public order. Community relations is a tool "to induce public cooperation with the police for the purpose of crime control . . . community organizations were organized and controlled from 'above'. This was an example of the police trying to participate in community life on their own initiative rather than responding to the needs expressed by local residents" [Murayama, 1980, pp.16,87-88].

The media constitute an additional institution that establishes important links between the police and Japanese society [Ames, 1981, pp.72-74. Advanced Course, 1989, pp.98-99]. The police not only uses a generally supportive press to improve its own image in the community. But the press is also a very useful instrument for publicizing regularly and prominently photographs and descriptions of criminals most wanted by the police. Furthermore, because a particularly important part of social control in Japan is the fear that, if arrested, one's name would be published in the papers, "violators often plead with the police to keep their names from the newspapers to avoid loss of face" [Ames, 1981, p.73]. The police thus are known to have created social pressures, especially in smaller communities, to combat specific offenses such as drunk-driving. Such social pressures created by the interaction between the police and the press, are accepted by the courts. Sentences are often reduced because the courts explicitly recognize the weight of social sanctions that the defendant has already experienced. Furthermore, it is quite typical that the names of suspects are revealed by the police and publicized by the media not only at the time of arrest but when a suspect is searched for even for minor infractions such as signing a lease under false identity or giving a wrong address. In many instances the search or arrest of political radicals has become headline news even if it involved only very minor offenses [Asano, 1987, 1990].

Private security firms give the police an additional channel of influencing society. While the Japanese police constitutes a monopoly over the exercise of legitimate force, it does not constitute the totality of such force. Private police forces in Japan have grown rapidly especially in the 1970s. The first private security firm after 1945, Sekomu, was founded by Makoto Iida in 1962. Ten years later this young industry consisted of 775 firms employing 41,146 guards, less than one fourth of the more than 175,000 police officers serving in the prefectural police force. In 1979 there existed 2,600 firms employing 105,000 private guards. And by 1988 these numbers had increased further to 4,896 firms with 218,880 employees, just about the same as the total number in the prefectural police [Advanced Course, 1989, p.271. National Police Agency, 1989b, p.65. Parker, 1984, p.180. Keisatsucho, 1972, 1973, 1977b, p. 834]. The number of private guards should surpass the number of public police officers by the early 1990s.

The dramatic increase in the number of private security guards has occurred under the supervision and regulation of the NPA [Advanced Course, 1989, p.271. National Police Agency, 1989b, p.65. Keisatsucho 1972, 1973]. In pushing for the Parliamentary adoption of the Private Security Business Law in July 1972 (S47 Law no.117), the NPA took advantage of several scandals in this unregulated industry. In 1972 it also encouraged the security firms to organize themselves in a professional association, the All-Japan Security Service Association. In its policy papers for the 1970s and 1980s the NPA designated private security firms as one of the pillars supporting the police strategy of crime prevention at the community level [Keisatucho, 1972, pp.72-73 and 1980, pp.53-57]. Private firms deal only with 1 percent of the crimes known to the police but work on 8 percent of all the cases that are cleared [National Police Agency, 1989a, p.65]. These are not overwhelmingly large figures. But it nonetheless remains true that private security firms are from the perspective of the police a "private crime-prevention system" [Advanced Course, 1989, p.275]. "The private security industry," concludes Setsuo Miyazawa, "provides the police with an enormous network of cooperating private persons which is better trained, organized, and equipped than any neighborhood citizen group and is almost as large as the police force itself . . . The closer control of private security services by the police may simply mean the expansion of the police network of public surveillance and of potential employers of retired police officers" [Miyazawa, 1991b, pp. 250,255].

The close relationship between the NPA and the private security industry means that many police bureaucrats and officers can look forward to remunerative retirement positions in the private sector. The establishment of the Urban Security Center in the mid-1980s, for example, provided an additional link between the NPA and the private security industry. To date the Presidents of the Urban Security Center have been the retiring heads of the NPA. This association legitimates the private security industry and also provides some flexible funding for special research purposes that the NPA cannot support from its regular budget [Interview no.1, Kobe, January 14, 1991]. In 1987 this system was further reinforced when the Diet passed legislation which gives the NPA the right to monitor also private detectives and firms specializing in investigative and surveillance work. The ties that link the Japanese police to various social sectors are not only concentrated in the private security industry but extend broadly throughout society. By 1989 a total of 768 retired senior police officers had been placed, through Japan's general system of amakudari, in private sector jobs after retirement. Table 14 illustrates the broad range of companies -- public and private, large and small, industrial and service-oriented -- that employed retired police officers. In short during as well as after their active careers Japanese police officers have access to the most important social sectors.

The close links between the police and society make police corruption a possibly growing problem in Japan. The instances of police corruption, it should be noted, have been very small and apparently have decreased sharply in frequency over the years. The number of police officers who were disciplined reached a postwar high of 962 in 1966. This figure declined to 465 in 1973 and fell further to 178 by 1979. Furthermore, between 1965 and 1984 the average annual number of dismissed officers was 28, and for the 1980s the figure was even lower [Tahara, 1986a, p.103. Jiyuhosoudan, 1986, pp. 186-199]. Despite a rash of well-publicized cases of police corruption in the 1980s, one of the leading students of the Japanese police, David Bayley, concludes that in Japan "the public thinks police behavior is exemplary; external interference, especially with respect to discipline, is both strict and legitimate; and police misbehavior is remarkably rare by world standards" [Bayley, 1985, p.179].

Police corruption thus is apparently not a matter of quantity. But for a number of reasons it has become more conspicuous since the beginning of the 1980s. First, police presence in society has spread in the last decade, and the scope of police action has widened, largely due to the new methods

Table 14: Police Networks and <u>Amakudari</u>

	Sept. 1984	June 1989
A.1. Politics (Diet)		
Representatives	6	6
Councilors	3	3
Diet Library	1	1
2. Bureaucracies		
1) Cabinet		
PM's Secretary	1	1
Chief Cabinet Secretary	1	1
Cabinet Secretariat		
Internal Affairs	(1)[d]	2
External Affairs	_[d]	0
Security Affairs	(2)[d]	4[a]
Information	4	15[a]
Public Relations	2	3[a]
Legislature Bureau	2	2
2) PM's Office		
Personal Authority	3[a]	3[a]
PM's Office	6[b]	1
Manag. & Coord. Agency	4	5
Environment Agency	1[c]	2[c]
Land Agency	1	1
Imperial House Agency	3	3
Defense Agency	6	6
Defense Facility Agency	1	
3) Ministries		
Ministry of Justice		
Pub. Sec. Inv. Agency	4	4
Prosecutors Office	1	
Ministry of Foreign Affairs	3	3
Japanese Embassies	13	2[c]
Ministry of Finance	1	1
National Tax Agency	2	1
Ministry of Health and Welfare	1	1
Ministry of Agriculture, Forestry & Fisheries		1

Table 14: Police Networks and <u>Amakudari</u>, continued

	Sept. 1984	June 1989
Ministry of Transport	2ᵉ	1
Ministry of Post. & Telecom.	1	1
Ministry of Construction	1	1
Ministry of Home Affairs	1ᵉ	1
L. Government & LG's pub. corp.	4	
B.3. Public corporation		
Automobile	(2)	76
Airport	2	4
Railway	(5)	2
Construction	8	6
Other	10	6
4. Judicial Branch		
Judge/Mediator	7	5
Lawyer	9	11
Other prof.	3	10
5. Education	10	11
6. Religion/Ethic	4	4
7. Politics	-	8
C.8. Transport/Traffic		
public association	28	79
private company	16	38
9. Construction/Housing		
public association	4	4
private company	17	30
10. Security Business		
public association	5	132
private company	12	20
11. PR, Information, Research		
public association	0	10
private company	14	22
12. Realtor, Building		
public association	0	0
private company	6	10
13. Amusement, Travel, Public Service		
public association	9	26
private company	2	13

	Sept. 1984	June 1989
14. Bank, Trust, Security		
public association	1	0
private company	12	16
15. Insurance		
public association	0	0
private company	19	42
16. Loan, Credit		
public association	0	0
private company	4	14
17. Commerce, Retails		
public association	0	0
private company	8	9
18. Energy		
public association	3	0
private company	9	8
19. Electronic Telecommunication		
public association	0	
private company	17	12
20. Automobile		
public association	0	
private company	2	2
21. Machine		
private company	6	12
22. Metal		
private company	2	8
23. Chemical, food		
private company	5	5
24. Other		
public association	7	34
private company	2	2
Total	352	768

Notes: a - including division chief.
        b - in addition three members of the advisory committee.
        c - in addition one member of the advisory committee.
        d - before 1986, these three were one office called the Cabinet
           Councillors' Office.
        e - other sources refer to as many as 20 police officers
           who were transferred to the Japanese embassies.

Source: Nikkan Keisatsu Shimbun-sha 1989, Nishio 1984.

adopted by the security police [Asahi Journal, 1989a, 1989b]. The private security industry, for example, has had many links to Japan's underworld. Private guards assisted the police in 72 cases in 1970; they also committed the equivalent of 95 felonies [Miyazawa, 1991b, p.249]. With the adoption of the Act of Security Business in 1972, amended in 1982, the NPA has sought to impose some controls over the daily operations of this industry. Furthermore, recent developments have strengthened the role of the administrative and security police more than that of the criminal police. Japan's organized crime, Yakuza, has always referred to what it calls "structural police corruption". With an increase in the jurisdiction of the police its tasks expanded to include the entertainment business broadly defined [Yomiuri Osaka, 1984. Kobayashi, 1986]. In the 1980s this trend has become stronger. Reports about a decline in the morale of the criminal and safety police have become quite frequent in recent years [Mizoguchi, 1986].

In 1982 and 1985 the former chiefs of the Osaka and Siga prefectural police headquarters committed suicide related, among others, to police corruption and police failures in crime investigation; at that time several books were published which criticized the anti-constitutional character of the security police, a secretive and unaccountable police force, and detailed numerous instances of illegal spending of police funds [Matsuhashi, 1984. Matsuhashi, Kobayashi, Harano 1986. Ohashi, Chiba, Matsuhashi, 1985]. Journalists and lower ranking police officers followed with a spate of publications [Matsumoto, 1987. Hosaka, 1986]. In October 1990 police corruption in Osaka led to the worst rioting in Japan in twenty years, leading to the arrest of 55 and the injury of about 200. The cause of five nights of rioting was the arrest of a policeman reportedly on the payroll of the Yakuza crime syndicate which had 45 known front offices from which it ran its illegal operation undisturbed by the police [Weisman, 1990c]. The "administrative and security-oriented police" in particular have become a favored target of the media.

The intertwining between police and society points to an osmotic relation between the police and rightest, organized crime. Best known perhaps was the Japanese government's plan to rely in the spring of 1960 on organized crime to staff an "irregular" police force of about 30,000 to protect the visit of President Eisenhower before that visit was eventually canceled [Kaplan and Dubro, 1986, pp.86-86] More generally "the police certainly get to know their adversaries well. When the Far Eastern Economic Review sent a reporter to talk to a gangster in 1984, the reporter found him 'having tea and a friendly chat with a highly placed official of the Osaka police'" [The Economist, 1990, p.20. Kaplan and Dubro, 1986. Vogel, 1979, pp.212-13. Kühne and Miyazawa, 1979, pp.63-69. Clifford, 1976, pp.117-24. Parker, 1984, pp.198-202. Ames, 1981, pp.105-29]. Organized crime counts about 80,000 gangsters or, according to different estimates, 4 to 20 times the membership of

America's Mafia [Iishiba, 1990, p.12. The Economist, 1990, p.20]. In industries like construction retired police officers and organized crime apparently often cooperate to facilitate the work of contractors [Heishman, 1990, pp.24-25]. Yet organized crime does not preoccupy the Japanese police. Only about one percent of the NPA staff is assigned to the section investigating the Yakuza, and nationwide only a few hundred policemen in a force in excess of 200,000 specialize in organized crime [Terzani, 1990a, p.109]. An informal advisory group meeting with NPA officials in May 1988 was quoted as saying "that round-the-clock stationing of officers by the road near a crime boss's residence gives the public an impression that the police were guarding mobsters rather than maintaining surveillance on them . . . It is a 'peculiar fact' that Japan was the only country in the world when outlaws are allowed to set up 'offices' in towns and overtly engage in 'businesses' of extortion and intimidation" [The Japan Times, May 17, 1988].

It may be coincidental that compared to the United States Japan has only one-twentieth as much crime but possibly as many as twenty times as many organized gangsters. But the coincidence reminds us of the important fact that the degree of self-organization of society has much to do with the problem of internal security. This crime cartel, according to a recent NPA study, "collects" funds from perhaps as many as one-third of Japan's major corporations [Der Spiegel, 1990]. And it helps maintain public order on its own terms. Organized crime actively cooperates with the police in trying to keep foreign drugs out, thus protecting its own business and keeping Japan's drug problem in manageable proportions [Iishiba, 1990, p.104. Mizoguchi 1986, p.184]. Similarly important is the cooperation of organized crime in preventing a flooding of the domestic market for prostitution through an uncontrolled influx of large numbers of foreign prostitutes who would not only ruin the price structure in domestic markets if they work independently but would also constitute a public health hazard [Terzani, 1990a, 1990b]. In Japan control through the active, informal supervision by normal families and "families" of gangsters, neighbors, and fellow workers, that is stable networks of named people, are essential [Bayley, 1976, pp.61-63. Kühne and Miyazawa, 1979, pp.91-98. Smith, 1983, pp.126-27].

Another illustration of the deep penetration between police and society is Japan's system of voluntary probation officers. Japan has less than one thousand full-time probation officials. With about 100,000 new probationers and parolees each year, their primary function is not to counsel individual clients but to supervise an army of almost 50,000 voluntary, part-time probation officers. Japan is divided into 884 probation districts, with each district assigned an authorized number of part-time officers serving on the average two clients [Miyazawa, 1991c, pp.242-43]. Heavily skewed toward retired farmers, the system is of diminishing relevance to urban Japan, a fact that is only partly compensated for by the growing number of women serving as part-time counsellors [Miyazawa, 1991c, p.246]. Rehabilitation of former convicts also relies on a large number of volunteers. The Women's Association for Rehabilitation Aid has about 800 local chapters with a total membership of about half a million [Clifford, 1976, p.107].

A variety of institutional links establishes close relations between the police and Japanese society that are of great importance for the effectiveness of the Japanese police. This fact explains why, by international standards, the Japanese police has been relatively cautious to invest in a variety of modern technologies facilitating police work, and why it deploys the technologies in a manner particularly well suited to its pervasive presence in society [Bayley, 1978, p.181]. In contrast to Europe in Japan the discussion of technology and communications issues affecting the police concentrates on rather traditional topics: the use of telephones by Japanese citizens and the reliance of the police on patrol cars [Ames, 1981, pp.67-72. Murayama, 1980, pp.22-25. Bayley, 1978, pp.72-73,180].

Japan's police uses modern technologies only on a limited scale to reinforce traditional police work. But it does so cautiously. Wire-tapping, for example, is restrained by the constitution. Informed oberservers of the police, however, without direct proof insist otherwise. A scandal in 1986 confirmed the suspicion that in unusual circumstances the police will seek information through illegal means and is not interfered with [Ogata, 1987. Ames, 1981, p.145. Miyazawa, 1989. Van Wolferen, 1989, p.199]. With the exception of some drug-related crimes, as specified in the Narcotic Control Law, Article 58, the use of undercover agents is not permitted.

As early as 1959 the police introduced a punch-card system to process criminal and traffic accident statistics [Clifford, 1976, p.82. National Police Agency, 1989b, pp.71-76. Rinalducci, 1972, p.xxviii]. All prefectural police headquarters were eventually connected with the NPA first through a teletype network later through the Electronic Data Processing System. After the enlargement of its core memory in 1965 this so-called A-line computer system initially stored information on 170,000 criminal arrests made and on 20,000 reported crimes. In 1969 a separate B-line computer system was set up recording driver's licenses as well as all traffic violations. In the mid-1960s 10,000 to 15,000 traffic cases were checked each day. Since 1974 these system have gradually been converted from batch to on-line service, and the data recorded have gradually been enlarged. Although the police links the computer systems of each prefecture in one centralized nationwide network, the more detailed data stored at the pefectural level may in fact not be fully accessible from the center [Interview nos. 4, 10, 12, 19 Tokyo, May 14-18, 1990]. The MPD does apparently, however, store in a central computer system at least some of the data collected by the security police at local and prefectural levels [Interview no.12, Tokyo, May 16, 1990].

Other government agencies have their own information retrieval systems not accessible to the NPA. The MOJ, for example, has not only a central data archive on all convictions which contains 10 million cases for the last two decades. It also stores off-line in personal computers data from the prosecutors office on individual cases. The Public Security Agency is in the early stages of developing its own data archives. The MPD stores the membership lists of Akahata (JCP's newspaper) and other left-wing organizations which, according to the unconfirmed assessment of one long-standing observer of the Japanese police, make possible the standard practice of some of the major Japanese corporations to screen the applications of new employees at the MPD [Interview, no.12, Tokyo, May 16, 1990]. These various sources of computerized information on individuals may soon become an additional useful technological instrument in Japan's policy of internal security [Interview no.2, Tokyo, December 8, 1988. Interview nos.4 and 18, Tokyo, May 14 and 18, 1990].

In the late 1980s the A-line system was used about 43 million times a year and stored information on about 6-9 millions individual citizens. The B-line system stored records on about 60 million drivers. The Automated Fingerprint Identification System is utilized about 3.5 million times a year [Interview no.4, Tokyo, May 1990]. By international standards these figures are not particularly large. As early as the late 1970s the West German police, for example, is reported to have used a computer system similar to Japan's A-line system about 70 million times a year. And the system stored information on indviduals estimated in the 1980s between "several million" on the one hand and "up to ten millions" on the other [Katzenstein, 1990, p.19]. The Japanese police relies on computer technology to supplement traditional police work. Bayley reports for the 1970s that in the course of the intrusive questioning of suspiciously looking individuals whom the Japanese police encounter on the streets, radio contact with police headquarters make it possible to check whether these individuals are in fact wanted. By the end of the 1980s about one half of Japan's 3,000 patrol cars were equipped with computers [Bayley, 1978, pp.37-38. Interview no.7, Tokyo, May 15, 1990].

By and large technological innovation in Japan's police work has been slow and cautious [Interview no.1, Tokyo, December, 1988]. The police has not been very interested in developing a high-technology strategy for gaining access to social information and thus seeking to enhance internal security. The number of officers assigned the the koban and footpatrol still remains four times as large as the number of officers working out of patrol cars [Interview no.7, Tokyo, May 15, 1990]. While some progress has been made in the areas of developing video sensors and while a computerized fingerprinting data archive has been built up since 1982 no separate data banks apparently exist for storing information on individuals suspected to be politically subversive or possibly involved in terrorist activities. Budget restraints in the 1980s have slowed the rapid development of a modern data retrieval system. In short, a variety of institutional channels provide the Japanese police with excellent access to very rich information about most important developments in Japanese society. In a country that celebrates technological advances, computer technology in the field of criminology is viewed, at best, as complementing traditional police work.

3C. Transnational Police Links

The link between Japanese and transnational state structures that encompass a variety of government bureaucracies is weak. This may possibly be related to the principles that inform Japan's "vertical society" [Nakane, 1973]. Many scholars have commented on the sharp distinction that the Japanese draw between those who belong to their group in Japan and those who do not. Indeed this distinction is much more important than the one between public and private. For public and private spheres are not fixed and clearly demarcated. They vary according to the particulars of specific vertical relationships [Ishii and Muramatsu, 1988]. The tenuous links between Japan and transnational structures and the odd mixture of extreme courtesy and rudeness in a Western sense that characterizes Japanese behavior domestically probably results from this organizing principle of Japan's social and political life [Smith, 1983, p.94. Nakane, 1973, pp.20-21,131. Kühne and Miyazawa, 1979, pp.96-97].

In contrast, for example, to the extensive connections between different European police forces that have intensified greatly since the mid-1970s, Japan's police still operates, for reasons of geography and history, in virtual isolation from the police forces of other states. This is in part just a matter of the homogeneity of Japanese society that, with the exception of Koreans, makes it virtually impossible for foreign terrorists to hide in Japan [Bermudez, 1990, pp.146-54]. And it is also the result of the geographic isolation of an island nation. With a population of about 15 million Netherlands registered more than 200 million border crossings in 1987 [Birch, 1989, p.11]. The Federal Republic, with a population of 62 million, counted about one billion border crossings in the same year, as compared to about 100 million border crossings for the United Kingdom [Katzenstein, 1990, p.4. Central Statistical Office, 1990, Table 10.36]. This compares with 10.8 million border crossings for Japan in 1988, a sharp increase from 5.2 million in 1980, 1.7 million in 1970 and 0.3 million in 1960 [Somucho, 1988]. In relative terms the number of foreigners living in Japan was less than one sixth of that of the Federal Republic in the late 1970s [Kühne and Miyazawa, 1979, p.69]. Japan simply lacks participation in transnational police structures that by now are quite widespread in Western Europe [Katzenstein, 1990, pp.23-27].

But in recent years Japan's growing internationalization has generated increasing contacts between its law enforcement officials and those of other countries. The MOJ, for example, instituted in the 1980s a variety of programs to afford especially junior officials the opportunity of travelling and learning abroad. A study program sends each year two bureaucrats abroad for a leave lasting up to two years; about seven officials are sent as interns to foreign governments for about five months each; another half dozen officials travel each year for a month on study tours that the ministry organizes for them. The Prosecutor's Office sends eight of its officials to serve at the Japanese embassies in the major Western countries, the Peoples Republic of China and the United Nations Crime Prevention Bureau. And in 1989 it set up a new program which sends forty young prosecutors abroad for two-weeks periods [Interview no.18, Tokyo, May 18, 1990]. The Public Security Agency has six of its officers stationed abroad, temporarily on loan to the MOFA, presumably involved in the gathering of intelligence. This provides at least some release from the strong opposition of the domestically oriented the MOJ to the gathering of foreign intelligence [Interview no.14, Tokyo, May 16, 1990].

The NPA and the prefectural police forces have strengthened their international capacities. Since 1985 the Police Academy of the NPA is offering special, intensive training courses at a newly created Institute of International Investigations [Asahi Evening, October 21, 1985]. The NPA and the prefectural police forces also delegate about 20 officers each to the MOFA to be stationed at Japanese embassies abroad. Although precise figures are not available, about half of them serve as liaison officers with foreign police forces and deal primarily with the physical security of Japanese; the other half is involved primarily in intelligence work. These officers build the links to foreign police forces that the NPA can activate when necessary in times of crisis. The number of embassies with at least one staff member from the NPA has increased from about 10 in the 1970s to 12 in 1984. By 1989 19 NPA officials were serving with 16 Japanese embassies around the world [Interview no.1, Tokyo, December 1988. Interviews nos.3, 15 and 16, Tokyo, May 14 and 17, 1990]. Two-thirds were chosen from among the elite career bureaucrats [Chiho Zaimukyokai, 1990]. The overseas training program of the NPA sends each year about 70 policemen, grouped into several teams, abroad for about a month to both observe foreign police systems and to receive practical training. Between 1973 and 1986 a total of 923 young police officers, about 1 percent of the relevant age cohort, were admitted into this program [National Police Agency, 1987a, p.34]. In addition a select number of officers is sent to American universities for longer periods of study. Between thirty and fifty of the police officers of the NPA and the prefectural police forces are serving abroad at any given period [Interviews no.15 and no.16, Tokyo, May 17, 1990]. According to one informed, rough estimate the total number of Japanese police officials annually travelling abroad on business has increased from about 120 in 1970, to 250 in 1980, and about 760 in 1989

[Interview no.3, Tokyo, May 14, 1990. Interview no.9, Tokyo, January 17, 1991].

In addition several Japanese organizations seek to gather economic information that may also be relevant for Japan's internal security. The Japanese Institute of Middle Eastern Economies which is affiliated with MITI and the Economic Planning Agency, does mainly general economic and political research, some of which with strategic implications. But occasionally that general information contains intelligence relevant to the tracking of the JRA [Interview no.6, Tokyo, January 16, 1991]. A small staff of researchers in Cairo receives assistance and briefings from Japan's diplomatic missions in the area; and the staff at the Institute's headquarter in Tokyo makes annual visits to the countries in the region. Other ministries, including the MOJ, have their own personnel stationed abroad for the purpose of gathering intelligence, including on the JRA. Compared to the early 1970s when only one person in the Japanese embassy in Beirut was collecting intelligence information the situation has probably changed quite dramatically, including the growing contacts between Japan and foreign intelligence services [Interview no.11, Tokyo, May 15, 1990]. But whatever intelligence is gathered is hoarded by individual ministries and shared only informally rather than being pooled systematically. Although the Japanese bureaucracy is a system that creates information redundancies, informal contacts make it likely that the important information filters upward to the top layers of different ministries and agencies.

Ad hoc coordination of policy with the United States confirms this impression of limited internationalization. A small number of Japanese police officers attend joint training programs held at the National Academy of the FBI. Since 1962 the FBI has admitted foreign police officials for training into its National Academy. By 1986 a total of 33 Japanese police officials, or less than two a year, had participated [National Police Agency, 1987a, p.35]. NPA officials also attend the annual Far East Training Program for Senior Drug Investigators that is organized each year by the Drug Enforcement Agency of the U.S. Department of Justice. And since 1980 the NPA organizes together with the United States US-Japanese conferences on countermeasures against organized crime. In 1986 the NPA sent for the first time some representatives to the Conference on Asian Organized Crimes, a meeting of American law enforcement officials dealing with the activities of Japanese and Asian organized crime in the United States. Personal contacts develop a trust that is essential for successful police cooperation. And that police cooperation has evidently grown over the years, especially between Japan and the United States [Yomiuri, July 29, 1985]. But the extent and depth of transnational links existing between Japan and other national police forces more generally, though also growing, still remains quite weak.

Japan's NPA has also accepted a small number of high-ranking foreign police officials for training in its general courses for new police inspectors. Participants must be proficient in Japanese and are expected to live in the same dormitories as Japanese trainees. Between 1953 and 1986 a total of 135 foreign policemen, primarily from South Korea, Thailand and the Philippines have been trained at the Academy [National Police Agency, 1987a, p.33]. With the assistance of the Japan International Cooperation Agency (JICA), the NPA also has organized regular short-term seminars for foreign police officials. These are held annually for about two to three weeks. The drug crime control seminar has existed since 1962 and, by 1988, had been attended by 544 foreign police officials drawn from 50 countries in East Asia, Central America, and South America. A similar program for the traffic police has existed since 1966 which, by 1988, had been attended by 139 police officers from 44 different countries. A series of international crime investigation seminars was set up in 1975 and by 1986 had been attended by 111 officials from 32 countries [Keisatsucho, 1987-1989].

In 1988 the NPA took additional steps towards forging stronger international links. It set up then the Japan Disaster Relief Organization, comprising 102 men for overseas service. This organization was legislated in September 1987, after Japan had been roundly criticized for failing to provide direct emergency relief after the massive Mexican earthquake in 1985 [Mainichi, March 30, 1988]. The NPA also organized additional conferences and provided technological assistance to other countries. It started a variety of seminars and conferences for foreign senior police officials and as a part of Japan's development aid policy also began to sponsor international police research. Two examples are the Counter Organized Crime Seminar for Asian Regions (1988) and the Conference for Patrol Police Systems (1989); new research has been conducted on anti-drug measures in 1988 and the technology transfer of transport management in 1989. It is probably no accident that the participants invited to these meetings are drawn from the same countries as those attending the Ministerial Conference on Security Matters for the Asia-Pacific Region in June 1988, the first high-level conference on internal security that the NPA has organized since 1945 [Interview 2, May 14, 1990. Nagamatsu, 1988. Keisatsucho, 1989a].

By the late 1980s the growing international contacts of the Japanese police and law enforcement system had led to a number of changes in organizational structure. A special research office dealing exclusively with the JRA was established in April 1978 with a staff of about 20. The NPA set up two additional research units for international terrorism in 1981 and 1984. Finally, on May 29th, 1988 some of the most important agencies and ministries dealing with terrorism established new divisions for international crime control, focusing primarily on JRA's international terrorist activities. A full eighteen years after JRA's first hijacking, the NPA established the 2nd

Foreign Affairs Division in its Security Bureau, with a staff of 32. The new division integrated two former subsections in the 3rd Public Security Division and the Foreign Affairs Division. The work of the new division covers all practical measures against the JRA and international terrorism more generally: gathering and analyzing information, maintaining international contacts, attending international meetings, overseeing domestic measures such as the prevention of terrorists infiltrating the country, and locating JRA suspects and JRA support groups [Kokusai Tero Mondai Kenkyukai, 1989. Yomiuri, June 29, 1989, Mainichi, June 29, 1989. Keisatsucho 1979, 1982, 1985].

A new division in the MOFA, the Division for the Prevention of Terrorism, also targets the JRA and international terrorism directly. Its purpose places more emphasis on information   retrieval and analysis to prepare the Prime Minister at the summit meetings and to support foreign ministers at other international meetings. It also exchanges relevant information with the Japanese Overseas Enterprise Assocation [Interview no. 9, Tokyo, May 15, 1990. Nihon Zaigai Kigyo Kyokai, 1987].

Finally, a new division of the MOJ, the International Division in the Criminal Investigation Bureau, formerly called the International Criminal Affairs Section with a staff of four, is not only in charge of international judicial cooperation, including extradition, but also of international treaties and agreements. Questions of international terrorism are evidently not unimportant; the first director of the new division was recruited from the Division of Public Security. Although there are no reliable data to evaluate the trend, the gradual internationalization of the Japanese police is probably slowly affecting also the organizational structure and capacities of Japan's prefectural police which does most of the practical police work.

At a first glance the United Nations Asia and Far East Institute for the Prevention of Crime and the Treatment of Offenders (UNAFEI) may also give the misleading impression of being bent on exporting Japan's judicial institutions and police practices [Twenty Year History, 1982. Criminal Justice in Asia, 1982. Suzuki, 1978. Interview no.3, Tokyo, December 7, 1988]. Founded in 1961 the Institute was conceived of as a regional training and research center initially funded and operated jointly by the United Nations and the Japanese government. At that time the MOJ rather than the NPA was chosen as the oversight agency of the Japanese government. Since the 1970s UNAFEI has been run under the auspices of the MOJ with the Overseas Technical Co-operation Agency, now the JICA, providing the funding for about 50 fellowships a year [Interview no.2, Tokyo, December 8, 1988]. While the director of the institute was originally appointed by the United Nations, since 1970 he or she is appointed by the Japanese government in consultation with the United Nations.

Under largely Japanese auspices the institute pursues its original objective of furthering the social development of Asia by promoting regional cooperation in the joint fight against crime and delinquency through training and research. With Japan and its low crime rate as a model UNAFEI has hosted more than 1,700 typically high-ranking participants in one of its numerous workshops and training courses. About 60 percent of the participants are foreigners [Twenty Year History, 1982, p.13]. Focusing on crime prevention and crime treatment these workshops and courses typically consist of comparative study and group workshop sessions. The courses are supplemented by visits to appropriate institutions in Japan and lectures by experts, many of whom are now Japanese rather than criminologists imported from the West [Clifford, 1982]. In particular UNAFEI has accepted quite frequently researchers from the National Research Institute of Police Science as participants or lecturers in its seminars. And the Institute of Police Science is regularly visited by UNAFEI participants as part of their training program. The research activities of the Institute are comparatively modest. But it does maintain close links with the Criminological Research Department of the Research and Training Institute of the MOJ.

Only very occasionally, as in 1989-90, do UNAFEI and other ministries in the law enforcement field get drawn together in an interagency process to define or redefine Japan's policy on an issue such as the preparation of a position paper for the United Nations Conference on Crime Prevention held in Cuba in August 1990. The conference dealt with five issues. UNAFEI was in charge of drafting four parts of the paper while the NPA was drafting the section on terrorism. Spurred by international developments such an interagency process may be useful but, by all accounts, with exception of the annual summit meetings of the G-7 heads of state, is rare in Japan [Interview no.3, Tokyo, December 7, 1988. Interviews nos.6 and 18, Tokyo, May 15 and 18, 1990].

Limited transnational links also characterize Japan's relations with the International Criminal Police Organization, commonly called Interpol [Fooner, 1973. Garrison, 1976. Meldal-Johnsen and Young, 1979. Igbinovia, 1984. National Police Agency, 1987a, pp.36-37]. Although it is, strictly speaking, a non-governmental organization, Interpol links designated national police organizations such as the NPA in an international network designed to facilitate and strengthen international police cooperation. De facto Interpol operates as an intergovernmental organization and has been recognized as such by the United Nations. In 1975 the NPA established an International Criminal Affairs Division in its Criminal Investigation Bureau which handles the routine exchange of information with Interpol [National Police Agency, 1987b, p.36]. The NPA has delegated three officers to serve with Interpol. Since 1985 Akira Kawada serves as head of Interpol's Police Division; in 1990 he was elected as one of the three Vice-Presidents of Interpol, the first Japanese citizen to hold such a high post in the organization. Two lower-ranking Japanese police officers serve in the sections for criminal affairs and for communication [Interview no.6, Tokyo, May 15, 1990. Anderson, 1989, p.52].

Interpol's central secretariat coordinates the exchange of information between national police bureaus on a worldwide basis. Japan's NPA acts as Interpol's central shortwave radio station in Southeast Asia. It is in direct contact with eleven police radio stations throughout Asia [National Police Agency, 1987b, p.60]. In 1986 the Tokyo radio statio handled about 17,500 messages, a fourfold increase compared to a decade earlier [National Police Agency, 1987a, p.39]. It can communicate directly with Interpol. Discussions about an Asian bureau of Interpol has been inconclusive for about a decade. Tokyo would be a natural and willing host for such a bureau. But since 1987 Thailand is already serving as Interpol's center for anti-drug investigations. It thus seems unlikely that a second Asian center will be opened in the near future [Interview no.6, Tokyo, May 15, 1990. Anderson, 1989, p.171].

Interpol's activity concentrates overwhelmingly on the investigation of crimes other than terrorism. In the mid-1980s about 50,000 of its two million files were searched actively each year [Katzenstein, 1990, p.22]. About eighty percent of the requests for information originate from Western Europe and the United States. Japan's role in Interpol is by comparison minor. Because of its insular geographic position, social homogeneity and tradition of isolation, it accounts for only a very small share of Interpol's total number of messages. Between 1977 and 1988 the total annual number of international messages concerning international crimes increased from about 4,500 to more than 7,800 with the NPA receiving in 1988 more than three times as many messages from abroad (5,509) as it was sending out (1,751). And in 1988 only 366 of these were direct requests acted upon under the provisions of the International Criminal Investigation Assistance Law [National Police Agency, 1987a, p.35. National Police Agency, 1989a, pp.49-50]. The volume of the NPA's international messages is by European standards extremely small. West Germany, for example, sends or receives each year more than 160,000 international messages concerning international crime [Katzenstein, 1990, p.22].

For reasons of security and political sensitivity information about terrorism is exchanged over a specially dedicated communication system that is not accessible to all of Interpol's 147 members. But Japan's NPA has access to this system and thus participates in the selective sharing of highly sensitive information among national police agencies. While no precise figures exist, we do know that the volume of information exchanged over these dedicated lines is very small in comparison to the total number of messages exchanged by Interpol members. And information relevant to Japan's anti-terrorist policy accounts probably only for a tiny portion of this small volume.

In sum, the transnational links between Japan's police system and foreign police forces are weak. In the era of Japan's internationalization the functional imperatives for the international coordination of police activities seeking to combat border-crossing crimes such as terrorism is growing. But the past isolation of Japan's police system is changing only very gradually.

IV.
THE NORMATIVE CONTEXT OF JAPAN'S POLICY
OF INTERNAL SECURITY

Japan's internal security policy is part of a broader normative context in which Japanese police officers, bureaucrats and politicians operate. Students of criminology concur that, in the words of Clifford, the secret to understanding Japan's approach to crime control lies "less in the structure than in the way in which the structure operates in practice. It is not in the form but in its interpretation, less the shape than the style and the meaning for people that the structure gradually acquires in a Japanese context" [Clifford, 1976, p.6]. The normative context of Japan's internal security policy in domestic politics consists of legal norms and their relation to broader social norms. And this context is also reflected in the approach Japan takes to questions of international law and the norms that influence its political choices in international society. In the words of Karel van Wolferen "whereas power in the West is masked by the illusion of principle, in Japan it is masked by the illusion of benevolence" [Van Wolferen, 1989, p.202].

4A. Domestic Norms

One social norm relevant to Japan's internal security policy, writes William Clifford, holds that "crime is a community phenomena [sic]. It is essentially defined by, detected by, prosecuted by, and determined by community involvement" [Clifford, 1976, p.97]. Japan's social norms are embedded in what Chie Nakane has called "vertical" groups that shape Japan's main institutions [Nakane, 1973]. Group allegiance is strong. "Rational judgement and universal rules defer to personal relationships. Even modern law and healthy public opinion have to compromise with such strong group manipulation . . . While a Japanese attaches great importance to concreteness and appreciates readiness to react to a changing situation, he does not trust nor establish a universal law, the nature of which is to be divorced from immediate actuality" [Nakane, 1973, pp.123,139]. The strength of these domestic social norms, all analysts agree, is a powerful factor which helps condition Japan's approach to questions of internal security. Legal norms are "subsidiary principles of social regulation" that become effective mostly when informal mechanisms of social control break down [Kühne and Miyazawa, 1979, p.19].

Recent studies of Japanese society have emphasized the integral aspects both of groupism and individualism as well as the interaction between legal and social norms. For example, Hamaguchi and Kumon have coined the concept of "contextualism" which seeks to describe both Japanese groupism and individualism. They defined its fundamental aspects as a combination of mutual dependence, an attitude of mutual trust and an understanding of human relations as the most essential part of human existence. They also recognized the strong group orientation of the Japanese and the role it plays in socializing individuals to group norms [Hamaguchi and Kumon, 1982, pp.223-23]. Contextualism puts an accent on the simultaneous existence of both legal and social norms, rather than emphasizing the priority of one over the other [Hamaguchi and Kuman, pp.222-26]. And this interaction makes it more difficult for Japan to participate actively in the evolution of legal norms in international society than is true for other states relying more exclusively on abstract, universal rather than contextual, social norms.

The normative context in which Japan's internal security policy is formulated and implemented is distinguished by a porous border separating formal and informal authority. In the words of David Bayley "formal and informal roles, legal and moral ones, interpenetrate in Japan because government is not considered a created entity -- it is not the result of an explicit act of fabrication by an existing community, the product of making a constitution. Government is not added on to community; it is intrinsic to community, as parentage is to family. Its role is larger than law, and consequently more difficult to circumscribe. Government officials, such as policemen, . . . are agents of the community's moral consensus as well as its statutory prescriptions. The homogeneity of the Japanese population has undoubtedly been important in allowing community and government, morality and law, informal and formal authority, to become combined" [Bayley, 1976, pp.65-66. Parker, 1984, p.87]. And as Robert Smith has argued, the distinction between state and society "cannot exist where the state itself is conceived to be a moral entity. Prior to the Greater East Asia War, the Japanese state never pretended to derive its authority from morally neutral, external laws. Instead, it based its control on the creation of a system of internal values, inculcated in its citizenry through its educational and military institutions" [Smith, 1983, p.130]. Indeed the distinction between state and society is problematic in a national setting where the very concept of "society" was encountered only in the early Meiji period as the Japanese came into contact with the West; for the Japanese it remains a difficult concept to articulate even today [Bayley, 1978, p.102]. In Japan, writes David Bayley, "there is no social contract. Government is an expression of community . . . Government is not a separable function grafted on to preexisting communities.

Therefore the dividing line between policemen and citizens are more vague than in the United States" [Bayley, 1978, pp.101-02].

This fusion between state and society occurred traditionally in the person of the emperor and in the institution of the imperial household. Before World War II, as Yanaga argues, one could not speak of a theory of the Japanese state but only of a "theory of morality, since the relationship of the people to the state and to the Emperor is dealt with not primarily through the medium of the study of politics but through what is known as national morality" [Yanaga, 1935, pp.1-2. Smith, 1983, pp.9-36]. The emperor made the abstract notion of the state concrete for the individual citizen. And through the person of the emperor the state was invested with a claim to an absolute moral rather than a legal authority [Smith, 1983, p.114]. Sovereignty was not a legal construct but the result of a process of historical evolution embodied in the person of the emperor. Obedience to the state was not based on any Hobbesian fear but on a sense of moral duty that each citizen holds in the realization of the foundation of the state [Yanaga, 1935, pp.52-53]. Traditionally this moral dimension helped constitute the almost sacred character of the Japanese state embodied by the emperor as a compassionate father of the national family.

After 1945 the emperor was stripped of all legal power and became no more than a symbol of the state and the unity of the people thus providing only an indirect avenue for social integration. In referring to himself as a symbol, Emperor Akihito affirmed this change during his enthronement ceremonies in November 1990 [Weisman, 1990b]. Instead of the emperor "the dignity of each person and popular sovereignty replaced the emperor and his state as the critical alloy, and a constitutional prohibition of militarism in 1947 fused with the new state vision" [Beer, 1989, p.68]. In the 1950s the split within Japan's conservative camp over the issue of constitutional revision opened the door to a possible, partial return to the prewar constitution. But it evolved eventually into a compromise that permitted a de facto partial rearmament of Japan while preventing the return to a more statist and less democratic constitution in which the emperor might have been granted again a more central role [Fukui, 1970, pp.198-226. Noda, 1973. 1976, pp.61-71].

But speaking generally in post-war Japan the fusion between formal and informal authority, between law and morality, is less personalized. It is the bureaucracy rather than the emperor that holds pride of place in public perceptions. Bureaucrats are typically thought of as disinterested actors who serve the common good. In contrast politicians are seen as self-interested and self-serving. In other words norms of the common good and the disinterested state are a central ingredient of the public's perception of the Japanese bureaucracy. And Japan's state bureaucracy, including the police, have since 1945 shunned to an unusual degree coercive methods of control [Pharr, 1990, p.146].

Japan's police illustrates that these state norms are always socially grounded. The patrol police, for example, is much less moved by traditional state appeals than was true before 1945 [Murayama, 1980, p.79]. Instead of cardinal importance is a pattern of Japanese society that gives pride of place to what one might call the social self [Smith, 1983, pp.70-74; 1985b]. The social context establishes the relationships that constitute individuality. "Both self and other can be expressed only in relational terms" [Smith, 1983, p.49]. Unusual about Japan is not the fact of social interdependence but the explicit acknowledgement of the importance of group affiliation and the awareness of the centrality of social institutions that are adaptable to modern forms of organizations [Smith, 1985, pp.40-41. Murakami, 1985, p.413]. Social order is not maintained and adapted primarily through legal and political means but through a web of reciprocal, complementary social obligations [Smith, 1983, pp.44-45]. This web establishes "connections" (kone) in networks that "exemplify the mutuality of power and compliance" [Smith, 1985, p.41]. These connections transcend narrow conceptions of short-term gain. Dore's analysis of "goodwill" and "relational contracting" underlines the importance of the social and normative context which embeds market-driven rational calculations of actors seeking to maximize their self-interest [Dore, 1986, pp.1-7,80-81; 1987, pp.16-17,169-92,227; 1988].

In Japan legal norms, morality and justice are not clearly differentiated in prescribing how individuals should act. As a doctrine of morality law is respected; as an instrument of adjudication in particular cases it is viewed with suspicion. A former Chief Judge of the Supreme Court, Ryohachi Kusaba stated, "it is characteristic of the Japanese that they seek to solve problems by talking as much as possible. Because of this preference it is by no means certain that Japan will become a litigious society" [Mainichi, November 11, 1990]. Estimates of the number of civil suits filed per capita in Japan lie only between 4 and 10 per cent of corresponding figures in other Western countries [Kim and Lawson, 1979, pp.505-06]. Legal sanctions are restricted by a variety of institutional barriers. West Germany, for example, with only one-half of Japan's population has in proportional terms six times as many judges, five times as many lawyers, three times as many private attorneys and a third more procurators [Haley, 1982a, p.274. Henderson, 1965, pp.195-96. Smith, 1983, p.43. Citizens Crime Commission, 1975, p.33. Oki, 1984, p.5. Oki, 1983, pp.233-43]. Henderson concludes that "the initial basic impression that emerges from the statistics on Japanese lawyers and lawsuits is that the Japanese courts are still relatively little used by the populace in litigation for the positive vindication of substantive rights conferred by the law" [Henderson, 1965, p. 205]. Formal legal sanctions are less important than in the United States or West Germany because of the prevalence of informal, extralegal sanctions that express a community consensus and the working's of a bureaucratically oriented and politically conservative judicial system [Van Wolferen, 1989, pp.202-26]. It thus comes as no surprise that in contrast to West Germany none of Japan's radical organizations have been declared illegal since 1952.

The mutual penetration of legal and social norms emanates from a Japanese tradition that combines elements of an East Asian legal tradition -- stressing public law, individual duties and dispute settlement especially in politically sensitive matters -- with elements of Western law -- emphasizing private law, individual rights and law enforcement on politically unimportant issues [Haley, 1984, pp.2-7. Noda, 1973]. Japan fuses an "embryonic private law system with the basic elements of traditional law in East Asia . . . The introduction of formal conciliation procedures in addition to the variety of informal mechanisms used to encourage parties to compromise their claims as well as institutional limitations on access to the courts -- mainly the dearth of judges and lawyers -- but one might also include requirements of proof and inadequate awards -- can thus be viewed as products of similar efforts to accommodate a private law emphasis within a public law order" [Haley, 1984, pp.10,15]. That tradition, furthermore, denied that law had divine origin or expressed morality as in the Western natural law tradition. Although law was seen to reflect Confucian norms of social harmony, legal commands were considered to be different from moral commands [Haley, 1984, pp.6-7].

Legal norms and processes are thus closely linked to social norms. For example, in developing her analysis of the importance of the structures of Japanese society Chie Nakane argues that legal contracts are fundamentally alien to Japan [Nakane, 1972, pp.79-82]. John Haley has written in a similar vein that Japan's dense system of social relations makes up for a "law without sanctions" [Haley, 1982a]. And Kim and Lawson title one of their articles on Japan "law of the subtle mind" [Kim and Lawson 1979]. Despite some important changes that have occurred in the 1980s Japan's legal framework for trade and finance can still be characterized as discretionary rather than legalistic [Smith, n.d.]. Rules are enabling rather than regulatory; the regulatory process is informal and depoliticized rather than formal and politicized; and courts play a marginal rather than a central role. And Frank Upham and Ezra Vogel have pointed to the flexibility with which legal norms are applied in Japan thus creating the administrative discretion that typifies Japan's bureaucratic informalism [Vogel, 1979, p.211. Upham, 1987, p.17].

The expansion of coercive conciliation during the interwar period illustrates the point. "From the first conciliation statute to the last, the central purpose . . . was to ensure that dispute outcomes reflected Japanese morals rather than law . . . Inherent in conciliation was the notion that the legal rights of the parties must give way to the conciliators' sense of morality" [Haley, 1982b, pp.137,139]. Since 1945 Japan operates three different forms of voluntary conciliation [Smith, 1983, pp.39-40]. A large, though declining, proportion of all civil cases reach a compromise (jidan) without going to court. And about 60 percent of all civil court cases are settled by two other forms of conciliation. A formal pre-litigation procedure (chotei) gives laymen rather than judges an important position in the process of dispute settlement. Alternatively, the judge assists the different parties to reach court settlements (soshojo no wakai). The net result of these three practices is to reduce sharply Japanese rates of litigation [Henderson, 1965. Henderson, 1978, pp.707,716. Haley, 1978, p.364 and 1984, pp.15-16. Ramseyer, 1988. Tanaka, 1987, pp.204-27]. Law reinforces other forms of social control. "The institutionalized legal system enables Japan to create new norms, to meet new demands, but their viability requires consensus and a process for sanctioning that continually reinforce the existing social structure" [Haley, 1982a, p.281].

This is true also in the area of criminal law where the role of the police is much greater than in legal cultures such as Germany. Since in Japan laws are rarely identical with social norms police officers typically do not enforce laws strictly but rely often on their judgement to solve especially small problems on the spot [Kawashima, 1963, p.55. Ames, 1981, pp.28-29. Enomoto, 1984, p.232. DeVos, 1984, p.242. Kuhne and Miyazawa, 1979, pp.18-19. Bayley, 1978, pp.39-41,134-38]. Furthermore in normal proceedings the police develops the file for the prosecutor who, typically, merely condenses it before seeking an indictment. Only in politically sensitive and visible cases, such as major corruption scandals, will the prosecutor conduct investigations independent from those of the police. Although they are in may ways weak and dependent on the police, public prosecutors play a much bigger role in court proceedings than do judges. Most importantly, prosecutors have a very wide range of discretion. Prosecutorial discretion appears to be used to follow the recommendations of the police and, it is often argued, aims at correction rather than punishment. Many crimes that must be brought to trial in other judicial systems, in Japan are not prosecuted. But more than 99 percent of all the cases brought to court end in conviction [Kühne, 1973, p.1079]. Japan's legal process centers on confession, repentance and correction of behavior rather than conviction, punishment and guilt.

This tendency derives in part from the nature of criminal law and in part from the tension between the prosecutors and the police. The penal code prescribes in relatively abstracts and general terms criminal behavior and offers a broad range of possible penalties. This gives the prosecutors much discretion and, in particular, a strong incentive to get a suspect to confess so that a sentence can be imposed which takes account of the particular social situation.

Contemporary scholarship on Japanese law focuses precisely on this complex intersection between social and legal norms. Takeyoshi Kawashima's original and controversial thesis was that the Japanese were distinctive because of their aversion to litigation. In Kawashima's view "the Japanese, unlike modern Europeans, do not conceive of their social relationships in terms of universal standards of rights and duties . . . Japanese expect the law to be indeterminate in both its content and in its status as a norm" [Miyazawa, 1987, p.222. Kawashima, 1963, 1967]. The revisionist thesis, first articulated by John Haley [1978,1982a] and subsequently developed by other scholars, held instead that the Japanese aversion to litigation was the result of institutional factors.

Survey research in the 1970s and 1980s has yielded results that are suggestive and also ambiguous. Responses to several items in a 1973 survey suggest "that the Japanese hold strict views about the formal legal system as an institution but at the same time expect flexible enforcement" [Miyazawa, 1987, p.224]. Furthermore the results indicate also that respondents expressed not only a clear aversion to litigation but also a keen appreciation of the costs and difficulties of litigation. The results of a second survey reinforce the view of a complex relation between social and legal norms. Problems between people with continuous social relations will rarely be settled in court; the situation is very different in cases involving actual or potential sizeable damage [Miyazawa, 1988, pp.227-28]. Another study concluded that the major reason for avoiding litigation was the cost involved rather than beliefs derived from traditional values. Court-sponsored mediation may become an acceptable alternative to litigation for pursuing legally justified interests rather than restoring social harmony [Miyazawa, 1987, p.231]. In a society where the hiring of professional legal advice is often exceedingly difficult or prohibitively expensive, mediation may be a well-considered attempt by individuals to enforce their legally protected interests [Miyazawa, 1987, pp.234-35].

The mutual penetration of social and legal norms creates a context for political action that resembles fully neither the European rule-centered model of rule by law nor the Anglo-Saxon judge-centered model of rule of law [Upham, 1987, pp.7-10. Takayanagi, 1963, pp.15,38]. Japan's "bureaucratic informalism", Upham argues persuasively, does not only reflect some ancient yearning for consensus. It is instead also the result of conscious political choices designed to impede litigation and to maintain the bureaucracy in a position to direct the pace and direction of social change. Japan's bureaucratic elite is willing to accommodate itself to inevitable pressures for change. But it retains a vital interest in maintaining control over the framework in which policy for change is discussed and implemented. In the area of industrial policy the system of administrative guidance is one well-known manifestation. In the area of crime control legal informality and the widespread practice of personal and institutional mediation play a similar role. And since repeated attempts by conservatives to revive the pre-war security law have failed, the systematic political use of of legal informality has become a central aspect of Japan's internal security policy.

From this vantage point consensus rule is the consequence of policy choices and institutional rules designed to conceal political conflicts by privileging bureaucratic informalism and administrative discretion. This pattern of bureaucratic informalism has deep historical roots. For in a system in which those who exercise authority control the legal process, as was true of Tokugawa Japan, legal rights are largely irrelevant. It thus would be a great mistake to see the non-litigious ethic of the Japanese only as the result of deep-seated cultural forces. Haley argues like Upham that the institutionalization of this ethic was the result of a conservative reaction against a rise of litigation in the 1920s and early 1930s that the government saw as threatening to Japan's traditional social hierarchies [Haley, 1978 and 1984, pp.14-15]. In many areas of law institutional barriers to granting easy access to the court system have been created consciously and are being maintained deliberately. Barriers to litigation "have helped to reinforce a nonlitigious ethos and have thereby played an important part in assuring the continued legitimacy of bureaucratic rule" [Ramseyer, 1985, p.605. Smith, 1983, p.43]. As Masao Oki argues "The development of the system of mediation in Japan was brought about by the success of private conciliation to offset the inadequacy of the Japanese judicial system" [Oki, 1984, p.5]. Bureaucratic informalism thus rests on policy choices and institutional structures as much as on cultural heritage. It acknowledges the central importance of reciprocal social obligations rather than of remedial rights. And reciprocity provides for the mutual self-interest that sustains and reinforces customs and traditional relationships [Haley, 1982b, pp.126-128,133].

Japan's bureaucratic informalism has its own vision of what the relation between law and society should be. "Law does not just regulate behavior; it interprets behavior and, in doing so, gives it significance and meaning" [Upham, 1987, p.205]. One importantant ideology of Japanese law is that it is an import of Western individualism which is alien to a consensual and harmonious Japanese society. Japan has freely imported different legal traditions and has easily accommodated what in other settings would be regarded as insurmountable contradictions in legal theory and practice [Tanaka, 1976, pp.163-253. Takayanagi, 1963]. After the Meiji restoration Japan introduced French and in particular German principles of law [Kitagawa, 1978]. Subsequent developments especially in penal law followed closely German developments [Kühne and Miyazawa, 1979, p.17]. But after the surrender to the United States at the end of World War II Japan grafted onto Japanese and continental legal traditions elements of Anglo-Saxon law. Japan thus operates, for example, with a penal code which in its is essentials is German and a code of criminal procedure which is Anglo-Saxon [Kühne and Miyazawa, 1979, pp.17,108-09. Upham, 1987, pp.11-12. Kroeschell, 1987].

What the Japanese ideology of law stresses is a method of dispute resolution which is informal and based on conciliation [Kawashima, 1963. Haley, 1978, 1982a, 1982b]. Such a system minimizes the challenge individuals or groups can pose to the dominant social consciousness of Japanese society as harmonious while at the same time enabling the legal system to satisfy concrete individual needs [Upham, 1987, pp.207-08]. Law as the affirmation of custom is a powerful vision in Japan because Japan's institutional frameworks create compromise in informal settings and through private pressures and sanctions. As John Haley argues in an important article, while this fact may not be unique, its institutionalization surely is [Haley, 1978, p.389]. Institutional arrangements largely succeed in making litigation unprofitable and political conflicts invisible. Since social norms do not enjoy any existential priority over legal norms questions of causality are not easily answered [Ramseyer, 1985, pp.637-45 and 1988]. But it is clear that for reasons of both history and institutional design law operates in a way that reinforces the Japanese ideology of social harmony. And, in the words of Frank Upham, "this ideology is at the heart of informality throughout the Japanese legal system" [Upham, 1987, p.212].

This is not to argue that the role of law is negligible in contemporary Japan. Legal norms are generally accepted as a context for political action. Indeed, historically the bureaucracy gained much of its prestige by developing the expertise to deal with Western law. The bureaucracy typically needs a legal basis to take proactive measures, such as the extension of police powers. But when such measures are stalled, as they often are for political reasons, the tradition of bureaucratic informalism asserts itself. This is as true of the police as it is, to name another example, of MITI's system of administrative guidance. Because everyone is aware of the blockages of the system, the discretionary power that accrues in the hands of Japanese bureaucrats thus is larger than for bureaucrats elsewhere. Yet innovations occur in a lawful manner. Bureaucrats adjust to changing social conditions cautiously and experimentally before their informal extension of power, often ratified by the courts which acknowledge the practical necessity for this style of bureaucratic action, becomes a new bureaucratic routine applied on a large scale. Japan's policy of internal security offers numerous instances of support for this conclusion.

Japanese informalism was shaped by political factors in post-war Japan. Under the provisions of the 1947 Constitution legislation passed by the Diet was necessary for strengthening the authority of ministries and bureaucratic agencies. But such legislation is not easily passed. Japanese bureaucracies still rely predominately on ringisei (more specifically hingisei), a bottom-up system of circulating succesive drafts requiring the agreement of all affected bureaucracies before a law is drafted by the government. The occupation reform, broke up the most important domestic ministry, the MOI. Political change could no longer be imposed in the name of the Emperor. And the potential for leadership by the Prime Minister was diminished greatly by the intense factional struggles inside the governing party. In the absence of flexible bureaucratic adjustment and strong political leadership it thus takes generally a very long time to prepare a law.

Bureaucracies thus prefer to rely on other techniques to perform their duties, especially after most important legislation had been enacted by 1960. One such technique is administrative guidance (gyosei-shido) developed in the 1960s. Others include yosan-hojyo (subsidy payments made by the government bureaucracy but lacking concurrent legislation passed by the Diet), and tsutatsu-gyosei (regulations issued by top bureaucrats that are binding not only on the lower echelons of the bureaucracy but also on clients in society) [Kyogoku, 1983. Itoh, 1980. Kato, 1980]. Having learned the same political lesson as the bureaucracy, the LDP elite, under the leadership of Prime Minister Hayato Ikeda, also moved increasingly from formal deliberations in the Diet to informal negotiations with the bureaucracy.

In comparison to European states such as West Germany Japan's legislative history is marked by the absence of specific laws dealing with questions of internal security in the 1970s and 1980s [Yutenji, 1989, pp. 46-55]. In this legal grey zone the police have been self-conscious in relying on Japan's bureaucratic tradition of giving flexible interpretations to legal restraints (un'yo). Literally translated this term refers to "mere administrative practice" or "the application of rules and laws." As a key concept for understanding the normative context in which the police operates, it describes on questions of internal security the practice of giving a broad interpretation to the legal restraints under which the police operates through a very flexible application of police powers. Although it bears a superficial similarity, it should be clearly distinguished from the arbitrary discretion that the police enjoyed before 1945 [Okudaira, 1977]. For since 1945 police powers have not been arbitrary in an individual sense but have been based on clear, though unwritten, rules that have evolved within the police bureaucracy [Interview no.2, Kobe, January 17, 1991]. In particular, while preparing for the anticipated crisis of a renewal of the U.S.-Japan Mutual Security Treaty in 1970, the police made a conscious choice in the early 1960s to systematically narrow the gap between existing laws and evolving police practices [Interview no.17, Tokyo, May 17, 1990].

The concept of un'yo has the connotation of strategic thought and behavior. In the words of a dictionary "laws and rules are not alive. Only those responsible, relying on their wisdom and the requirements of specific situations, know how to apply laws and rules. Strategic thinking respects the creative application of laws and rules" [Shinmura, 1955, p.219]. Generally speaking, un'yo is the most important norm that guides police practice under the provisions of the Japanese Constitution. And it is also to the hon'ne (real intentions) of police officials [Kato, 1980, p.179].

This norm is rooted at least to some extent in the history of prewar Japan as well as the history of the 1950s. The prewar police, after all, had no legal basis for many of its everyday practices, including its infamous house calls [Interview no.2, Kobe, January 14, 1991 and no.12, Tokyo, January 18, 1991]. The discrepancy between law and practice arose also in the early 1950s when the GHQ, converted to Cold War thinking, favored tough police measures against the JCP and the Korean League, going at times beyond the limits imposed by law. But until the late 1950s and 1960s the police retained its general adherence to the prevailing legal norms [Hatakeyama, 1984, pp.92-92]. The failed revision of the Police Duties Execution Law in 1958 and mass unrest of the Ampo movement in 1960 finally led the police to change its strategy.

The police has developed un'yo systematically into two different directions. It applies systematically a number of minor laws and ordinances, to cover the deficit created by the lack of proper legal instruments. In addition the police also interprets broadly the small number of security and police laws that do exist, particularly the Police Duties Execution Law. Furthermore Article 2 of the Police Law of 1958 prescribes in very general terms the responsibilities of the police. This has unexpectedly turned into a potent instrument for justifying many police practices that appear as questionable in light of existing legislation [Fujita, 1988].

A former Commissioner General of the NPA, Arai (1965-1969), has explained that "without the Summary Procedure Law for Minor Police Offenses and the Administration Execution Law which the prewar police could rely on, new police techniques and a new approach to public relations were necessary. It is necessary to persuade the public that all police efforts are only aimed at the people's security and welfare" [Arai et. al, 1979, p.20]. And Arai argued elsewhere that for a proper functioning of the police "the principle of law or legalism is not enough" [Tahara, 1986b, p.145]. Community relations and other techniques are used to interpret broadly the intentions of various laws. "According to Arai's explanation, un'yo does not mean being passive; it operates in many ways and manages to accomplish its purposes even when specific legislation does not exist" [Tahara, 1986b, p.145]. And these techniques have typically, though not always, been backed by the courts.

After the successful revision of the Police Law in 1954, the government and the ruling LDP tried several times to further strengthen the legal position of the police. In 1958 a revision of the Police Duties Execution Law suddenly became a policy issue in the deliberations of the Diet and received the support of Prime Minister Kishi, a leader of the constitutional revisionism faction of the LDP as well as a few of the NPA's top officials [Hatakeyama, 1984]. The revision that was proposed created an enormous amount of resentment in the streets. Four million Japanese demonstrated and staged strikes to signal their strong opposition [Weinstein, 1971, pp.90-91. Packard, 1966, pp.101-105. Tsuji, 1966]. And the liberal members of the LDP were also reluctant to agree to it. The protest groups adopted the catchy slogan: "Deito mo dekinai Keishatu-ho" (say no to the revised Police Duty Execution Law so that the police force won't interfere with you dating your girl friend), a clear reminder of the bad memories of the intrusive prewar police.

In a second attempt the government took advantage of the 1960 assassination of a socialist leader, Inejiro Asanuma, by a right-wing terrorist, and introduced into the Diet a draft for Seibo-ho (Law for the Prevention of Political Violence). Even though the LDP had an absolute majority of the seats in the Diet at the time, neither the 1958 nor the 1961 bill passed. Opposition against both bills centered on the reactionary politics of the constitutional revisionists who were proposing them. Moderate conservatives in the ruling factions of the LDP were simply not prepared to back these political forces [Hatakeyama, 1984]. Subsequently LDP politicians did not seize on several political opportunities to press the case for passing new security laws. Since the laws which existed sufficed to contain any serious threat to Japan's internal security when applied flexibly by the police, any reform proposal simply lacked appeal for the moderate conservative majority of the party. The most recent illustration was the failure to enact the National Secrecy Protection Law in 1984-85.

The relationship between the Supreme Court, the MOJ, and the Japanese Federation of Bar Associations (Nichibenren) is also noteworthy for the way it has reinforced legislative passivity. While Nichibenren has been an active supporter of the Court, the Supreme Court itself has been reluctant to see its own strength augmented [Suekawa, 1966, pp.395-99,404-05]. Lawyers have been one of the strongest constituency for Japan's progressive parties. But, paradoxically, lawyers also have a strong interest, shared with the MOJ, to keep the legal profession small and well-paid [Tanaka, 1987, p.247]. These complex relationships have impeded a systematic review or revision of Japan's most important criminal laws. The Penal Code and the Prison Law are two examples. The revision of the Penal Code has been an important political issue at least since 1975 when the Legal System Advisory Committee presented its report to the Minister of Justice. Many of the proposed articles dealing with questions of internal security have been dropped in the subsequent process of political negotiations. In short, the power of the liberal members inside the LDP, the strong opposition of the JSP and the JCP, the cautious attitude of the NPA, and the stable relationship within the legal profession have prevented the drafting and passage of new laws which might have strengthened the hands of the police or, alternatively, have protected civil liberties on questions of internal security [Asahi Nenkan, 1976-1989. Horitsujiho, 1975].

The rise of terrorism and violent social movements did not lead to a frenzy of legislative activity designed to adjust Japan's criminal code to new social conditions [Hoshino, 1984, p.208. Steinhoff, 1984, pp.190-91]. But since the late 1950s a small number of security laws designed to control or suppress radical social movements were passed, as were laws that had an indirect bearing on internal security (Tables 15 and 16). Legislation passed in 1958 and 1964 aimed at countering the growing influence of organized crime; but in spite of the initial opposition by the MOJ since the late 1960s the police has relied on these laws to counter radical social movements and terrorist organizations [Suzuki, 1978, pp.154-55].

Since they do not fall under the jurisdiction of the MOJ or the NPA but of the Ministries for Education and Transport, the law on university disputes (1969, still in effect today although it was adopted in 1969 for a provisional period of only five years) and the law concerning the security of Narita airport (1978) cannot be called security laws in the strict meaning of the term. But the law on university disputes did have great substantive importance in that it threatened university administrators to resolve campus disputes successfully or face the closing of their campuses. The law concerning the security of Narita airport provides the Ministry of Transport and the police with the authority to guarantee the safety of airport operations. Like the local ordinances passed in the 1950s [Maki, 1964, pp.84-117] and the law against the use of Molotov cocktails in 1972, this piece of legislation was clearly aimed against leftwing radicals. Furthermore, penalties against hijacking were increased sharply. The grounds for refusing to issue passports were broadened. And in May 1978 the Diet passed a new Law to Punish Extortion Acts through Use of Hostages [Nishimura, n.d., p.9]. But in comparison to other states suffering from a spate of terrorism in the 1970s, such as West Germany, Italy or Britain, what is remarkable about Japan is the relative dearth of legislative changes.

Changes in legal norms evidently were not very important in the evolution of Japan's internal security policy. With the exception of the 1958 legislation (see Table 16) all of these are special laws or ordinances. Compared to the Penal Code their scope is limited and their legitimacy is less secure. Legislation passed in 1958 and 1972 were very effective until the period of mass demonstrations ended in the mid-1970s. Subsequently their importance has diminished. The so-called Narita law passed immediately after the spectacularly successful attack which radicals had staged against the airport's new control tower in May 1978. However, this law had been used in only two instances both occuring in 1978 before, in 1989, the government finally decided to invoke it once again. The reason was the passive attitude of the Ministry of Transport which is in charge of enforcing the law [Asahi

Table 15: Anti-Terrorist Legislation Amendments and Ratification of Treaties since 1970
[TR=Treaty; L=Law]

A (TR) 1970 6/1 Treaty on Crimes and Certain Actions aboard Airplanes ("Tokyo" Treaty, S45 Treaty-45) --S45 Law-112

B (L) 1970 5/18 Law on Punishment for Hijacking [6/7 executed] S45 Law 68 Rev. by (G) 1977

C (TR) 1971 10/11 Treaty on Prevention of Illegal Hijacking (Hague" Treaty, S46 Treaty-19)

D (L) 1972 5/14 Law on Punishment for Using Molotov Cocktails S47-Law 17 M. of Justice

E (TR) 1974 6/19 Treaty on Prevention of Illegal Actions against civil Aviation--(C) ("Montreal" Treaty, S 49 Treaty-5)

F (L) 1974 7/12 Law on the Punishment for Endangering Aviation S49-Law 87 M. of Transport; Re. by (G) 1977

G (L) 1977 12/19 Law on Strengthening Related Laws for the Prevention of Hijacking S 52-Law 82 (Revision of B, F, and Passport Law)

H (L) 1978 5/16 Law on Punishment for Coercion and Taking Hostages S 53-Law 73

I (L) 1980 10/1 Law on International Cooperation for Criminal Investigation S 55 Law 93

J (TR) 1987 6/18 Treaty on Prevention of and Punishment for crimes Against the Internationally Protected (Including Diplomats) ("International Representative Protection" Treaty, S62 Treaty 3)

K (TR) 1987 6/18 International Treaty on Taking Hostages--(J) (Hostage Prevention Treaty" Treaty S 62 Treaty-4)

L (L) 1987 Law on Partial Revision of the Criminal Law and Other Laws (Law on Punishment for Violent Action and (H))

Table 16: Legislation Affecting Social Movements and Protest Activities

1. 1948-60s Local Ordinances for Public Safety

2. 5/20/58 Amendment prohibiting gathering of weapons
    (penal law 205-2)

3. 7/14/64 Revision of Punishment Law for Mass Violent Action

4. 8/17/69 Resolution Promotion Law on University Disputes

5. 5/14/72 Law on Punishment for Using Molotov Cocktails
    S 47-Law 17

6. 5/13/78 Emergency Measure Law on the Security of the New Tokyo International Airport (Navita Law)
    S 53 Law 42

7. 6/15/78 Special Measure Law on Preparation for Earthquakes

8. 12/18/88 Law on Maintaining Quiet and Calm around the National Diet and Foreign Embassies
    S 63 Law 110

Nenkan, 1979, p.285. Suzuki, 1978, p.238]. This passivity fits the evident reluctance that even the NPA has shown in applying the security laws that do exist. During the mass demonstrations of 1960 and in the late 1960s the government rarely invoked the Subversive Activity Prevention Law, shied away from using the prohibition against rioting written into Japan's Penal Code, and did not invoke some of the relevant clauses in the Self Defense Forces Law. Yet with no apparent lack of self-confidence the NPA declared in its policy paper for the 1970s, that it "will equip our security forces to handle all police affairs at all times" [Keisatsucho, 1972, p.109].

Generally speaking Japan's judicial system has supported the police in its quest for an effective strategy of internal security. Yutaka Arai, a former Commissioner General of the NPA, openly acknowledges that police informalism can be "troublesome when cases are taken to the courts" [Tahara, 1986b, p.145]. Courts after all are unpredictable in their rulings. In the late 1950s, for example, lower courts had made a number of important rulings that declared as unconstitutional several local public safety ordinances adopted in May 1958, August 1958, August 1959, and October 1959. But in a case decided in July 1960, just after the big Ampo 1960 demonstrations, the Supreme Court reversed these rulings by declaring the Tokyo public safety ordinance to be constitutional, one instance among many which has gained the court a reputation "for overturning decisions against the government made by lower courts" [Van Wolferen, 1989, p.217. Oide and Fujiwara, 1987, pp.391-92]. In fact, the constitutionality of the process by which the Police Law itself had been revised in 1954 was challenged in court in the same year; but the Supreme Court upheld the Police Law in a decision handed down in March 1962 [Hironaka, 1973, p.234-35].

The legal system was occasionally embroiled in intense political conflicts in the late 1960s when serious disputes arose (in June 1967, July 1967, October 1968, February 1969, and March 1969 involving the Tokyo local courts, the Prime Minister's office, the Minister of Justice and the LDP leadership) over the decisions of the court in cases involving political demonstrations. And because of the direct intervention of the Director of the Sapporo Local Court, Kenta Hiraga, in the Naganuma case of 1969 (which centered on the constitutionality of the Self Defense Forces), a highly-charged political dispute also broke out between the Supreme Court, the MOJ, the LDP, the Youth Lawyer Association (Seihokyo), and several left-wing parties [Odanaka, 1973, pp.126-45. Van Wolferen, 1989, pp.216-20. McNelly, 1975, pp.105-08].

Yet these were exceptions occurring in exceptional times. Generally speaking, after the controversial Sunagawa case (and the positive ruling on the constitutionality of both the presence of the U.S. military in Japan as well as the U.S.-Japan Mutual Security Treaty) the Supreme Court has avoided ruling on highly politicized issues or has followed a conservative and restrictive line in its decisions. The Secretary General of the Supreme Court, Moriichi Kishi, warned judges in 1970 "not to participate in political organizations" [Odanaka, 1973, p.15]. This injunction was interpreted by a judge sitting on the bench of the Tokyo Advanced Court, Haruo Nakamura, to include participation in Seihokyo, an organization dedicated to the protection of the Constitution. In May 1970 the Chief Justice of the Supreme Court, Kazuto Ishida, warned again that "extremist students, militarists, anarchists, and ardent communists, are not suitable to perform the duties of judges" and insisted that "the execution of the power of the Constitution requires a very prudent cast of mind" [Odanaka, 1973, p.152. Hogaku-semina 1971, p.255. Van Wolferen, 1989, p.218]. After issuing these warnings, the Supreme Court formally refused to reassign several judges. And in the 1970s several young lawyers were not permitted to become judges. Discrimination against judges who are members of Seihokyo reportedly continues [Odanaka, 1973, p.150. Higuchi, 1979, pp.164-83. Mainichi, March 11, 1987].

The Supreme Court has adhered to a stance of judicial passivism and an attitude of barely concealed hostility toward progressive and radical political forces especially in constitutional decisions and rulings affecting the operation of public facilities, such as airports [Itoh, 1989]. The passivity of Masao Okahara, Director of the Supreme Court in 1978, typified this attitude. In his speeches he favored judicial self-restraint for he repeatedly warned Japanese judges to be aware of the complex consequences of their decisions [Tanaka, 1987, p.42]. The attitude of the Supreme Court affected lower courts in three different ways: (1) it encouraged conservative rulings on questions of substance as well as procedure in cases involving New Left activists [Odanaka, 1973, pp.207-35]; (2) it lowered the barriers for the police to acquire warrants [Harano and Takada, 1989]; and (3) it speeded the disappearance of rulings against the police on constitutional grounds in lower courts and provided for an increase in rulings backing questionable police behavior [Oide and Fujihara, 1987]. The Court's passivity was reinforced by the judicial politics of its General Secretariat. Over time the Secretariat has developed the practice of organizing conferences with lower court judges in which general policy lines are articulated. The review of the decisions of lower courts tends to be short-circuited by a political process that can threaten dissident judges with relocation [Miyazawa, 1988, pp.74-75]. In this way the informal exercise of police powers on questions of internal security has basically been supported by the courts since the 1970s.

This is also illustrated by the fact that the police has remained virtually shielded from any effect of the compulsory prosecution of the abuse of authority under Articles 262-269 of the new Code of Civil Procedure [Matsuhashi, Kobayashi and Harano, 1986, p.261]. Between 1948 and 1977 of the 1,785 charges brought against the police only 7 cases were prosecuted; of these only four ended in convictions. "Not only is the small number of cases being prosecuted conspicuous, but so is the low conviction rate, especially in view of the fact that the average conviction rate of all Penal Code violations has been more than 95% in Japan" [Murayama, 1980, p.69].

The informal extension of the Policy Duties Execution Law has enlarged the scope of police action dramatically. Political attempts to strengthen the law had failed in 1958, including provisions to give the police the right to inspect personal belongings, and to expand the scope of the provisions for protective custody, restraint, and entry. But the informal strategy of the police has made up for this failure. It has become actually quite normal for suspects to answer police questioning, and the police is now permitted to apply some restraining force while questioning suspects. Moreover, in their rulings the courts have increasingly permitted police inspection of a suspect's belongings. This shift occurred in the late 1960s when the courts were dealing with numerous cases of student radicals, and it was formalized under conditions which the Supreme Court specified in a ruling handed down in 1978 [Mitsudo, 1987, p.237. Tsunakawa and Handa, 1981. Fukunaga, 1974]. NPA Commissioners Mitsui and Yamada argued in public, in speeches held, respectively, in June 1982 and May 1986, that the police strategy of providing "comprehensive security" was very self-conscious in making intelligent use of the police's investigatory authority under all existing laws and ordinances. [Kawasaki, 1987, p.251. Mainichi, June 7, 1986].

The ambiguous restrictions imposed by the courts and legal norms on the police are reinforced by the pressure of public opinion. Kumon argues that Japanese political behavior is shaped by the constraints of multiple social contexts rather than by legal documents which prescribe certain forms of behavior. "This explains, at least partially, the peculiar attitude that most Japanese have vis-a-vis the present Constitution. They simply do not care much about its applicability to reality. The actual behavior of the Japanese is not really determined according to laws like this" [Kumon, 1982, p.15]. The reinforcement of public opinion and legal norms is, however, contingent rather than necessary [Bayley, 1984, pp.185-86]. Public opinion was sanctioned by the first Imperial Edict during the Meiji restoration as a special factor shaping the conduct of national politics [Yanaga, 1935, p.263]. As Japanese history amply illustrates, public opinion has by no means always expressed morally impeccable standards of political conduct. In the words of David Bayley "the reinforcement that Japanese culture supplies to today's lawful social order is fortuitous, and could perhaps change abruptly if other goals were substituted" [Bayley, 1984, p.186]. But since 1945 at least its pervasive power has aided the police in defending the internal security of a democratic state.

Public opinion is a potent sanction constraining not only potential criminals but also the courts and the police. Public opinion as reflected in the five major dailies weighs heavily in the decisions of Japan's powerful prosecutors. The same is true of judges and lawyers. Van Wolferen thus concludes that "the social sanctioning role played by the Japanese press must be seen in the perspective of the practical shortcomings of the Japanese legal system" [Van Wolferen, 1989, p.225. Beer, 1984, 1989. Yamamoto, 1989. Whittemore, 1961]. While legal restraints are not unimportant it is the informal mechanisms of social control that have primarily conditioned police behavior. Public opinion is one such mechanism which acts as a brake on the excesses of police and more generally executive power. Before 1945 police behavior was often capricious and brutal. As a consequence the police has been covered by a watchful and critical press and is constantly challenged by a legal profession which has a sizeable wing critical of state authority [Interview no.20, Tokyo, May 19, 1990]. But even when public opinion does not constrain the police bureaucracy or the courts, it can still be invoked as the ultimate arbiter in contentious issues. When the Supreme Court affirmed the decision of a lower court in one of the most celebrated wire-tapping scandals in postwar Japan, the JCP issued a statement in which it claimed that "the party will appeal to public opinion until it can win indemnity from the state" [Mainichi, March 15, 1989].

During the last forty years the public's perception of the police has changed dramatically [Bayley, 1984, pp.190-93]. This is undoubtedly due to a very self-conscious policy of the police to cultivate public opinion and not to act against public sentiments. [Interview no.9, Tokyo, January 17, 1991. Hatakeyama, 1984, p.96]. While the security police is very guarded in the information that it makes available to the public, the general police and the riot police have learned to go to great lengths to maintain public support for their policies even in the face of severe provocation. This was true of police reaction to student demonstrations in the late 1960s as much as of the political incidents in the 1970s and 1980s. The police delayed a crackdown on radical students for as much as two years until 1969, at which time it sensed that public opinion had swung away from the students and toward the police [Steinhoff, 1984, p.191. Farrell, 1990, pp.181-84]. "When students occupy buildings, or the Red Army takes over villas, or Japanese terrorists hold international hostages, the Japanese police tend to be patient, maintaining psychological pressure around the clock for days to encourage mass resisters to give in voluntarily and in order to avoid direct violent confrontations that might create or increase sympathy for potential martyrs. They could have cleared the Narita Airport field early in the 1970s but hesitated because of widespread popular support for the demonstrators" [Vogel, 1979, p.219]. A consistent policy pursued over forty years has led to stunning results. "All accounts agree that people now come to the police largely because they want to and not because they feel they have to. Furthermore, even people who tend to have a skeptical attitude toward the police . . . admit that abuses of power by the police are minimal" [Bayley, 1984, p.192]. The number of complaints lodged against the police with the civilian review boards of the MOJ has declined steadily since 1948, to about 100 a year in the 1980s, in a population of more than 110 million [Smith, 1983, p.125].

It is in fact an axiom of the contemporary Japanese police that its success depends on a public opinion favorable to police work. Public opinion is typically measured and expressed by the mass media, and the mass media are considered by many members of the political elite to be among the most influential political institutions [Kabashima and Broadbent, 1986. Kabashima, 1990]. Most analysts agree that the public standing of the police hit an all-time low around 1960, a time which many analysts see as the beginning of the extraordinary importance of public opinion in Japanese politics [Interview no.17, Tokyo, May 17, 1990. Asahi, June 28, 1978. Kamishima, 1989, pp.136-37]. But in subsequent years the public standing of the police has improved sharply before a series of major corruption scandals, especially in Osaka, significantly tarnished the public image of the police in the 1980s [Haberman, 1984. Yumiuri, May 11, 1988].

Based on three national surveys conducted in 1983, Kabashima concluded that among eight major public institutions, the police was rated most favorably, ahead of the big newspapers, big business, and government. Significantly, public support for the police did not differ among respondents who had conservative or progressive political preferences [Kabashima, 1988, pp.33-34]. A more recent public opinion poll reveals that two-thirds of the respondents had generally a good impression of policemen and three-fourths evaluated positively the crime investigations of the police (Table 13, (7)(8)). In a crossnational survey, however, Japanese trust in the police ranks relatively low. In a sample of six industrial countries, the proportion of people who trust police institutions varied between a high of around 80 percent for the United Kingdom, 70 percent for the United States and West Germany, and 60 percent for France, Italy and Japan, with Japan holding last place [Nishihara, 1987, pp.81-82].

Shigeaki Tanaka's data illustrate how the police succeeded in improving its public image. According to a NHK survey conducted in 1974, the police ranked second as an institution that protects human rights (26 percent) while it ranked a low 7th among respondents seeing it as violating human rights. Reinforcing these findings is a survey conducted by researchers at Kyoto University in 1978 which concluded that the police ranked first (31.9 percent) as protectors and ninth (2.8 percent) as violators of human rights. In both surveys many people classified the mass media and big business as violating human rights, while the protectors included, besides the police, the family and the courts. Tanaka's explanation for the high esteem the police enjoys in the public eye is very plausible. It focuses on the daily activities of the police in community life, through counselling, koban activity, and residential area patrols [Tanaka, 1987, pp.21-23]. Throughout the 1970s and

1980s the police has emphasized these very activities in order to create a favorable climate of opinion.

The normative context in which the Japanese police operates is also influenced strongly by the hostile attitude that the Japanese public holds against radicals on both the left and the right. In their centrist leanings the Japanese lead even the West Germans. In response to the question, "choose any of the eleven types of people with whom you wouldn't like to be neighbors," 61 percent of the Japanese respondents answered "left radicals" (West Germany 51 percent, Italy 37 percent, United States 30 percent, United Kingdom 27 percent, France 10 percent), and 60 percent of the Japanese also named "right radicals" (West Germany 45 percent, Italy 40 percent, United States 23 percent, United Kingdom 22 percent, France 14 percent) [Nishihara, 1987, p.75].

On many policy questions Japan lacks a rigid system of due process to protect individual rights. Conciliation and mediation is more important than litigation. This makes it very difficult for individuals to seek redress when the government fails in engaging in the lengthy negotiations to hammer out a compromise acceptable to all concerned. Because the legal system cannot produce an authoritative and final decision which would end the dispute, dissident groups can find themselves locked in irreconcilable conflict with the government when established social practices for reaching an acceptable compromise have failed. This was probably the case in the protracted struggle over the construction of the Narita International Airport. The government chose not to mobilize the overwhelming force that it surely commanded to end the protest. The violent protests of farmers and students may have been anathema to those in power; but as acts of sincerity they commanded respect, even approbation [Smith, 1983, pp.97-98,131-32]. "Where due process is lacking, the alternative is a politics of principle, which can quickly become the politics of no compromise. And the politics of no compromise requires one to turn one's back on the legitimacy of the state itself" [Apter and Sawa, 1984, p.209].

The social stalemates to which the absence of due process contributes is one possible explanation for the ambiguity in Japanese attitudes towards social revolution, reform, radicalism, and terrorism. Along with the West Germans, the Japanese are the least willing to change society through revolution (2 percent) while strongly favoring gradual reform (40 percent). But in contrast to the West Germans (38 percent), only 15 percent of the Japanese believe fighting against radical forces is an act of bravery; this is the lowest number in any of the six major industrial countries. Moreover, the Japanese were less willing than any of the other national samples (58 percent) to condemn terrorism unconditionally [Nishihara, 1987, pp.75,88]. In the early 1970s, for example, public opinion polls recorded a sharp increase in the percentage of people who expressed a lack of trust in government and supported breaking the law at certain times, especially among the young [Steinhoff, n.d., pp.112,114].

Legal principles articulate what is professed to be occurring in society rather than describing what actually occurs. This difference between principle and rule (tatemae) on the one hand and intention and practice (hon'ne) on the other, between superficial formalism and essential realism, is self-evident to the Japanese who live in both spheres and accept the inevitable contradictions between principle and practice. Although they are part of the world of practice, legal principles do not direct practice. They are not superior to it. The guides informing action are not derived from explicitly stated norms but from specific circumstances. Indeed Japanese language is rich in ambiguities which are ill suited to the conceptual clarity and precision which is a necessary ingredient of German and French legal reasoning. What matters is not an abstract consistency between norms and action but the ability to arrive at a consensus in specific cases [Ames, 1981, pp.2-3. Kühne and Miyazawa, 1979, pp.106-09]. "The interesting and perhaps unique feature of the Japanese case is the apparent separation of this legitimizing function from enforcement. It is as if law need not be enforced to remain vital . . . legal norms are left to private informal enforcement. In a system in which social not legal controls provide the most important mechanisms of enforcement, law must always be tatemae" [Haley, 1984, pp.19-20]. Thus the tatemae of formal controls imported from abroad and imposed on the police after 1945 lives side by side with the honne of a powerful and independent police organization controlled only indirectly by mechanisms such as public opinion which are in agreement with Japan's indigenous social structure and practices [Ames, 1981, pp.227-28].

4B. International Norms

In fashioning their anti-terrorist policy Japanese officials unavoidably have been involved with developments abroad. Genuine internationalism has been impaired by Japan's informal approach to legal norms and the lack of a sense of 'rights' [Van Wolferen, 1989, p.211]. In a technical sense though Japanese policy agrees with the evolving international human rights foundation of the anti-terrorist policy of the major Western democracies. Japan, for example, has opposed strongly Third World states that have defended certain acts of terrorism as integral political components of national liberation struggles. The Japanese government signed or acceded to the three major international conventions of the International Civil Aviation Organization (ICAO) concerning the hijacking of airplanes that were passed in Tokyo (1963), Hague (1970) and Montreal (1971). And in the preparation for the Economic Summits which has brought together the leaders of the major capitalist countries, Japan has favored taking up the issue of terrorism [Interview no.4, Tokyo, December 7, 1988].

The political pressures of Japan's membership in an international society of nations thus have had legal consequences. Facing emergency situations in the aftermath of several hijackings in the 1970s, the Japanese government enacted six laws targeting international terrorists, including members of the JRA, so that it could ratify five international treaties which the government had signed previously (Table 15). But the effect of these security laws is largely symbolic and has had little bearing on the practical work of the police and the legal profession on questions of internal security.

It certainly remains true that to date Japan has never been forced to act on the strength of the international conventions it has signed and ratified and thus demonstrate that it regards them in fact as binding. In the ICAO as well as in the United Nations Japan has never taken on this issue, as on any other, a leading role. In 1973, for example, it voted together with France in the ICAO's legal committee against a proposal, supported by the United States, Britain and Canada, that backed collective action against states refusing to interrupt airservice with countries granting safe haven to terrorists [Fingerman, 1980, p.141]. And even though it sponsored one of them, in the 1980s Japan has not ratified two conventions dealing with the security of airports (which it would be prepared to ratify if the convention had a chance of being adopted) and of oil drilling platforms (which for a variety of technical reasons it is not prepared to ratify) [Interview no.4, Tokyo, December 7, 1988. Interview nos.9 and 18, Tokyo, May 15 and 18, 1990]. Furthermore, in contrast to Western Europe, East Asia simply has not evolved international organizations that have helped Japan in articulating new international norms or reinforcing established ones. Thus on questions of human rights as on many other issues "in Asia there are neither regional norms nor decision-making procedures" [Donnelly, 1986, p.628].

In pursuing its anti-terrorist policy Japan has thus taken a relatively passive stance in the development and furthering of international legal norms regarding terrorism. This passivity reflects Japan's relative isolation from international society and the system of international law. While foreign lawyers had been permitted to work in Japan during the Allied Occupation, no additional foreign lawyers were accredited after 1955. This barrier finally fell in 1987 [Japan Law Journal, 1987]. Furthermore, Japanese officials, especially at the NPA and in the MOHA, must still be counted, together with the staff of the Imperial Household, as belonging to the most domestically-oriented of Japan's major public bureaucracies.

Japan's passive attitude in the evolution of international legal norms has deep historical roots [Taijudo, 1975]. In the middle of the 19th century the Japanese found intuitively plausible the universal philosophical principles of natural law embodied in the "law of nations"; but they did not accept "international law" as a series of concrete steps evolved to deal pragmatically with concrete problems. First-hand experience with international adjudication as well as the Japanese attempt to renegotiate the unequal treaties had changed Japanese attitudes dramatically by the early 20th century. Henceforth the Japanese favored a technical approach to international law and sought it as a tactic to defend their national interests. Ronald Dore, for one, argues that this condition has not fundamentally changed during the postwar period. "Should Japanese opinion switch to a general gloomy belief that the world has basically changed, and should a siege mentality set in, then there is very little underlying internationalism to counteract it -- internationalism in the sense of identification with the international commumnity, with human kind as a whole, that is, rather than in the sense of 'good neighbour' punctiliousness about international obligations -- which the Japanese have in good measure" [Dore, 1986, p.245].

Both the early philosophical and the subsequent tactical approach reflect the fact that in contrast to the United States and Britain, for example, Japan views international law not as a process but as a product, not as part of the evolution of its domestic law but as a given attribute of international society to which it must adjust. Japan views international law as a tool of diplomacy. In contrast to the United States and Britain it lacks a dynamic conception of international law which accepts the creation of norms that bind the initiator. And in contrast to West Germany's commitment to the normative import of international legal doctrines Japan has a narrower conception of the role of international law. This static and narrow orientation of Japan as a late-comer to the Western state system differs, however, also from the stance of many of the late-late comers of the Third World which joined the international system not in the middle of the 19th century in an era of imperialism but in the middle of the 20th century at the height of decolonization. In contrast to Japan Third World states espouse norms -- on terrorism, the new international economic order, and the global commons -- which are often at odds with those of the capitalist West.

Japan appears to lack a positive conception, cast in universalist terms, of what international society should look like. The reason for this state of affairs, as Robert Smith argues, may well lie in "the awful sense of isolation from the rest of the world"; after all of their international experiences the Japanese may have concluded that "their compatriots are not much preoccupied with assessing the right and wrong or good and bad of things on the basis of abstract principles" [Smith, 1983, p.112].

Japan's passivity on these issues is also revealed on other questions of international law. In the law of treaties, for example, Japan insists on the cumbersome unanimity rule that prevents multilateral treaties from going into effect until the objections of all signatories have been accommodated by all other partners to the treaty. In the law of recognition Japan adheres to a schematic formalism. On questions of human rights Japan tends to lag international developments and, with the exception of the use of substitute detention houses (or police jails) for prolonged interrogation and forced confession, not necessarily for reasons of domestic abuse [Yomiuri, January 27, 1989. Asahi Nenkan, 1989, p.119]. And in international trade Japan has until very recently only thought about the interests of its exporters.

This is not to argue that Japan lacks any conception of international norms. Like other states it seeks to generalize to the international realm the domestic institutions and practices that shape the evolution of norms. But it lacks in the international realm what it has in the domestic, an ideology of law and a moral vision of the good society. "As to Japan, in few if any other industrial societies are formal legal sanctions so weak and social sanctions so strong . . . The social order in Japan is maintained therefore not by law and legal controls but by social coercion . . . modern forms of traditional village sanctions remain far more real than penal code penalties or formal sanctions in law" [Haley, 1984, p.17-18]. Without the dense set of social interactions that characterize domestic society what remains in international society is a world of "connections", of interests and reciprocity, that looks opportunistic and self-interested when stripped of its thick domestic social context. International responsibility means to the Japanese doing what is expected of a country whose international influence and stature is rapidly growing. And it also means conceiving of Japanese interest in longer terms. But it does not mean conceiving of the "self" in new and broader terms based on a moral vision that resembles the self-confident assertiveness of the Anglo-Saxon brand of liberal imperialism. For the Japanese to transcend an exclusively interest-driven approach to questions of international norms would require nothing less than a fundamental domestication of international society by Japan, the extension of its deep social fabric abroad. While such changes are beginning to be observable throughout the Western world in both small ways (exchanging name cards among professionals) and large ones (organization of work in the automobile industry) any substantial change along these lines would constitute a fundamental break in the history of the international system.

In an era of rapid change and contested international norms, Japan's passive stance on questions of international norm change, for example on questions of anti-terrorism policy, is indeed notable. And it is not an exception. Japan's approach is conservative and aims at maintaining the status quo on other issues as well. Japan passed its Equal Employment Opportunity Law in 1985 largely because of the international pressure crystallized during the UN Decade of Women (1975-85) [Gelb, 1990, p.1]. Japan's conservative stance is also very much in evidence in environmental issues that are affected greatly by Japan's industrial prowess. In the fall of 1989 speakers at an international conference of 1,000 environmental activists from 15 countries dubbed Japan an "eco-outlaw" because the effects of its development policies, it was claimed, were causing the destruction of the tropical forest and other natural resources of the Amazon and in Asia; Japan accounts for 40 percent of imports of wood from the world's jungles. Japan is contributing to the destruction of several endangered species. It is also the world's largest consumer of ivory. It continues to kill whales for scientific purposes. And its fishing industry continues to use nets that cause each year the death of hundreds of thousands of dolphins, porpoises and seals [Vogel, 1990, pp.23-24]. And at a time when many industrial states were using various forms of economic pressures to change South Africa's system of apartheid, the appreciation of the yen made Japan South Africa's most important trade partner in the late 1980s.

National and international norms both affect the conduct of Japan's policy of internal security and more generally its exercise of power. Throughout the last two decades Japan's social norms have not been challenged in any significant way by the rise of terrorism or violent social protest. Since legal norms played a less important role than, for example, in West Germany, it has been much more difficult for Japan to participate actively in the evolution of international norms affecting policies of internal security in all of the major capitals around the world. Japan's domestic successes in combatting terrorism and its capacity to live with violent social are also a severe handicap in how it approaches and participates in the evolving norms of international society.

V.
JAPAN'S POLICY OF INTERNAL SECURITY

Japan's internal security policy has had a domestic and an international component. Challenged by mass protests at home that in the 1970s and 1980s often turned violent the police has continued to perfect tactics of crowd control and selective intimidation which it learned in the late 1960s. This continuity contrasts with two embryonic changes in the international aspects of Japan's policy of internal security. Confronted with the JRA operating largely outside Japanese territory, Japan's policy has changed from substantial indifference to international concerns about terrorism to a hesitant involvement with the police forces and law enforcement officials of other countries. Furthermore, although it remains to be tested in real life, at least in principle Japanese policy in dealing with terrorists has changed from being "soft" to being "hard". Ever since the Bonn summit of 1978, the Japanese government has been committed, at least on paper, to a policy which refuses, even at the risk of human life, to cave in to terrorist blackmail.

5A. Domestic Policies and Internal Security

Internal security policy was a hotly contested issue in the late 1950s and early 1960s. Despite the political offensive by the "revisionists" in the conservative camp, several major attempts to strengthen state power through enlarging the jurisdiction of the police failed. These attempts included the failure to revise the Police Duties Execution Law in 1958, to enact the Political Violence Activity Prevention Law in 1961, and to get a supportive political response to a series of reports by the Research Council for Revision of the Constitution and the Ad-hoc Committee for Administrative Reform in 1964. The latter aimed at a centralization of the bureaucracy built around a strengthened Prime Minister. With the growing emphasis on creating domestic social stability through high economic growth in the 1960s no subsequent attempts at introducing any further structural changes were undertaken. This was true even during the tenure of Prime Minister Sato (1964-72), supposedly a proponent of constitutional revision. This status-quo policy has continued throughout the 1980s.

The failure to have the Diet adopt a security law in 1958 and again in 1961 as well as the mass demonstrations in 1960 have made the Japanese police lose their nostalgia for the powerful position that it enjoyed before 1945. Henceforth the police has based its operations on two pillars: utilizing public opinion and flexible interpretations of legal restraints (un'yo). Since 1960 the security police has assumed a low profile while the civilian police has acted in the public eye. The procedures used to obtain confessions and information were based on time-honored notions of identifying the criminal and on the old-fashioned community "police boxes". Both procedures were criticized by the modernizers inside the police and as well as some scholars [Watanabe, 1985]. But the police strategy was not to shed tradition but to integrate it with some modern techniques to further its informal powers. In the late 1960s, for example, the community relations (CR) approach integrated some traditional, decentralized police arrangements organized around the koban with modern techniques of public relations, with the assistance of Dentsu and other public relations companies [Tsumura, 1976. Nishio, 1976].

The leadership of the police interpreted legal restraints in a flexible manner, thus achieving a viable midway point between the constitutional revision that looked increasingly unlikely after 1958 and 1964 and strict adherence to existing laws and regulations that in the eyes of the police made it difficult to implement an effective policy of internal security. It was in line with this approach that in 1969 the NPA opposed strongly proposals of the LDP Research Committee for Public Administration aiming at strengthening the position of the police through the creation of a portfolio for a police minister, downgrading the role played by the Public Safety Commission, creating a special state riot police force, and passing a number of new security laws. The NPA opposed these proposals not only because it wanted to avoid the appearance of being subordinate to the LDP, but also because it feared a hostile public reaction to this proposed expansion of its powers [Suzuki, 1980, pp.236-37. Asahi Nenkan, 1970, p.305].

With the support of the courts the police developed a system of specific techniques for conducting security investigations. The police favored two types of informal investigation techniques: a systematic application of minor, miscellaneous laws, ordinances, and rules to cover the deficit created by the absence of proper legal instruments, and a systematic expansion in the interpretation of the small number of relevant laws that did exist, particularly the Police Duties Execution Law.

This reformulated police strategy dates back to the first half of the 1960s. The new consensus inside the LDP on a policy tolerating a reinterpretation of the existing constitution was, according to Hironaka, reinforced by two rulings of the Supreme Court in 1960 and 1962 that touched on the constitutionality of the Public Safety Ordinance and on the 1954 revision of the Police Law. In both instances the Court encouraged the police to work without the legal backing of new security laws and without a revision of the constitution. The police learned these political lessons quite quickly. Jiyuhosodan (the Liberal Lawyers Association) reports, for example, that since 1964 regulations prohibiting the display of political posters on lampposts and other public property were more strictly enforced. To this end the police used the Local Billboard Regulation Ordinance. On the basis of this regulation 52 people were arrested in Osaka between 1964 and 1968 [Jiyuhosodan, 1986, p.65]. One of the few senior police official who turned against the police in his retirement, Matsuhashi, admitted that he himself began to apply minor laws in Fukuoka in 1962, such as traffic and public building regulations and rules regulating mass demonstrations [Matsuhashi, 1984, pp.283-84]. Hironaka has analysed the change in policy in the 1960s in some detail and named it the "no-need of legislation" strategy [Hironaka, 1973, pp.228-74].

Consistent with these developments the NPA's 1980s Policy Paper emphasized the importance of the "active application of existing laws" in security investigations [Keisatsucho, 1980, p.88]. The police has utilized many minor laws during the last two decades. Among these particularly noteworty is the Minor Offenses Law [Keihanzai-ho]. A weakened version of the Minor Police Offense Law of the prewar era, this law is used with growing frequency against social movements, despite an explicit provision that prohibits its abuse. For example, the Tokyo headquarters of Kokumin-kyuenkai (a legal support association for defending political activists) reported that in the court cases it defended in the decade 1975-85, 130 street campaign cases out of 202, and 226 arrests out of 359 were based on the Minor Offenses Law [Jiyuhosodan, 1986, p.88].

Political discretion provides the executive branch of government with ways of stifling political dissent especially among members of radical sects suspected of engaging in violent social protest or terrorist activities. Apter and Sawa, for example, recount a rather ordinary and tragic tale of a woman who had been swept up in the periphery of the Sanrizuka movement protesting the Narita airport construction project. Once she was arrested she had to wait for over a year before her case came up in court. In the meantime her former life -- job, friends and family -- collapsed around her [Apter and Sawa, 1984, pp.148-50]. The organization of Japan's prison system offers several opportunities for isolating political radicals. Japan's pre-trial detention system, organized around more than 1,200 centers run by the police, eight times as many as the formal detention houses run by the MOJ, permits keeping arrested suspects in police cells, separate from regular prisons, for up to 23 days. After three and thirteen days a judge must authorize continued detention for additional questioning, usually a routine formality. And the method of questioning, including techniques, which show some striking similarities to police methods relied upon in the 1930s [Steinhoff, 1988b and

1991] aim primarily at breaking the will of the individual rather than infiltrating opposition movements. Suspects are kept in the police centers primarily for extracting confessions, under conditions that according to a 1984 report can only be described as shocking [Kühne, 1973, pp.1083-84. Murayama, 1980, p.89, note 24. McCormack, 1986. Igarashi, 1986. Van Wolferen, 1989, pp.188-90. Mainichi, September 17, 1989]. While the statistical average for the length of stay of natural criminals is well below twenty-three days, political radicals, like JRA member Maruoka, have been held in some cases for up to a couple of months [Interview no.11, Tokyo, January 18, 1991].

One of the preferred legal techniques the police uses in order to detain political radicals for as long as possible is bekken taiho (arrest for lesser offenses rather than arrest for the serious charges which are often levelled against radicals). For example, using several articles in the Penal Code such as the Obstruction of Official Duties (Article 95), and Larceny (Article 235), some suspects were reported to have been arrested, detained, released and rearrested several times over a period of several months or more [Asano, 1990. Maruoka 1990. Oono and Watanabe, 1989]. Once arrested on a minor offense suspects are known to have been interrogated around the clock [Interview, no.9, January 17, 1991].

This police detention system was an issue in the UN Human Rights Committee in 1988 [JSP, 1989, p.441]. After an indictment has been handed down the accused are held in the Tokyo detention house of the MOJ for the duration of the trial as well as all appeal procedures. While conditions in the house are better than in ordinary prisons (no work, permission to receive daily visits, availability of reading material, and relatively unrestricted correspondence with the outside world) communications with the defendant's lawyers are very restricted and, most importantly, the defendant is put in solitary confinement. The procedures of the judicial system are therefore organized in a way that in some instances has permitted keeping political radicals isolated up to a decade before the final verdict. "In effect, the leaders of the most extreme protest groups have been treated within the letter of the law, but legal maneuvers have been contrived to keep them out of society for long enough to destroy the effectiveness of their leadership. The limits of acceptable dissent have been set primarily by bureaucrats trained in the law, who are clever enough to uphold it and still accomplish their aims" [Steinhoff, 1989b, p.190].

The gradual expansion of police powers has broadened the range of activities that are covered by a law prohibiting the obstruction of public officials in the performance of their duties. Charges brought by the police under this law are a good indicator of fluctuations in the general level of political activism as analyzed in Chapter 1 (Figure 3). On average half of all of the arrests based on this law occurred in Tokyo, a figure that peaked at 70 percent in 1969. Furthermore Chiba prefecture, which includes Narita Airport, records a much lower though still substantial number of arrests (5 percent) as does Osaka. In contrast to the Ampo 1960 demonstrations, the number of arrests in 1969 and 1971 were far larger than the increase in the number of demonstrations. The figures support the inference that the police, for political reasons, has used a flexible application of this legislation (un'yo) in its effort to control challenges to the Japanese state. Furthermore, the evolving police strategy of informalism has been much more important for investigating and arresting suspects than for actually convicting them [Hironaka, 1973, pp.339-41].

The extension of informal police powers thus serves the explicitly political purpose of strengthening the hands of the police. Crime and court statistics illustrate the sharp increase in the police powers of investigation since the early 1970s. Figure 4 shows that despite a declining rate in the 1960s and a constant rate in the 1970s and 1980s in the number of crimes (B), and in the number of arrest warrants (C,D), since 1975 warrants for attachment, investigation, and inspection (A) and warrants for body searches (F) have increased sharply. In addition, the dismissal rates for all warrants, already low originally, have fallen still further -- from 0.33 percent to 0.17 percent for (A), 0.32 percent to 0.10 percent for (C), and 0.17 percent to 0.06 percent for (D). Although the increasing reliance on court warrants appear to suggest a growing role of the judicary, in fact the issuing of search warrants has become no more than a bureaucratic formality involving the police and the courts in routine interactions.

A similar trend is noticeable in the policy of detention. Warrants for detention (E) follow the changing crime rate. The number of persons detained by the police has, however, not decreased since the early 1970s, since it has been more difficult for suspects to be released by posting bail. During the last twenty years the police and the prosecutors have evidently become more aggressive in the number of warrants they issue and the number of suspects they refuse to release on bail. Judges, furthermore, have also become harsher in their treatment of defendants. Since the early 1970s judicial statistics show an uninterrupted decline of those found innocent in court proceedings, from 0.60 percent in 1971, to 0.53 percent (1972), 0.39 percent (1976) and 0.14 percent (1984 and 1986). After having examined a broad array of data, former High Court Judge Yasuo Watanabe concluded that the number of trumped up charges has probably increased over time [Watanabe, 1989, pp.422-23].

Before major public events house searches with or without warrants have been reported frequently [Hosaka, 1986, pp.186-209. Nishio, 1984, p.162. Interview no.15, May 17, 1990]. For example, in preparation for the funeral of Emperor Showa the police searched without a warrant 200,000 apartments three times during the week before the funeral procession.

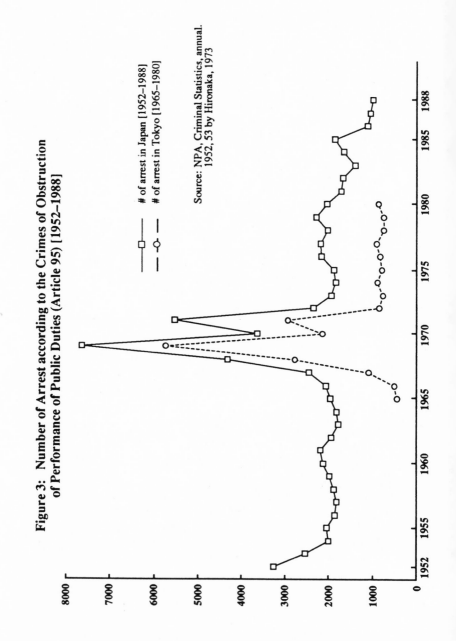

Figure 3: Number of Arrest according to the Crimes of Obstruction of Performance of Public Duties (Article 95) [1952–1988]

# of arrest in Japan [1952–1988]
# of arrest in Tokyo [1965–1980]

Source: NPA, Criminal Statistics, annual. 1952, 53 by Hironaka, 1973

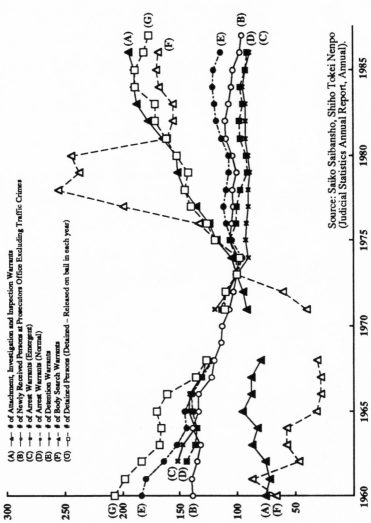

Figure 4: Police Warrants and Detentions (1960–1986) (Index 1973=100)

(A) ──┼── # of Attachment, Investigation and Inspection Warrants
(B) ──┼── # of Newly Received Persons at Prosecutors Office Excluding Traffic Crimes
(C) ──┼── # of Arrest Warrants (Emergent)
(D) ──┼── # of Arrest Warrants (Normal)
(E) ──┼── # of Detention Warrants
(F) ──┼── # of Body Search Warrants
(G) ──○── # of Detained Persons (Detained – Released on bail in each year)

Source: Saiko Saibansho, Shiho Tokei Nenpo
(Judicial Statistics Annual Report, Annual).

Compared to the precautions taken at the Tokyo summit of 1986, this was a vast increase in numbers. A knock at the door, a polite request, a quick search of the apartment and virtually universal compliance were the norm. Citizens who were hesitant or opposed to the police, by opening their doors still afforded the police the opportunity of at least a quick scanning of their typically small quarters. In any case only a few law suits were filed protesting the search method the police was employing even though this Apartment Roller Operation, which utilizes door-to-door questioning of residents, might be in violation of Article 35 of the Constitution.

This particular police tactic is not new. As early as 1971, in response to a wave of bombing attacks by radicals, the police adopted a policy called "Apartment Roller Operation" (Table 3). Targeting 40 suspects thought to have been involved in these attacks, as well as 200 members of radical organizations like the Red Army, Keihin Ampo Kyoto, RG and a number of anarchist groups, the police organized two such operations. The first (between December 29, 1971 and February 29, 1972) involved 1,600 policemen searching 260,000 apartments and contacting 10,000 realtors; the second (between March 1, 1972 and April 30, 1972) was staffed by 800 policemen who searched 74,000 apartments and talked to 7,000 realtors. As a result of this large operation the police discovered about 50 hideouts, identified 250 radicals and collected more than 2,000 pieces of information relevant to questions of internal security [Takigawa, 1973, pp.120,215. Steinhoff, n.d., p.228]. The massive reliance on this particular tactic illustrates dramatically how the police strategy of informalism, operating with public support, has drastically enlarged the scope of Japan's policy of internal security.

The community relations (CR) approach which the police developed fully in the 1970s and 1980s became a new source of police power by extending the informal contacts of the police in the community. Initially adopted for the patrol police to complement the system of police boxes, it has become a key concept of informing the entire policy approach of the police since the early 1970s [Nishio, 1976, p.223]. The extension of the CR approach was not primarily motivated by the specific threat that political radicals posed in the 1970s and 1980s. It reflected, rather, a more basic policy orientation that agreed with, and was supported by, the devAlH@ment of Japan's internal security policy during the last two decades. The CR policy aimed at a mutual penetration of police and society. Through numerous initiatives the police opened itself up to society, backed heavily by modern methods of public relations. One police officer of the Guard Division in the MPD described the CR approach as "a dialogue that differs from the one-way communication of traditional public relations" between local residents and the police. "Its aim is the anticipation [of radicals' activity], the separation [of radicals from the society] and the isolation [of radicals]" [Takigawa, 1973, pp.63-65,20].

Furthermore, in an effort to create a favorable climate the police went beyond a self-conscious media policy that courted public opinion. For example, the police began in 1973 with the publication of its annual White Papers. An unintended consequence of the decision to put the police's case more explicitly and self-consciously before the public was to reinforce the greater role which leading police officers have played in electoral politics. By giving the annual White Papers to some extent a programmatic focus the NPA's bureaucratic leaders created political issue -- among others on terrorism, foreigners, organized crime -- with which they were identified and which could help them after retirement to launch a political career in the LDP. And in 1973 the police also reemphasized the development of a variety of small community services not related to the investigation of crime, such as the police news notice, community consultations and police welfare service, particularly visiting old people living alone [Keisatsucho, 1972, pp.20-26; 1986]. Conversely, the police promoted vigorously a greater degree of integration between the patrol police and the security police [Keisatsucho, 1972, pp.109-11. Fukunaga, 1988, p.36]. A variety of social networks have been created in the communities that tie the police closely to residents. Former NPA Commissioner General Gotoda (August 1969-June 1972) was an active champion of this policy. Although advocates of modernization had questioned these traditional methods inside the police in the 1960s, a series of bombings of the homes of senior police officials in the early 1970s restored the household survey to its preeminent instrument as a standard police check on the people.

Traditional police methods were reivigorated once again in the late 1980s. The sharp increase by over 100,000 in the number of local crime prevention checkpoints was due to the concerted efforts of the police to broaden the social base of the crime prevention system by including larger numbers of women and younger people [Interview no.5, May 14, 1990]. The growing anonymity of Japan's urban life and a gradual decline in the clearance rate of Japanese crime, from the perspective of the police, required an adaptation and renewed effort in extending existing institutional practices. In a similar vein in its programmatic policy paper for the 1980s the NPA reemphasized the importance of the patrol police and the methods of the 1960s and 1970s while articulating also a new approach that puts a major accent on the safety police. The safety police is in charge of what it calls a policy of "comprehensive crime prevention", including maintaining effective social and police networks in the community and at the workplace, supervising the adherence to security regulations by business, providing social counselling, overseeing entertainment businesses as a likely source of crime, and attending to other administrative police functions. This is the only subject matter on which the 1980's Paper offers a more detailed description on more pages than did the 1970's Paper [Keisatsucho, 1980b, pp.21-24,53-66].

At the same time the police has developed the CR approach into more systematic forms. CR policy has been extended to include many CR cooperative organizations, including private security businesses, a variety of private institutions, and even individual buildings. And in the 1980s the police has tried informally to make crime prevention a consideration in the modernization of roads and the construction of apartment complexes. Particular localities can now be surveyed with technologically sophisticated TV-monitors and the computerized "area information control" system. This system divides areas into squares of 250 meters and all relevant information is computerized for each square [Keisatsucho, 1980b, p.29]. A less sophisticated airial surveillance system has also been put into effect. Since President Chun's visit in August 1984 a police blimp monitors closely all developments in and around Tokyo during all major public events. All buildings which are over four stories high have identification numbers on their rooftops which are easily visible from the air [Nishio, 1984, p.162. Yamada, 1986]. In general it is fairly clear that the police has shifted away from supplying the public at least with some information in the 1970s to gathering information from the public in the 1980s. Compared to the policy paper for the 1970s the section on supplying the public with information was deleted from the policy paper for the 1980s; instead, considerable attention was paid to the establishment of police information systems and networks. This is especially true of information relevant for the security police [Yomiuri, July 29, 1989. Yomiuri, 1986, pp.185-194].

The public's tolerance of and cooperation with the police thus remains a key ingredient to Japan's policy of internal security. It is true that some of the major security risks during the late 1980s have been managed largely by the police alone. For example, before and during the Olympic Games held in Seoul in 1988, the police protected Korean targets throughout Japan. And it is now standard operating procedure of the police that in preparation for a major event thousands of manholes in Tokyo are searched for explosives and then sealed. More important though is the fact that the police actively seeks and promotes public support, among others through well-orchestrated media campaigns. In many instances the massive security checks that the police has run especially in Tokyo since 1985 work only with the active cooperation of the public. Roadblocks manned by the police to protect the foreign dignitaries attending the funeral of the Emperor, for example, were effective because the public heeded the urgent pleas of the police and left its cars at home. And it did not object either to the fact that many subway exits were closed so that a larger than usual crowd could, through a smaller than usual number of subway exits, pass by police officers inspecting their bags [Interview no.16, Tokyo, May 17, 1990].

The approach of the police was set forth in a lecture that the Commissioner General of the NPA, Hideo Yamada, delivered before the

Foreign Correspondents Club of Japan in May 1986 [Yamada, 1986, p.337]. Yamada made three main points. First, an effective campaign against political radicals requires that the police extend the issue of defense to the air as well as underground. Secondly, the Japanese police has relatively limited powers to perform its duties, for example, in organizing public security during major political events such as the Summit. Finally, the Japanese police operates by Japanese methods, that is, supported by and in cooperation with the public at large. The success of the police depends largely on the public backing that it receives.

With the abatement of terrorist attacks and the waning of violent mass demonstrations after 1972 the police needed new reasons for sticking to its policy of a further build-up of the riot police. Although in the 1970s Interim Policy Report the NPA had proposed the creation of a new joint police force of 15,000 preparing for natural disasters, the MPD decided to maintain a large riot police [Asahi Nenkan, 1971 p.312. Asahi Nenkan, 1972, p.313]. The predicament the police found itself in justifying this build-up was resolved by international developments. Beginning with President Ford's visit to Japan in November 1974, the riot police has been busy preparing international public events that, with increasing frequency, have been staged in Tokyo. Two police failures in 1975 were the turning point from a security police that, as in the 1960s, operated at large public events behind the scenes to a highly visible security police deployed massively at large public functions: the assassination attempt of Prime Minister Miki in June and the attack on the Crown Prince in July [Suzuki, 1980, pp. 114-120. Tahara, 1986a, pp. 321-322. Interview no.17, Tokyo, May 17, 1990]. In later years an internationalizing Japan hosted not only two economic summit meetings in 1979 and 1986 but also welcomed PLO leader Arafat in 1981, President Reagan in 1983, and President Chun in 1984. And Japan celebrated the sixtieth anniversary of the Showa Emperor's reign in 1986, planned the Emperor's visit to Okinawa in 1987 as well as his funeral 1989, and staged the new Emperor's enthronment in 1990.

Mobilization for these events has increased sharply over the years. In the 1960s a maximum of about 5,000-10,000 policemen were estimated to have been mobilized by the MPD for protection of events such as the Tokyo Olympics in 1964 or USSR Vice-Prime Minister Mikoyan's visits in 1961 and 1964. However, at the occasion of President Ford's visit in 1974 the MPD mobilized 23,000 policemen on a daily basis. This number increased to 26,000 at the Tokyo summit in 1979, and 30,000 at the 1986 summit and the Emperor's anniversary; and it increased still further to 32,000 in 1989 at the time of the Emperor's funeral, and 37,000 in 1990 at Emperors's Akihito's enthronment. Indicating a sharp increase in the extent of police precautions taken, the total number of "policeman-days" mobilized during these events increased from 16,000 during President Ford's visit, to 412,000 at the first summit in 1979, and 810,000 at the second summit [Asahi Nenkan 1962, 1965, 1975, 1980, 1987. Keisatsucho, 1975, 1980a, 1987a. Weisman, 1990a].

These figures illustrate that when it is necessary the police mobilizes on a scale and with a thoroughness that reminds us how important internal security is being taken in Japan. The 1984 visit of South Korean President Chun Doo Hwan, for example, inspired the police to stop cars, a month before the event, on Tokyo's crowded super-highways for so-called 'practice' searches [Van Wolferen, 1989, p.199]. And during the 1986 Tokyo Summit an army of policemen protected conference halls and hotels in Tokyo, and, over a period of several days prior to the meetings, was manning checkpoints throughout Japan and inspecting vehicles in an effort to forestall terrorist attacks. Interpol, the MOFA, the Immigration Bureau and the customs-houses cooperated for several months prior to the Summit in seeking to interdict the smuggling of weapons and ammunition and to prevent people who might be a security risk from entering Japan [National Police Agency, 1987a, p.121]. Similarly in preparation for Emperor Hirohito's funeral in February 1989 the police sealed thousands of manholes, constructed a steel wall around the inner courtyard of a park in which the foreign dignitaries assembled, inspected subway tunnels, without warrants searched several hundred thousand apartments along the four-mile route of the funeral procession, banned domestic cargo flights several days before the funeral, circled the city in a blimp, and closed off so many roads and set up so many checkpoints that car traffic in the central districts of Tokyo came to a virtual standstill [Sanger, 1989a, p.A7; 1989b. Nickerson, 1989, p.8].

These large-scale public events as well as the Narita struggle provided the police with the opportunity to develop the new key concept of a "comprehensive security policing" in domestic politics that soon thereafter found also a programmatic expression in Japanese foreign policy. According to this concept a comprehensive policy of internal security must be preventive and involve not only the various departments of the police but also other public bureaucracies, such as public corporations and related organizations, in supporting the police [Tahara, 1986b, pp.164-70]. Before the 1986 summit, for example, the Superintendent of the MPD called a meeting of the leaders of 213 business associations and asked for their cooperation in helping to reduce traffic congestion for the duration of the summit. And the MPD distributed one million leaflets to ask the general public for support and assistance [Hosaka, 1986, p.190]. This approach has evolved from the CR measures taken in the early 1970s. The MPD has become very eager to elicit a broad array of information from the general public. The policy paper which the National Police Agency issued for the 1980s thus argues among others that "in dealing with security matters, it is required to adopt 'comprehensive preventive policing' broadly defined and in cooperation with related administrative authorities and other organizations in order to gain a timely and well-informed assessment of the possible causes of social disturbances" [Keisatsucho, 1980b, p.87].

By the late 1980s this emphasis on a comprehensive security policy had become unmistakeable. Commissioner Yamada's official notice of May 7, 1986, following the second Tokyo Summit, stressed that the police had acquired substantial powers that had permitted a considerable strengthening of its surveillance of radicals and the monitoring of particular localities without losing public support. It was thus only natural that the MPD and other prefecture police forces doubled their manpower dealing with radicals. Moreover, the NPA required other public bureaucracies to examine the behavior of 9,000 radical public servants, and encouraged them, using various obscure bureaucratic regulations, to investigate buildings and homes in an extended search for radicals. Finally, local police stations were reportedly also encouraging their local assemblies to issue proclamations against political radicals [Mainichi, June 8, 1986. Yomiuri, June 11, October 20, 1986. Asahi, September 4, 1989. Yamada, 1986, p.342].

The close ties which the police has to the public and the great weight that it attaches to public opinion explain why the imperative of Japan's internal security policy -- "thou shall not kill" -- has not changed substantially since police power reverted back from the American occupation force to the Japanese government in 1952. This has been evident in the police's restrained reaction to many of the pitched battles which a coalition of groups and social movements have waged against the construction, operation and enlargement of Narita Airport, the symbol for many of the violent demonstrations in the 1970s and 1980s [Smith, 1985, p.131]. But the imperative was most clearly displayed in February 1972 when the police, having pushed radicals into rural Japan, cornered five of them and one hostage in a lodge in central Japan. Thus began an extraordinary ten-days drama: the siege of Asama-Sanso. The last ten hours of the siege were carried live by all major TV channels and watched by 95 percent of the Japanese viewing public [Steinhoff, n.d., p.112. Ames, 1981, pp.159-60. Bayley, 1976, pp.160-62. Kühne and Miyazawa, 1979, pp.121-22. Farrell, 1990, pp.19-28. Keisatsucho, 1977b, p.1154. Interview no.15, Tokyo, May 17, 1990].

The police orders were unambiguous: save the hostage alive, capture the terrorists alive, do not exchange hostages, maintain good relations with the media and do not incur any police casualties. Over the next ten days the police used a variety of methods in trying to break the psychological resolve of the terrorists. Finally on the tenth day, with the hope of saving the hostage alive dwindling, the police decided to take the building by storm. With a huge armor-plated crane breaking down the walls a police unit armed only with pistols, which it was under strict orders not to use, staged an assault in the early morning hours. Supported by eight armored cars, nine water cannon-trucks, about 140 other automobiles and trucks, and 1,600 other policemen the unit forced its entry into the building before noon. Inside the building a policeman was shot and killed by one of the radicals within the hour. Only then was the police granted permission to use firearms in self-defense but without the intent to kill. After another six hours of fighting the radicals surrendered and the hostage was found unharmed. Two policemen and one TV cameraman were killed, and, depending on the source, either sixteen or twenty-four policemen were injured. Although it was confronted by a group armed with several rifles and two thousand rounds of ammunition, during the entire drama the police had fired only fifteen rounds from their pistols. It did use a wrecking crane, high pressure water hoses dispensing at least 50 tons of water, twelve smoke bombs and 1,400 cannisters of tear gas [Farrell, 1990, p.27. Steinhoff, n.d., p.112, Takigawa, 1973, pp.164-79].

Since an additional 14 members of the United Red Army were still at large the police was intent on avoiding at all cost of making it in the eyes of the public a group of martyrs. Soon afterwards one of the captured members took the police to the grave of one of twelve United Red Army members that had been tortured and killed in a brutal process of self-criticism and purges within the group [Steinhoff, n.d. Farrell, 1991, pp.1-19]. Revelations of these facts signalled the end of the Red Army's operations in Japan, as a horrified public turned against it. The police strategy of patient non-violence had scored an impressive triumph.

The controlled violence which the Japanese riot police uses is, by international standards, remarkable even if one considers that virtually no citizen in Japan owns or carries a gun. The principle of avoiding bloodshed at almost all costs explains why the police adamantly opposed the demands of politicians in 1960 and 1970 that the Self-Defense Forces be used as a back-up force to defend Japan's internal security at the height of mass protest against the renewal of the Security Treaty and the Vietnam war. And it makes intelligible why even at the height of the protest movement in the 1960s the police never seriously pushed demands for a force of 200,000, consisting in equal parts of the normal and the riot police [Suzuki, 1980, p. 250]. In fact the largest concentration of police in the last two decades has never exceeded 37,000. At the height of what came to be known as the 990 days of mass protest -- between October 8, 1967 and June 23, 1970 -- there occurred not a single death among the protesters while the police made 15,000 arrests and suffered itself 12,000 injuries in more than 2,000 encounters with radicals [Interview nos.15 and 17, Tokyo, May 17, 1990. Farrell, 1990, p.182].

To accomplish this feat the tactics of the riot police where honed in the 1960s. Brutal police intervention against the 1956 mass demonstrations at Sunagawa had elicited public criticism that was so strong that the police fought the mass demonstrations against the Security Treaty in 1960 with a minimum of defensive equipment such as shields or vests. Preparations for the resumption of diplomatic relations with South Korea in 1965 embodied what the police had learned from the 1960 demonstrations and became a trial run for dealing with the large-scale campus demonstrations and riots of the late 1960s [Interview nos.13 and 17, Tokyo, May 16 and 17, 1990]. Police equipment -- helmets with plastic face masks and long shields -- were improved. Policemen were not equipped with clubs, an offensive weapon that in media coverage might undermine the hoped-for image of the police as a disciplined force that was being put on the defensive by a hostile mob. But policemen trained to use the shield as an offensive weapon, not only to push demonstrators back but to incapacitate them for a while by slamming the heavy shield down on their ankles and toes.

In addition the police enforced as strictly as possible a security ordinance requiring the organizers of demonstrations to inform the police about the location and timing of any planned demonstrations. And it made maximum use of its power to arrest demonstrators hoping to create a deterrent against future involvement in demonstrations. It succeeded in limiting the amount of public space available for political demonstrations in the center of Tokyo. High-level contacts with the Japanese construction industry convinced one of the largest companies to store large amounts of building material on one site. And the police succeeded in convincing the leadership of the JSP to hold rallies in Hibiya Park thus eliminating another potential site for mass demonstrations, while at the same time creating conflict between the the JSP and the JCP which favored the mass protests. In addition the police learned from many of the tactical mistakes it had made in 1960. Police cars were refitted to make them secure against rocks; strong search lights were installed at the sites of major planned demonstrations; the food supply and sanitary facilities for the police were improved while vendors as potential source of supply for the demonstrators were not permitted to do business for the period in which demonstrations were anticipated; injured policemen were rushed to the best hospitals in the area while injured demonstrators had to wait their turn; photographers and journalists were provided with escorts and what in the parlance of 1980s-style American politics came to be known as "picture opportunities", vantage points, that is, most favorable to the police; editors and commentators were invited to lectures sponsored by the police which provided background information and were intended to break the coalition between radicals and ordinary citizens. Six months before the anticipated peak of demonstrations in November 1965, the police started to train in earnest, and the normal system of personnel rotation was temporarily halted. In short the police made innumerable small adjustments in preparation for demonstrations which in the end did not materialize, as November 1965 passed without mass demonstrations. But the police was ready when campus protest erupted on a large scale in 1967. Over the next twenty years there have been few changes in the tactics of the riot police. With less frequent mass demonstrations since 1975 the mission of the riot police has been adapted to include the protection of buildings and the securing of important public events.

The interim report of the police for the 1970s revealed considerable clarity about the goals and instruments of policy. The preface of the report states that "from now on, more than ever, we are planning to strengthen the bond between citizens and the police. Although Japan's growing urbanization will be detrimental to this task, we are confident that we can forge an enduring link between citizen and police" [Fukushima, 1972, p.10]. In looking back over the postwar period, the report listed ten important tasks that the police had accomplished. Five of these were related directly to the surveillance of left-wing radicals by the security police. Speaking generally, Japan's policy of internal security has not led to large-scale structural changes in police or society as much as a set of incremental adjustments over time. The slogan which the police adopted in the wake of the catastrophic defeat of 1945 still was an apt summary of its basic mission in the late 1980s: "respect human rights, keep alert, always be kind and popular" [Steiner, 1965, p.90]. By opting for the politically compelling path of constitutional "revision by interpretation" and by relying on its considerable informal powers, the police has been able to gradually change its political practices in ways that would have been deemed impossible two or three decades ago. Without any conspicuous organizational changes or great political debates, the police has enhanced greatly its capacities to deal with violence-prone social movements, guerrilla attacks and acts of terrorism. And it has done so without endangering its political legitimacy.

5B. International Policies and International Security

In contrast to its domestic side the international dimension of Japan's internal security policy has shown greater changes. The imperative of "thou shall not kill" governed Japan's policy until 1978 and explains why the government was blackmailed by the JRA after each of a series of spectacular hijacking operations in the mid-1970s. A change in policy occasioned by the Bonn Summit of 1978 committed the Japanese government to stand fast in the face of terrorist blackmail, a change that until the summer of 1990 had not yet been tested in reality [Interview no.4, Tokyo, December 7, 1988. Interview nos.1 and 15, Tokyo, May 14 and 17, 1990]. A second change was the government's hesitant but nonetheless growing international involvement in the international coordination of anti-terrorist policy.

Compared to Israel, the United States, Britain and West Germany, the Japanese government was accommodating to terrorist blackmail in the 1970s [Miller, 1986, pp.409-10]. The policy was defined by the governments reaction to the very first hijacking of a Japan Air Lines flight in 1970. Intent on avoiding the loss of life, after days of arduous bargaining, the government basically acceded to the hijackers' demands, thus encouraging the JRA to plan additional hijackings [Angel, 1990, pp.40-41]. The government's accommodating stance was very much in evidence, for example, when Palestinian terrorists seized the Japanese ambassador in Kuwait in 1974 to effect the release of Japanese and Palestinian terrorists trapped on a ferry in Singapore harbor after bungling an attempt at setting fire to an oil refinery. And it was also evident when a JRA team of terrorists hijacked a Japanese airplane to Dacca in 1977; the Japanese government eventually acceded, after agonizing deliberations, to the demand to release six prisoners and to provide a six million dollar ransom as well as a supply of blank passports [Farrell, 1990, pp.185-91]. Here perhaps lies the kernel of truth in the caustic joke that in the 1970s the Japanese were good at exporting TV sets, automobiles and terrorists. It was thus less than consistent when in response to Israeli's shocking reversal of policy -- the exchange of 1,500 PLO fighters, including the lone survivor of the Lod airport attack, Kozo Okamoto, for three Israeli soldiers in May 1985 -- the Japanese government "expressed official irritation that it had not been consulted, and asked that Okamoto remain in Israel to serve out his sentence" [Steinhoff, n.d., p.64].

In the initial attacks the government misjudged the significance of the fact that some of the terrorists were Japanese. For example, "when the Government learned that two of the four guerrillas who struck in Singapore on January 31 were Japanese youths, the Foreign Ministry's reaction was one of disinterest. It remained cool and aloof to guerilla demands for an aircraft, arguing that settlement of the incident was within the competence and authority of the Singapore Government" [Nakamura, 1974, p.22]. Similarly at the time of an attack on the diplomatic offices of the United States and Sweden in Kuala Lumpur in August 1975, Japanese government and security officials were reportedly caught by complete surprise. "They had been under the impression that the estimated 30 members of the JRA who were reportedly based abroad had been forced to remain quietly underground, having been integrated into larger groups in which their presence was said to been 'rather insignificant'"; the link between the Popular Front for the Liberation of Palestine (PFLP) and the prominent role of the JRA was, according to police officials in Tokyo, "more than we have ever expected" [Nakamura, 1975].

But by 1977-78 opposition in Tokyo against the government's accommodating stance had grown significantly. As early as 1974 top police officials let it be known in public that they thought the government's policy unwise in that it would encourage further attacks leading to the release of additional members of the Red Army who were being held in jail [The Economist, 1974]. In 1977 the Minister of Justice, Hajime Fukuda, was strongly opposed to acceding to the demands of the terrorists, refused to be involved in the release of jailed members of the JRA, and resigned together with his deputy at the end of the Dacca hijacking crisis [The Economist, 1977. Hielscher, 1977]. These signs of disarray in the executive branch of government were also reflected in the Diet. The Diet considered but did not act on legislation which proposed making it more difficult for the government to issue passports and easier to continue court proceedings against accused terrorists in the absence of defense councils, as long as that absence was dictated by a strategy of the accused to prolong the trial [Crome, 1978b].

As early as 1974 government policy showed some signs of shifting. The international base of operation of the JRA ineluctably drew the Japanese police and government away from indifference to international developments toward an internationalization of its operation. After the JRA had taken the Japanese ambassador in Kuwait hostage all embassies judged to be high-risks for a terrorist attack were partially rebuilt to provide greater physical security. And after the 1977 Dacca hijacking the NPA and the MPD began stationing at major Japanese embassies officers with the mission to collect intelligence information. By 1980 about 10 officers were serving abroad [Interview no.11, Tokyo, May 15, 1990]. In the 1980s the PSIA has also, in coordination with the NPA, begun to collect on a limited basis intelligence data abroad [Interview no.14, Tokyo, May 16, 1990]. The pattern which has emerged in the 1980s is for a number of different ministries and agencies -- among them MOHA, MITI, MOJ and the Defence Agency -- dealing with different facets of internal security to generate their own intelligence on Japanese radicals operating abroad.

The incipient changes in Japanese policy received a major boost from an agreement reached by the heads of state of the major democratic states at the Bonn summit of 1978. It provided the Japanese government with an opportunity to back some of its general rhetoric favoring international cooperation with a more specific commitment. In response to the wave of terrorist attacks that Japan experienced in the early 1970s the NPA, for example, had stressed in its annual report as early as 1974 the need for international cooperation to deal with the internationalization of crime [Clifford, 1976, p.27]. In the evolution of Japan's policy the Bonn declaration on terrorism was an important historical accident. Since no prior staff work had been done on the issue, Prime Minister Fukuda found himself in the uncomfortable position of having to respond to an idea which emerged literally over lunch. The occasion demanded a show of international solidarity, a political opportunity which the MOFA seized in order to reshape Japanese policy [Interview no.9, Tokyo, May 15, 1990]. In accord with the resolution passed at Bonn, a cabinet decree issued in September 1978 committed the Japanese government to stand firm in the face of future terrorist blackmail.

The implementation of this policy was, however, slow and tortuous. The Tokyo summit of 1986 held at a time of heightened threats from Libyan and Syrian terrorism found the Japanese government only a hesitant supporter for the activist stance of the United States and several European countries. But as host and chair of the meeting the Japanese government was forced to coordinate the different national viewpoints and thus to support a policy which a narrow conception of Japan's foreign policy interest might have rejected. But in part because of the continued emphasis on the importance of a coordinated anti-terrorist policy, the 1987 Venice summit finally translated the broad principles of the Bonn declaration into more operational measures [Interview no.9, Tokyo, May 15, 1990].

Difficulties of implementation were also evident on the domestic side. In September 1978 the cabinet allocated the necessary resources to equip and train a 53-members strong special anti-terrorist unit [Asahi Nenkan, 1979, p.286. Suzuki, 1980, p.131]. Staffed equally by the police (28) and by the Self-Defense Forces (SDF) (25) it was to be deployed at selected Japanese diplomatic missions abroad. By 1990 the staff had doubled to 115 officers [Mainichi, September 11, 1990]. In fact no such unit was ever created, possibly because of the precedent it would have set for involving the SDF on questions of internal security. Instead special anti-terrorist squads have been training in each of the prefectural police forces as well as in the MPD. These units can be deployed singly or in combinations at very short notice. It was illustrative of the problem of implementing the new policy that the bulk of resources was allocated to the establishment of two other units: a small unit protecting Japan's 34 nuclear power plants and a much larger one dealing with Japan's organized crime [Crome, 1978a]. The change in Japan's anti-terrorism policy was thus partly packaged in a more general move to beef up some of the government's security measures not directly related to the threat of terrorism. While the shift in policy was welcomed by Japan's allies abroad, it received a mixed review in Japan. Although the measures adopted were rather modest by European standards, the press argued forcefully that the government's past policy of the inviolability of innocent lives should not be equated with political weakness.

The gradual increase in the importance of the international dimension of Japan's policy of internal security is noticeable especially in the 1980s. This has become a constant theme in policy pronouncements in recent years. In the words of the 1987 White Paper "the police are not immune to the recent waves of internationalization that are affecting every aspect of our life. To cope with the challenge, efforts will be made to increase cooperation in investigations with foreign police and train international investigators. Technical cooperation to [sic] foreign countries will also be stepped up, while personnel exchange with other countries will be promoted" [National Police Agency, 1987a, p.1]. In fact the special issues of the 1987 and 1990 White Papers are devoted to the increasing importance of international interdependence for Japan's internal security and the problems posed by foreign labor.

Translating this general commitment to internationalization into policy terms has been a slow and difficult process. It seems, for example, entirely plausible to assume that through a variety of channels the Japanese government may have used its foreign aid policy to influence Syria to restrict the movement of the JRA at certain times, for example, around the time Emperor Hirohito was planning foreign travels. We do know that the Emperor travelled in Europe in the fall of 1971 and in the United States in the fall of 1975. But there is no definitive proof that the sharp increases in Japanese aid to Syria in 1972 and 1975 were directly related to these trips [Organization for Economic Co-operation and Development, 1978, p.222]. However, official briefings of reporters on Japanese aid policy in 1989-90 listed as one of five reasons for continued aid to Syria Japan's interest in having the Syrian government keep track of the JRA stationed in Lebanon's Biqua Valley under the protection of the Syrian army [Interview no.11, Tokyo, January 18, 1991]. In fact, because it contains, in the judgement of Japanese bureaucrats, quite reliable political intelligence on the terrorist scene in the Middle East, the newsletter of the JRA -- which is written in Syria but produced and distributed to a private list of subscribers in Tokyo -- is apparently a valued source of information. The MOFA, for example, has a standing order for six copies [Interview no.11, Tokyo, January 18, 1991].

Speaking more generally in recent years Japan has become a more important source of information and technology for the police forces of other Asian states. The automated fingerprint identification system that the police developed in the 1980s have made Japan an increasingly important and attractive partner for countries in Southeast Asia as well as Central and Latin America [National Police Agency, 1987a, p.28]. In 1986 a total of 150 police study groups visited Japan, 55 from Asia, 26 from the United States and Canada, 25 from Western Europe, and the rest from other countries [National Police Agency, 1987a, p.32]. The National Research Institute of Police Science has accepted 42 foreign trainees between 1977 and 1986 [Advanced Course, 1989, p.25. National Police Agency, 1987a, p.30]. Occasionally Japan is sending police officials to other countries to offer specialized training in the use of "comprehensive information and communication systems" [National Police Agency, 1987a, p.29]. The Philippines, for example, have become an important partner for the Japanese police seeking to contain the activities of Japan's organized crime groups and the smuggling of firearms and drugs and, potentially, the JRA's activity in Asia, as shown by the Wakaoji case in 1986-87. Traditionally aid to foreign police forces was granted under the auspices of JICA in the name of "economic assistance". But since 1988 the growing self-confidence of the NPA, the availability of more funds for economic assistance, and perhaps a lessening public sensitivity to the international operation of the Japanese police all led to a change in policy. In 1989 the NPA for the first time ran its own small (72 millions yen) new program of foreign aid [Interview no.4, Tokyo December 7, 1988. Interview no.2, Tokyo, May 14, 1990]. The political salience of this issue is likely to grow in the coming years, especially if in times of acute crisis Japan were to seek the active cooperation of governments which in the past it has supported through targeted forms of police assistance.

A symbol of this process of internationalization was the convening, under the auspices of the National Police Agency in June 1988, of the Ministerial Conference on Security Matters for the Asia-Pacific Region. It was the first such high-level meeting that the NPA had convened since 1945. The meeting dealt with a broad array of law enforcement issues but focused among others also on questions of terrorism and some pressing security questions of the 1988 Olympic Games in Seoul, South Korea [Interview no.1, Tokyo, December 6, 1988. Interview no.6, Tokyo, May 15, 1990. Nagamatsu, 1988]. This kind of international police cooperation is organized by NPA's anti-terrorist division. An internal study group explained in a recent report that "anti-terrorist equipment should be deployed internationally because it would not be effective if only Japan performed them. "In line with this change in policy Japan is now considering to provide equipment free of charge, as part of its development aid budget dfor international technological cooperation, to areas where terrorists concentrate, like the Mid-East countries" [Kokusai Tero Mondai Kenkyuka, 1989, p.72].

Between Japan and South Korea practical police cooperation on questions of terrorism has also increased in recent years. Such cooperation had ceased since 1973-74. But with 35 Olympic teams training in Japan and 130 travelling through Japan, the 1988 Olympic Games posed great security risks not only for South Korea but also for Japan [Yomiuri, April 20, 1988]. Both countries thus began again to actively cooperate in 1986, especially in the areas of immigration and surveillance [Interview no.15, Tokyo, May 17, 1990. National Police Agency, 1989a, pp.125-26]. For Japan the issue had acquired great urgency ever since it had become clear in 1986-87 that the JRA had begun to relocate from the Middle East back to Asia. At the time it appeared probable that the JRA, seeking to disrupt the Games, would prepare terrorist attacks either alone or in cooperation with North Korean agents. But the problems Japan encountered in venturing into the field of multilateral diplomacy on questions of internal security became evident very quickly. When the time came to issue a final communique about the need for providing strong security measures for the Olympic Games, a number of governments were simply unwilling to choose sides publicly between South and North Korea or to be seen as backing the Japanese government against the JRA.

The conference illustrated, however, that Japan's international contacts on questions of internal security, limited and problematic as they are, extend naturally first to Asia. The International Association of Chiefs of Police (IACP), originally founded as an organization of police officials in the United States, has gradually turned into an organization with some potential for broader regional appeals in Asia. In 1974 the IACP was recognized as an advisory organ of the United Nations. Its aim has been to "enrich the training and equipment of police mainly around the Pacific basin. Because of this, ICAP is expected to pay a role supplementary to ICPO in view of its regional basis and objectives" [National Police Agency, 1987a, p.37].

The activities of UNAFEI point in the same direction of an incipient opening toward Asian cooperation [Interview no.3, Tokyo, December 7, 1988]. With the funding, faculty, curriculum, case material and participants heavily skewed to Japan, UNAFEI has exported Japanese institutions and police practices, such as voluntary probation officers or Japan's system of police boxes to a few states including Hongkong, Singapore, Indonesia, Papua New Guinea and Malaysia. The export of the koban system to Singapore deserves mentioning precisely because it appeared to be so successful and yet was so limited [National Police Agency, 1987a, pp.29-30. Bayley, 1984, pp.193-94. DeVos, 1984, pp.240-41. Asahi Evening News, November 30, 1982 and January 3, March 22, August 29, October 17, 1983. Mainichi, March 18 and October 26, 1982. Yomiuri, February 21, 1990].

In the early 1980s Singapore sent in short succession three study commissions to Japan to evaluate the possibilities of importing the koban system to Singapore rather than struggling with sharp increases in urban crime [Bayley, 1984, p.193]. And at the request of the government of Singapore the Japanese police sent a survey team to Singapore. In February 1982 the Japanese police made a proposal for the introduction of a police box system in Singapore. Eight provisional boxes were introduced in the jurisdiction of the Toa Payoh police station. The experiment was so successful in reducing crime (reportedly by about 50 percent) that Singapore decided in 1984 to go ahead with the introduction of a full-scale koban system. Singapore's willingness to imitate Japan is noteworthy because it was the first time that a Japanese government institution dealing with security had become a model for the world. "In effect, the Japanese are engaged in a demonstration of the utility of their hallowed koban system in another country . . . The new element, which grew throughout the 1970s, is not only an awareness of what they are doing in world perspective but a willingness to show it to the world" [Bayley, 1984, pp.194,196].

But this episode is so noteworthy precisely because it is a striking exception to a general pattern of Japanese isolation from international developments in the area of international crime control. In fact UNAFEI has not been successful in providing a ready Japanese copy for the police and justice administration bureaucracies of other Asian states. The reason is quite obvious. It was after all not entirely clear whether Singapore's Prime Minister was primarily interested in improving the efficiency of the police in controlling criminal behavior, or whether he was attracted by the possibility to establish "a Japanese-type surveillance system" [DeVos, 1984, p.241. Asahi Evening News, August 29, 1983]. While Japan may be a model for other Asian countries in containing crime at home, the historical memory of

Japanese atrocities committed during World War II throughout Asia has not yet been erased. It tempers the willingness of any Asian state to emulate Japanese police practices.

Furthermore, in contrast to Western Europe there exists no indigenous legal framework shared easily by most of the Asian states. Instead Japan, with its amalgamated legal system of French, German and American residues lives side-by-side, for example, with India and the Philippines shaped by the heavy influence of the English and American judicial and police systems. The legal basis for regional cooperation in Asia on questions of internal security thus is very weak.

Yet Japan is slowly but inevitably drawn into international society. The pattern by which this process is occurring in the realm of policy has a remarkable similarity with the adaptation to changing conditions that distinguishes Japan's domestic police practices. In the wake of the 1977 hijacking of a Japan Airline jet at Dacca, for example, the NPA, MOF and MOI began considering legislation that would facilitate international policy coordination with other countries. A draft bill that was prepared by 1980 proposed giving the Japanese police the power, enjoyed by most other police forces around the world, to arrest, rather than just observe, suspected foreign felons sought by foreign police forces or the International Criminal Police Organization (ICPO). This would have strengthened the hand of the Japanese government in seeking the extradition of Japanese criminals, like the members of the JRA, who had fled abroad, rather than negotiating with foreign governments through diplomatic channels on a case-by-case basis [Mainichi, January 9, 1980]. However, for a variety of reasons, including a strong hesitation to increase the formal powers of the NPA, the bill was not enacted. But when the JRA issued a statement on January 7, 1989 calling for a fight against the Emperor system, the NPA wasted little time to change its policy by requesting the General Secretariat of Interpol to stop issuing the less urgent blue international enquiry notices and asking instead for the international red wanted notices as the single step preceding extradition requests [Farrell, 1990, p.219]. The change in policy occurred in part because the Japanese government had become convinced that strict reciprocity was no longer the norm in the international coordination of anti-terrorism policy. Even though Japanese law still prohibits the government from arresting foreign suspects who had been listed on the international red wanted notices, the Japanese police started to request other countries, with tougher domestic laws, to post red notices on fugitives from Japan, in particular members of the JRA [National Police Agency 1989a, pp.49,127. Interview no.6, Tokyo, May 15, 1990. The Japan Times, January 21, 1989]. In short, without changing Japanese law, the NPA had enlarged its scope of action in seeking to secure Japan's internal security.

Interpol is from the Japanese perspective very useful for disseminating information and for receiving back-up information on suspected terrorists. But Japan relies on bilateral contacts rather than multilateral cooperation to deal with any sensitive issue such as terrorism. For the Japanese government police cooperation may be strengthened by occasional conferences held between government officials; but it is best left uninstitutionalized. In practice this means that Japanese police officers will occasionally travel abroad since virtually no foreign police officials come to Japan for conducting serious business [Interview no.1, Tokyo, December 1988].

As is true of other aspects of internal security policy, extradition policy reflects Japan's relatively high degree of isolation from international crime and the international police system [Advanced Course, 1989, pp.182-91]. Between 1945 and 1985 Japan responded to five formal and four defacto requests for extraditing fugitives. In the same forty-years span Japan made six formal and twenty-four defacto requests to other states [Nishimura, n.d., pp.4,ii-v]. This adds up to a total of thirty-nine requests in forty years or about one a year. Although the numbers have increased significantly in recent years [Interview no.18, Tokyo, May 18, 1990], corresponding figures for the Federal Republic of Germany are several magnitudes larger. Between 1980 and 1985 the annual figure was about 750 [Katzenstein, 1990, p.59].

Like other states operating within the civil law tradition Japanese police practice is based on the principle of reciprocity rather than the existence of extradition treaties. "Thus, no extradition can be expected when a suspect is found in any other countries in which the existence of a treaty is a prerequisite for extradition. Moreover, even when a suspect is located in a country which does not require the existence of extradition treaty and extradites fugitives on the basis of the assurance of reciprocity by the requesting country, extradition is still impossible if that country adopts the principle that its own nationals are not extraditable" [Advanced Course, 1989, p.182]. In fact Japan has concluded an extradition treaty only with the United States. First signed in 1886 it came into force again in 1953. About as many suspects are being deported from Japan in the 1980s as are being extradited, in part because of the absence of extradition treaties and in part because of the flexibility which deportation hearings offer to bureaucratic agencies in comparison to the complicated, formal process of extradition [Interview no. 2, Tokyo, December 8, 1988].

The increasing importance of international crime, including terrorism, and in particular a series of spectacular international hijackings staged by the JRA in the mid-1970s convinced the Japanese government that the scope of the extradition treaty with the United States needed to be broadened. A new treaty was signed in 1978 and entered into force in 1980 [Ministry of Justice, 1988, pp.1-13. Nishimura, n.d., pp.8-16]. As the number of extradition requests has risen in the last decade, Japan is now contemplating signing treaties with states other than the United States, including those that make extradition conditional. And in the same spirit as the 1977 European Convention on the Suppression of Terrorism Japan favors narrowing the scope of the political offense exception to extradition. On the other hand, Japanese law stipulates that extradition cannot be granted unless the person in question has been convicted in a court of law [Interview no.2, Tokyo, December 8, 1988. Interview no.18, Tokyo, May 18, 1990]. But in recent years international judicial cooperation handles the issue of reciprocity with more flexibility. This grants Japan's police greater opportunities in seeking the extradition of fugitives who have fled abroad [Advanced Course, 1989, pp.182-83]. However, the Japanese government is selective in its approach. It chose, for example, not to request the extradition of an alleged member of the Japanese Red Army, Yu Kikumura, from the United States in the late 1980s. In a Japanese court Kikumura could have been charged only with minor violations of Japan's passport law. In the United States the federal prosecutor in New Jersey charged the possession of pipe bombs as nine separate crimes resulting in a thirty-years jail sentence [Kuby and Kunstler, 1990. Interview no.18, Tokyo, May 18, 1990]. This sentence was considered much too harsh by an appeals court which subsequently remanded the case back for re-sentencing.

Japan's relative isolation from international society was also reflected in a prolonged conflict between the MOJ and the MOFA. At stake was the applicability of Japan's penal code in different settings. The Penal Code covers crimes committed by any person in Japan (Article 1), crimes committed abroad by foreign nationals that constitute a risk to Japanese security such as counterfeiting Japanese currency, participating in insurrection against Japanese authority or rendering assistance to Japan's enemies (Article 2), and crimes by Japanese nationals committed outside Japan (Article 3). But the MOFA insisted that, in addition, Japan was bound by the principle of universal jurisdiction which obliges states to prosecute specific crimes judged to infringe on universally held norms such as the prohibition against piracy, the slave trade, genocide, hijacking and certain acts of terrorism. This universal principle was not recognized by the MOJ which rejected the interpretation of the MOFA for many years before eventually acceding to a change in Japan's Criminal Code in 1987 [Interview no.18, Tokyo, May 18, 1990].

Japan's policy of internal security has been marked by continuity in its domestic component and embryonic, though still untested since the Bonn summit of 1978, change in its international dimension. Most significantly there appears to be underway a gradual process of internationalizing Japan's policy approach to questions of internal security. It is important, however, to put this process in perspective. Its undeniable importance lies in the fact that it signifies a rising importance of the internationalist factions in what must arguably be counted among the least international political institutions in contemporary Japan, the police and the judiciary. But important as it is, the kind of internationalism that is emerging in policy and politics is restricted to the level of exchanging liaison officers with other countries and organizing study tours. In contrast to the European industrial states we do not find any significant instances of an institutionalized, operational cooperation with the police of other countries [Interview nos. 11, 14 and 20, Tokyo, May 15, 16 and 19, 1990]. The depth of Japan's internationalization remains relatively shallow. In fact the Japanese police was utterly surprised and confounded by the attacks which the JRA has staged in Asia since the mid-1980s. Its intelligence in Europe and the Mideast was much stronger than in Indonesia and the Philippines [Interview 11, Tokyo, May 15, 1990]. In light of the heterogeneity of Southeast and Northeast Asia, the legacy of Japanese imperialism and Japan's overwhelming relative influence in these two regions, it is unlikely that Japan's internationalization will deepen quickly in the coming years.

VI.
CONCLUSION

Has the Japanese police been effective in its policy of internal security? As Miyazawa has shown for Japanese crime statistics in general, this question is not easily answered [Miyazawa, 1990]. In the area of internal security the issue is probably even more complex. The statistical data summarized in Table 17 and Figure 4 above is of only limited use in answering the question. As a percentage of total arrests, security-related arrests declined from 1.60 percent in 1969, to 0.39 in 1975 and 0.17 in 1985. Excluding arrests for traffic crimes, the corresponding percentage figures were 4.20, 0.90, and 0.39. But does this declining trend mean that the Japanese police has become more or less effective in coping with threats to Japan's internal security. Either of two answers appears to be at a first glance inherently plausible. The police has become more effective; it has succeeded in arresting most of those who are threatening the security of the Japanese state. Alternatively we could also argue that the Japanese police has become less effective in arresting those who constitute a security risk to the Japanese state, especially in view of the rise of terrorist and guerilla attacks after 1984. The question is inherently difficult to answer and may in fact conceal divergent trends in a fight against the JRA which, in light of a series of arrests in recent years, may have been more successful than the fight against groups operating well-concealed in the Japanese underground.

In the early 1970s Japanese policemen had a difficult time understanding European terrorism. In Japan, the police believed, it was virtually impossible to hide from the police for as much as a week and even more so for a group of suspects holding another person hostage [Kühne and Miyazawa, 1979, p.127]. Radical groups initially operated in the open as was evident from the time that Japan's radical students began forming organizations in the 1960s that would eventually end up engaging in terrorist practices and violent social protests. "Sekigun [the Red Army] was the object of intense police surveillance from the moment of its debut. The organization's first public meeting, held at a public hall in Tokyo in early September 1969, featured a massive display of state authority. In addition to the ring of uniformed police surrounding the building, plainclothes police

167

Table 17: Statistics on Arrests of Political Activists

	Arrests in security crimes		Total Arrests
1969	Total (approx.)	15,800	999,981
	New left	14,748	(377,826)[a]
	Labor (approx.)	1,000	
	Right	100	
1975	Total	3,267	830,176
	New left	1,761	(364,117)[a]
	Labor	1,016	
	Right	490	
1980	Total	1,665	970,369
	New left	934	(432,250)[a]
	Labor	258	
	Right	473	

Notes: [a]Excluding arrests for traffic crimes

Source: Police Statistics and White Papers. Security crime arrests defined as arrests due to the crimes in the new leftist movement, labor movement, and rightist movement.

photographed the three hundred people who entered, and more police stood around the back of the hall watching. Onstage, Sekigun's leaders made rousing speeches with black ski masks covering their faces so they could not be identified. Nobody got arrested that day because the gathering and the talks were perfectly legal. Yet the tone of the relationship had clearly been set" [Steinhoff, 1989a, p.727]. Soon after they had begun their attacks in Japan Sekigun found itself the target of intense police surveillance. Known members of the organization were put under "round-the-clock police surveillance, sometimes with two or three plainclothesmen surrounding one person whenever he stepped outside" [Steinhoff, n.d., p.98]. With virtual no place to go in Japan and with Sekigun leadership's ideological inclination toward the principle of internationalism firmly in place, Japan's terrorists saw great advantage in relocating abroad [Steinhoff, 1989a, pp.729,732].

The JRA has operated since 1972 outside Japan. "While in the late 1980's it is no longer surprising to find a network of Japanese circling the globe, the concept of a Japanese multinational revolutionary organization may still seem like a contradiction in terms. In fact, Japan's multinational corporation employees and its multinational revolutionary group, the Japanese Red Army, have similar social origins and a strikingly similar organizational style" [Steinhoff, 1988, p.2]. The Japanese Red Army continues to make front-page news. It is "a small group, but its members are seasoned professionals with the entire world as their field of operation. There is simply no way to stop them completely" [Steinhoff, 1988, p.16]. While the NPA suspects that a relationship may exist between the JRA and some of the hostage crises of the 1980s, such as the Wakaoji case of November 1986, it remains uncertain about the precise connections and new movements of the JRA [Takagi 1988, p.195]. But in November 1987 the Japanese police uncovered the Anti War Domestic Front (AWDF) as a domestic support group of the JRA. A movement document which the police recovered argued that the JRA had moved into the second phase of a five-phase struggle that would bring it back closer to the Japanese homeland [Farrell, 1990. Interview no.1, Tokyo, December, 1988].

A long-term perspective and patience are an essential part of the policies of internal security that the Japanese police has developed over time. Fifteen years elapsed between the height of the anti-Narita movement in the mid-1970s and the final removal in 1990 of the watch-towers that radicals had erected. Specific legislation passed in the Diet in 1978 that gave the police special powers to deal with radicals occupying airport land was invoked only twice in the years 1978-80 and again several times in 1989-90 as the police waited patiently for the radical movement's strength to wane. In the intervening decade the underground train station designed to speed passengers to Tokyo remained closed for security reasons. The police has shown similar patience in dealing with the cadres of violence-prone domestic groups as well as with some of Japan's most prominent terrorists.

Although it has become increasingly difficult for the police to identify the militant cadres of domestic protest groups, the security police persists in its traditional method of long-term surveillance. And the police is very patient in tracking down some of the terrorists which had been on its most wanted list for many years. The arrest of one of the leaders of the JRA, Osamu Maruoka, in November 1987 occurred fifteen years after the attack on Tel-Aviv's Lod airport, the first of a series of spectacularly cruel acts of terrorism abroad in which Maruoka is suspected to have been involved at least indirectly [Chira, 1987]. Other prominent members of the JRA were also arrested after many years either in Japan or while planning new attacks abroad: Yu Kikumura (in the United States, April 1988), Yasuhiro Shibata (in Japan, May 1988), and Hiroshi Sensui (in the Philippines, June 1988) [Farrell, 1990, pp.200-04].

But these success stories can be disputed quite easily. Early successes have turned into a history of failures. Since moving abroad the JRA has been able to operate with impunity for many years from a foreign base that the Japanese government and police has had very little influence over. The internationalization of crime whittles away at the geographic isolation of Japan and undermines national attributes like public cooperation, strict gun control and a generally effective police organization. Some of the police suspects brought to court after years of investigations have been found not guilty in subsequent court proceedings. And the capture of Yu Kikumura on the New Jersey turnpike can hardly be credited to the efficacy of the Japanese police. Furthermore, even in Japan the capture, for example, of JRA members Osamu Maruoka and Yasuhiro Shibata illustrates the importance of luck rather than persistent police work [Interview no.1, Tokyo, May 14, 1990. National Police Agency, 1989a, pp.125-26. Maruoka, 1990, p.116]. Furthermore, the police lacks the legitimacy to wage a concerted campaign to reduce the role of the major organized protest groups now operating in Japan. And it has found it virtually impossible to penetrate radical sects which have moved underground. It knows, for example, little that is specific about the operation of the military cadres of the Chukaku [Interview nos.12 and 13, Tokyo, May 16, 1990]. And the relatively high efficacy of the MPD contrasts starkly with the weakness of the police forces in other prefectures to keep track of radicals [Interview nos.1 and 12, Tokyo, May 14 and 16, 1990].

It thus would be wrong to overestimate the efficacy of Japan's policy of internal security. Since the late 1970s the police has in fact experienced great difficulties in infiltrating the militant core of radical groups such as the Chukaku and Kakumaru [Parker, 1984, p.131]. Thus the clearance rate of crimes committed by and among different radical political sects falls well below the clearance rate for general homicides and violent crimes [Parker, 1984, pp. 192-93. Tachibana, 1975]. Illustrative of the inability of the police to prevent attacks was the Tokyo summit of 1986. Despite the full mobilization of Japan's police forces members of the Chukaku staged with home-made rockets an unsuccessful attack on a palace residence in downtown Tokyo where the Western leaders were being welcomed. Fired from a distance of three kilometers the rockets overflew their target. Based on the technological sophistication of home-made rockets employed in previous attacks, the police had searched about 50,000 apartments and buildings in a radius of only two kilometers of the conference site. The incident humiliated Japan's police which had arrested 900 leftist activists with no clear reason, sealed off downtown Tokyo within a two-kilometer radius of the conference and lodging sites, mobilized 30,000 policemen, tried out 40 million dollars worth of new equipment, and spent an additional 17 million dollars [Schiller, 1986, p.39. National Police Agency, 1987a, p.121. Van Wolferen, 1989, pp.199-200. Interview no.16, Tokyo, May 17, 1990].

For Japanese ears the concept of strategy has unwelcome military and authoritarian connotations, painful reminders of the 1930s and 1940s. According to virtually all police officers Japan's internal security policy is not based on a sense of strategic mission but emerged instead by trial and error in reaction to social developments [Interview no.1, Tokyo, December 6, 1988. Interviews nos.1 and 17, Tokyo, May 14 and 17, 1990]. To the outside observer, though, there exists a discernible pattern in the policy response during the last two decades. The police has increasingly relied on un'yo, a flexible interpretation of the legal restraints under which it operates. In the initial phase in the late 1960s and early 1970s the Japanese police succeeded in closely monitoring the moves of the Red Army Faction and, within a short period of time, pushing it outside the country. In the hope of gradually strangling the organization of the JRA a patient and long-term policy has sought to narrow its operational base and resources abroad and at home; since the mid-1980s that strategy has been rewarded by the arrest of several key suspects.

Such long-term approach also informs the police approach to radical groups operating inside Japan. After their failure to mobilize the Japanese public for mass protests, various radical groups have moved underground since the late 1970s. Since Chukaku and other radical groups face growing difficulties in finding new recruits and experience a general decline of support in urban areas, the police tries to contain their operations rather than to eliminate them altogether [Tachibana, 1975]. The MPD maintains that it is so effective in protecting important events in Tokyo that radicals move outside of Tokyo for their duration; but by most accounts the MPD lacks the information and resources to seriously curtail the operations of radical groups in normal times [Interviews nos.1 and 12, Tokyo, May 14 and 16, 1990]. While the police is, by comparative standards, extraordinarily restrained in its reliance on violent tactics, it would be wrong to underestimate the pressure it exerts through surveillance and the extension of the informal powers it has succeeded in acquiring.

In contrast to the general pattern of crime control in Japan the evidence thus is too ambiguous to permit us to answer the question of police effectiveness in combatting terrorism and violent social movements. Is the fact that the police has not succeeded in eliminating deadly, interfactional strife among radical sects indicating a failure of penetrating the hard-core of underground organizations, or is it testimony to a clever policy of presiding over a bloody self-liquidation of the Left [Interviews nos.10 and 18, Tokyo, May 15 and 18, 1990]? Is the fact that, in contrast to the mid-1970s, the NPA in the 1980s is no longer attempting to define a minimum crime security standard for Japan signalling a victory against the forces threatening Japan's internal security, or is it an admission that events have simply become too complex and unpredictable [Interviews nos.13 and 16, Tokyo, May, 16 and 18, 1990]? The answer to these questions is that we simply do not know.

We do know, however, that Japan's policy of internal security reflects the structures and norms that shape how Japanese officials think and act. The head of the NPA, Hideo Yamada, summarized the issue in the following terms: "The police in foreign countries have taken various measures to suppress acts of terrorism. For example, security officers have been augmented in the number of men and arms used while on patrol in the U.S. and Europe. Naturally, working conditions for these security officers have been improved, including pay. In addition army troops have also been mobilized to guard international conferences. In Japan, however, the police are not allowed to take similar measures; but I am very proud that the Japanese police have been successful in maintaining order and security in this country. I hope they will use their wisdom 'native to the Japanese' in curbing violence in full cooperation with the people" [Mainichi, April 21, 1988].

Structures and norms both have dictated to the Japanese police a strategy aspired to, less successfully, also by some urban guerrillas in Latin America: to swim like little fishes in the warm sea of the people. The police are part of one system which is predictable, eschews violence if at all possible, and engages only in extremely carefully controlled processes of escalation. It has "turned the habit of leniency into a kind of second nature. But a condition is attached: the recipient must in turn acknowledge the goodness of the established social order; political heterodoxy elicits tough measures" [Van Wolferen, 1989, pp.182-83]. The police is able to mobilize totally, often working unpaid overtime shifts, to make the security arrangements for the major events that since the mid-1980s have occurred at least once a year in Tokyo. It does so relying on a cooperative public. But it lacks the support of the political parties for a resumption of a sustained campaign against terrorist organizations or violent social movements, as some police officials have occasionally demanded [Interviews nos.13, 14, 19,

Tokyo, May 16 and 18, 1990]. Instead the police has adopted a long-term strategy of attrition that aims at reducing the scope of operation and the resources available to the radical movements operating both inside and outside Japan. Meanwhile it collects as much information and intelligence as possible and waits patiently for the aging of radicals and the lack of new recruitment to gradually sap the strength of radical movements [Interviews nos.1 and 15, Tokyo, May 14 and 17, 1990].

Culture and geography explain why internationalization has come later and more haltingly to Japan than to other industrial states. Internal security policy is no exception to this generalization. Japanese terrorists have not operated in proximate areas of Japan. After its move to the Mideast in the early 1970s, it took the JRA more than a decade to set up the logistical infrastructure in Asia to permit its members to operate at closer range to Japan. In doing so the JRA has underlined the fact that even Japan's NPA can no longer neglect the international dimensions of its internal security policy. With the rise of Japan's international position Japanese embassies, corporations and nationals will become more attractive targets for international terrorists. And as Japanese terrorists are beginning to move closer to Japan, other Asian states from whose territory these terrorists are now operating are likely to develop a stronger interest in cooperating with the Japanese police. Japan's greatest political challenge thus will lie in learning how to manage the unavoidable tensions between the resilience of adapting institutions, norms and practices which contain violent crimes at home and the fragility of evolving institutions, norms and practices in an international society to which it must accommodate.

APPENDIX

The Incident of Japanese and German Terrorism: Statistical Comparisons

Table A-1: Distribution of Incidents* in FRG and in Japan, by Modus Operandi

Table A-2: Distribution of Incidents* in FRG and Japan, by Nature of Target (persons/facilities)

Table A-3: Distribution of Incidents* in FRG and in Japan, by Major Perpetrating Group

Table A-4: Number of Incidents* in which Victims Were Killed in FRG and in Japan, by Major Perpetrating Groups

Table A-5: Number of Victims Per Year in FRG and in Japan

Table A-6: Distribution of Incidents* in FRG and in Japan, by Affiliation of Victims to Political Blocks

Table A-7: Distribution of Incidents*, by Nationality of Target Victim, in FRG and in Japan

Table A-8: Frequency of Incidents Per Year, in FRG and Japan (1983-mid 1989)

Table A-9: Distribution of Incidents** outside FRG and Japan, by Site of Incident: Country (1970 - September 1989)

Table A-10: Distribution of Incidents** outside FRG and Japan, by Site of Incident: Region (1970 - September 1989)

Table A-11: Distribution of Incidents** outside FRG and Japan, by Nature of Target (persons/facilities) (1970 - September 1989)

Table A-12: Distribution of Incidents** outside FRG and Japan, by Major Perpetrating Group (1970 - September 1989)

Table A-13: Distribution of Incidents by Year, outside FRG and Japan (1983 - September 1989)

*   German data cover the period between 1970 to the end of September 1989. Data before 1979 are incomplete as they include only incidents in which Palestinian terrorist organizations were the target of assaults. Japanese data cover the period between 1979 to mid 1989.

**   Data cover the period between 1970 and the end of September 1989. Data before 1979 are incomplete as they include only incidents in which Palestinian terrorist organizations were involved.

Source: Project on Low Intensity Warfare, The Jaffee Center for Strategic Studies, Tel-Aviv University, Israel, 1989.

Table A-1: Distribution of Incidents in FRG and in Japan, by Modus Operandi

Modus Operandi*	West Germany**		Japan***	
	Number of Incidents	Percentage of Total	Number of Incidents	Percentage of Total
Bombing or Arson	404	66.5	131	72.0
Armed Assault	100	16.5	40	22.0
Specific Threat	7	1.2	3	1.6
Kidnapping	4	0.6	-	-
Sabotage	47	7.7	5	2.7
Barricade Hostage	8	1.3	-	-
Letter Bomb	22	3.6	2	1.2
Hijacking	11	1.8	1	0.5
Unknown	5	0.8	-	-
Total	608	100.0	182	100.0

* Incomplete/thwarted incidents are classified according to their intended modus operandi.

** The period: 1970 to the end of September 1989. Statistics for years before 1979 are incomplete as they include only incidents in which Palestinian terrorist organizations were the target of assaults. It should also be noted that records of attacks perpetrated during 1979-1980, the first years of the data base, may not be full.

*** The period: 1979 to mid 1989. It should be noted that records of attacks perpetrated during 1979-1980, the first years of the data base, may be incomplete.

Table A-2: Distribution of Incidents* in FRG and Japan, by Nature of Target (persons/facilities)

Nature of Target	West Germany**** Number of Incidents	Japan***** Number of Incidents
Political & Adversary**	319	58
Random Public	107	12
Economic	206	104
Diplomatic***	32	8
Unclear	11	1

*   Some of the incidents include more than one type of target.

**   Government officials and facilities, political rivals.

***   Embassies, Diplomats, Consulates.

****   The period: 1970 to the end of September 1989. Statistics for years before 1979 are incomplete as they include only incidents in which Palestinian terrorist organizations were the target of assaults. It should also be noted that records of attacks perpetrated during 1979-1980, the first years of the data base, may not be full.

*****   The period: 1979 to mid 1989. It should be noted that records of attacks perpetrated during 1979-1980, the first years of the data base, may be incomplete.

Table A-3: Distribution of Incidents in FRG and in Japan by Major Perpetrating Group

Perpetrating Group	West Germany[***] Number of Incidents	West Germany[***] Percentage of Total	Perpetrating Group	Japan[****] Number of Incidents	Japan[****] Percentage of Total
RAF	135	22.2	Chukaku-ha	118	64.8
RZ	88	14.5	Senki-kyosando	15	8.2
Unspecified German[*]	68	11.2	Leftist Japanese	14	7.7
Leftist German	67	11.0	Kakurokyo	9	4.9
Rightist German	30	4.9	PCJRI[**]	4	2.2
Provisional IRA	24	3.9	Unknown Japanese	4	2.2
RZ and RAF	24	3.9	JRA	3	1.6
Other	172	28.3	Other	15	8.2
Total	608	100.0	Total	182	100.0

[*]   Unclear political orientation.

[**]   Patriotic Corps of Japanese Racial Independence.

[***] The period: 1970 to the end of September 1989. Statistics for years before 1979 are incomplete as they include only incidents in which Palestinian terrorist organizations were the target of assaults. It should also be noted that records of attacks perpetrated during 1979-1980, the first years of the data base, may not be full.

[****] The period: 1979 to mid 1989. It should be noted that records of attacks perpetrated during 1979-1980, the first years of the data base, may be incomplete.

Table A-4: Number of Incidents in which Victims were Killed in FRG and in Japan by Major Perpetrating Groups

Perpetrating Group	West Germany**				Perpetrating Group	Japan***			
	No Deaths	Incidents with Deaths	Number of Deaths Unknown	Total		No Deaths	Incidents with Deaths	Number of Deaths Unknown	Total
RAF	113	12	10	135	Chukaku-ha	92	4	22	118
RZ	83	1	4	88	Senki-kyosando	9	-	6	15
Unspecified German*	65	1	2	68	Leftist Japanese	13	-	1	14
Leftist German	66	-	1	67	Kakurokyo	3	-	6	9
Rightist German	27	2	1	30	PCJRI	2	1	1	4
Provisional IRA	20	4	-	24	Unknown Japanese	4	-	-	4
RAF and RZ	24	-	-	24	JRA	2	-	1	3
Total	388	20	18	436	Total	125	5	37	167

* Unclear political orientation.

** The period: 1970 to the end of September 1989. Statistics for years before 1979 are incomplete as they include only incidents in which Palestinian terrorist organizations were the target of assaults. It should also be noted that records of attacks perpetrated during 1979-1980, the first years of the data base, may not be full.

*** The period: 1979 to mid 1989. It should be noted that records of attacks perpetrated during 1979-1980, the first years of the data base, may be incomplete.

Table A-5: Number of Victims Per Year in FRG and in Japan (1983 - September 1989)

Year	West Germany			Year	Japan		
	Killed	Wounded	Total		Killed	Wounded	Total
1983	1	-	1	1983	2	1	3
1984	9	25	34	1984	-	12	12
1985	9	92	101	1985	-	-	-
1986	5	202	207	1986	-	63	63
1987	2	32	34	1987	1	2	3
1988	1	29	30	1988	-	24	24
1989*	2	11	13	1989*	-	-	-
Total	29	391	420	Total	3	102	105

*   Updated to early September 1989.

Table A-6: Distribution of Incidents in FRG and in Japan, by Affiliation of Victims to Political Blocks

Political Affiliation of Victims*	West Germany**** Number of Incidents**	Japan***** Number of Incidents***
Nato	66	1
Arab League	19	-
Warsaw Pact	5	-
Other	61	12

*   Victims include killes, wounded, and kidnapped (whether or not released by captors).

**   The total number of incidents with victims was 111; some of the incidents involved victims of more than one political affiliation.

****   The total number of incidents with victims was 12; some of the incidents involved victims of more than one political affiliation.

****   The period: 1970 to the end of September 1989. Statistics for years before 1979 are incomplete as they include only incidents in which Palestinian terrorist organizations were the target of assaults. It should also be noted that records of attacks perpetrated during 1979-1980, the first years of the data base, may not be full.

*****   The period: 1979 to mid 1989. It should be noted that records of attacks perpetrated during 1979-1980, the first years of the data base, may be incomplete.

Table A–7: Distribution of Incidents, by Nationality of Target Victim, in FRG and in Japan

West Germany****		Japan*****	
Nationality of Target Victims*	Number of Incidents**	Nationality of Target Victims	Number of Incidents***
FRG	46	Japan	10
USA	26	Pakistan	1
Great Britain	14	Thailand	1
Iran	8	USA	1
International Organizations	5		
Israel	5		
Libya	4		
Yugoslavia	4		
Poland	3		
Syria	3		
Turkey	3		
Other Countries	15		

*   Comprises only countries that were the target of 3 or more attacks. Victims include killed, wounded, and kidnapped (whether or not released by captors).

**   The total number of incidents with victims was 111 - some of the incidents involved target-victims of more than one nationality.

***   The total number of incidents with victims was 12 - some of the incidents involved target-victims of more than one nationality.

****   The period: 1970 to the end of September 1989. Statistics for years before 1979 are incomplete as they include only incidents in which Palestinian terrorist organizations were the target of assaults. It should also be noted that records of attacks perpetrated during 1979–1980, the first years of the data base, may not be in full.

***** The period: 1979 to mid 1989. It should be noted that records of attacks perpetrated during 1979–1980, the first years of the data base, may be incomplete.

Table A-8: Frequency of Incidents Per Year, in FRG and Japan (1983 to mid 1989)

Year	West Germany Number of Incidents	Japan Number of Incidents
1983*	8	3
1984	44	9
1985	105	47
1986	80	37
1987	27	24
1988	28	17
1989**	23	7

*   From mid 1983.
**   Updated to mid 1989.

Table A-9: Distribution of Incidents Outside FRG and Japan, by Site of Incident: Country (1970 to September 1989*)

(Countries in which three or more incidents took place)			(Countries in which two or more incidents took place)		
West Germany			Japan		
Country	Number of Incidents	Percentage of Total	Country	Number of Incidents	Percentage of Total
Lebanon	15	14.8	China	5	14.3
Colombia	10	9.9	Peru	5	14.3
Portugal	10	9.9	Philippines	4	11.4
Peru	8	7.9	France	2	5.7
Greece	7	6.9	South Korea	2	5.7
France	5	4.9	Other	17	48.6
Israel	4	4.0			
Nicaragua	4	4.0			
Turkey	4	4.0			
Belgium	3	3.0			
Italy	3	3.0			
Other	28	27.7			
Total	101	100.0	Total	35	100.0

* Statistics for years before 1979 are incomplete as they include only incidents in which Palestinian terrorist organizations were involved. It should also be noted that records of attacks perpetrated during 1979-1980, the early years of the data base, may not be in full.

Table A–10: Distribution of Incidents outside FRG and Japan, by Site of Incident: Region (1970 - September 1989*)

Region	West Germany		Japan	
	Number of Incidents	Percentage of Total	Number of Incidents	Percentage of Total
AMERICA				
North	–	–	1	2.8
Central	5	4.9	1	2.8
South	20	19.8	5	14.3
CARIBBEAN	–	–	–	–
EUROPE				
Eastern	–	–	–	–
Western	35	34.6	7	20.0
AFRICA				
North	5	4.9	1	2.8
Subsaharan	8	7.9	1	2.8
South	–	–	–	–
MIDDLE EAST	24	23.8	3	8.6
ASIA				
South	2	2.0	2	5.7
Southeast	–	–	2	5.7
FAR EAST	2	2.0	11	31.4
OCEANIA	–	–	1	2.8
Total	101	100.0	35	100.0

*Statistics for years before 1979 are incomplete as they include only incidents in which Palestinian terrorist organizations were involved. It should also be noted that records of attacks perpetrated during 1979–1980, the early years of the data base, may not be in full.

Table A-11: Distribution of Incidents* outside FRG and Japan, by Nature of Target (persons/facilities) (1970 - September 1989)****

Nature of Target	West Germany Number of Incidents	Japan Number of Incidents
Political & Adversary**	23	1
Random Public	38	11
Economic	43	27
Diplomatic***	12	5
Unclear	-	-

*   Some of the incidents include more than one type of target.

**   Goverment officials and facilities, political rivals.

***   Embassies, Diplomats, Consulates.

**** Statistics for years before 1979 are incomplete as they include only incidents in which Palestinian terrorist organizations were involved. It should also be noted that records of attacks perpetrated during 1979-1980, the early years of the data base, may not be in full.

Table A–12: Distribution of Incidents outside FRG and Japan, by Major Perpetrating Group (1970 - September 1989*)

Perpetrating Group	West Germany No. of Incidents	% of Total	Perpetrating Group	Japan No. of Incidents	% of Total
FP=25	10	9.9	JRA	6	17.1
Hizballah	10	9.9	Unspecified Chinese or Rightist Japanese	5	14.3
ELN	8	7.9	MRTA	3	8.6
SL	7	6.9	NPA	3	8.6
ASALA	3	3.0	Hizballah	2	5.7
FDN	3	3.0	Separatist Japanese	2	5.7
PKK	3	30.0	SL	2	5.7
RPA	3	3.0	Other	12	34.3
ETA	2	1.9			
FRC	2	1.9			
MNR	2	1.9			
Polisario	2	1.9			
PRS	2	1.9			
SPLA	2	1.9			
Unita	2	1.9			
Other	40	39.6			
Total	101	100.0	Total	35	100.0

*Statistics for years before 1979 are incomplete as they include only incidents in which Palestinian terrorist organizations were involved. It should also be noted that records of attacks perpetrated during 1979–1980, the early years of the data base, may not be in full.

**Table A-13: Distribution of Incidents by Year,
outside FRG and Japan (1983 - September 1989)**

West Germany		Japan	
Year	Number of Incidents	Year	Number of Incidents
1983*	6	1983*	1
1984	8	1984	5
1985	23	1985	2
1986	18	1986	5
1987	7	1987	8
1988	12	1988	2
1989**	5	1989**	7

*   Incidents recorded since mid 1983.
** Updated to early September 1989.

REFERENCES

Advanced Course for Senior Police Administrators. 1989. Tokyo: Japan International Cooperation Agency and National Police Agency.

Aichiken-Boren no Jigyo An'nai (Aichi Prefecture Federation Crime Prevention Association: An Introduction to Its Business). 1990. Aichiken: Aichiken Bohankyokai Rengokai.

Akagai, Suruki and Inakawa, Shoji, 1983. Seisaku Kettei Kiko to Naikaku Hojobukyoku (Policy Decision-Making Mechanisms and Bureaus Supporting the Cabinet). Tokyo: Gyosei Kanri Modai Kenkyu Kai.

Akahata, Daily. Tokyo: Japan Communist Party.

All Japan Crime Prevention Association. n.d. Zenboren: Promotion of Crime Prevention Hand in Hand Together! Tokyo: All Japan Crime Prevention Association.

Ames, Walter L. 1981. Police and Community in Japan. Berkeley: University of California Press.

Anderson, Malcolm. 1989. Policing the World: Interpol and the Politics of International Police Co-operation. Oxford: Clarendon Press.

Angel, Robert C. 1990. "Japanese Terrorists and Japanese Countermeasures," in Barrey Rubin, ed., The Politics of Counterterrorism: The Ordeal of Democratic States, pp. 31-60. Washington, D.C.: Foreign Policy Institute.

Apter, David E. and Sawa, Nagayo. 1984. Against the State: Politics and Social Protest in Japan. Cambridge: Harvard University Press.

Arai, Yutaka. 1979. "80 nendai no Keisatsu" ("Police in the 1980s"), Keisatsu Kenkyu (Police Studies) 589 (January): 28-36.

Arai, Yutaka et al. 1979. "Wagakuni Keisatsu no Ayumi" ("The History of Japanese Police: A Roundtable)," Keisatsu Kenkyu (Police Studies) 589 (January): 3-27.

Archambeault, William G. and Fenwick, Charles R. 1983. "A Comparative Analysis of Japanese and American Police Organizational Management Models: The Evolution of a Military Bureaucracy to a Theory Z Organization," Police Studies 6: 3-12.

Archambeault, William G. and Fenwick, Charles R. 1985. "Differential Effects of Police Organizational Management in a Cultural Context: Comparative Analysis of South Korean, Japanese and American Law Enforcement," Police Studies 8,1 (Spring): 1-12.

Asahi, Daily. Tokyo: Asahi Shimbunsha.

Asahi Evening News Daily. Tokyo: Ashahi Shimbunsha.

Asahi. 1978. Shin Jyoho-sen (A New Intelligence War). Tokyo: Asahi Shimbunsha.

Asahi Journal. 1976. "Tokushu: Seiji Tero" ("Special Topics: Political Terrorism"), (30 January): 4-33.

Asahi Journal. 1977. "Tokushu: Uyoku Hantaisei Tero no Shundo" ("Special Topics: Rightist Anti-Establishment Terrorism Astir"), (18 March): 6-17.

Asahi Journal. 1978a. "Tokushu: Chiankyoka e no Kiken na Yuwaku" ("Special Topics: A Dangerous Temptation to Strengthen the Security Laws"), (26 May): 10-26.

Asahi Journal. 1978b. "Tokushu: Narita Kaiko" ("Special Topics: Opening Narita Airport"), (2 June): 10-26.

Asahi Journal. 1987a. "Keisatsu yo Ogoruna" ("Police! Don't be Arrogant! Case Studies"), (26 June): 6-13.

Asahi Journal. 1987b. "Ibaruna Keisatsu" ("Police! Don't Be Arrogant! Case Studies, Parts II-IV"), (7 August): 6-12; (25 September): 6-13; (6 November): 6-12.

Asahi Nenkan (Asahi Almanac). 1960-90. Tokyo: Asahi Shiumbunsha.

Asano, Ken'ichi, 1987. Hanzaihodo to Keisatsu (Crime News Report and the Police). Tokyo: San'ichi Shobo.

Asano, Ken'ichi, 1990. Kagekiha Hodo no Hanzai (A Crime News Report on Radicals). Tokyo: San'ichi Shobo.

Bayley, David H. 1975. "A Comparative Analysis of Police Practices," Resource Material Series No.10, pp.3-27. Fuchu, Tokyo: United Nations Asia and Far East Institute for the Prevention of Crime and the Treatment of Offenders (UNAFEI).

Bayley, David H. 1976. "Learning about Crime -- The Japanese Experience," Public Interest 44 (Summer): 55-68.

Bayley, David H. 1978. Forces of Order: Police Behavior in Japan and the United States. Berkeley: University of California Press.

Bayley, David H. 1984. "Police, Crime and the Community in Japan," in George DeVos, ed., Institutions for Change in Japanese Society, pp.177-98. Berkeley: Institute of East Asian Studies, University of California.

Bayley, David H. 1985. Patterns of Policing: A Comparative International Analysis. New Brunswick: Rutgers University Press.

Beer, Lawrence Ward. 1984. Freedom of Expression in Japan: A Study in Comparative Law, Politics, and Society. Tokyo: Kodansha.

Beer, Lawrence Ward. 1989. "Law and Liberty," in Takeshi Ishida and Ellis S. Krauss, eds., Democracy in Japan, pp. 67-87. Pittsburgh: University of Pittsburgh Press.

Bermudez, Joseph S. 1990. Terrorism: The North Korean Connection. New York: Crane Russak.

Bestor, Theodore C. 1989. Neighborhood Tokyo. Stanford: Stanford University Press.

Birch, Roger. 1989. "Policing Europe in 1992." London, Royal Institute of International Affairs, 19 April.

Campbell, John C. 1984. "Policy Conflict and Its Resolution within the Governmental System," in Ellis S. Krauss, Thomas P. Rohlen and Patricia G. Steinhoff, eds., Conflict in Japan, pp. 294-334. Honolulu: University of Hawaii Press.

Central Statistical Office, 1990. Annual Abstract of Statistics. London: Her Majesty's Stationary Office.

Chiho Zaimu Kyokai. 1990. Naisei Kankeisha Meibo (Directory of Civil Servants Working in Home Affairs). Tokyo: Chiho Zaimu Kyokai.

191

Chipello, Christopher. 1991. "Mr. Ogawa's Tale: How Sweet Potatoes Grounded an Airport," The Wall Street Journal, April 12: A1, A7.

Chira, Susan. 1987. "Terrorist Leader is Seized in Japan," The New York Times (25 November): A8.

Chiyomaru, Kenji. 1982. "Keisatsu Kokka no Genjyo" ("The Present Situation of the Police State in Japan"), in Minshuno Hyogen no Jiyu o Kakuritsu surukai, ed., Ukeika no Kozo (The Structure of Rightist Tendencies). Tokyo: JCA Shuppan.

Citizens Crime Commission of Philadelphia. 1975. Tokyo: One City Where Crime Doesn't Pay. Philadelphia: Citizens Crime Commission.

Clifford, William. 1976. Crime Control in Japan. Lexington, Mass.: Lexington Books.

Clifford, William. 1982. "The Development of Comparative Criminal Justice in the Asian Region," in Criminal Justice in Asia: The Quest for an Integrated Approach, pp.72-90. Tokyo: United Nations Asia and Far East Institute for the Prevention of Crime and the Treatment of Offenders (UNAFEI).

Criminal Justice in Asia: The Quest for an Integrated Approach. 1982. Tokyo: United Nations Asia and Far East Institute for the Prevention of Crime and the Treatment of Offenders (UNAFEI).

Crome, Peter. 1978a. "Japan sorgt sich zunehmend um Extremisten, Atomkraftwerke," Frankfurter Rundschau (13 September).

Crome, Peter. 1978b. "Noch eine Blamage will der Polizeichef nicht," Frankfurter Rundschau (18 May).

Darlin, Damon. 1989. "Japanese Fear New Juvenile Violence is Sign of Spreading 'American Disease'", The Wall Street Journal (2 August): A10.

Deacon, Richard. 1982. A History of the Japanese Secret Service. London: Muller.

DeVos, George. 1984. "The Post-War Police: Discussions, Conclusions and Comparative Implications," in George DeVos, ed., Institutions for Change in Japanese Society, pp.236-44. Berkeley: University of California Press, Institute of East Asian Studies.

Donnelly, Jack. 1986. "International Human Rights: A Regime Analysis," International Organization 40,3 (Summer): 599-642.

Dore, Ronald. 1986. Flexible Rigidities: Industrial Policy and Structural Adjustment in the Japanese Economy 1970-80. Stanford: Stanford University Press.

Dore, Ronald. 1987. Taking Japan Seriously: A Confucian Perspective on Leading Economic Issues. Stanford: Stanford University Press.

Dore, Ronald. 1988. "Goodwill and the Spirit of Market Capitalism," in Daniel I. Okimoto and Thomas P. Rohlen, eds., Inside the Japanese System: Readings on Contemporary Society and Political Economy, pp.90-99. Stanford: Stanford University Press.

Dörmann, Uwe. 1984. "Interpolstatistik: Kein wahrer Spiegel der tatsächlichen Kriminalitätsbelastung," Kriminalstatistik 8-9: 414-20.

The Economist. 1974. "Very low Profile," (16 August): 44.

The Economist. 1977. "Bitter Aftermath," (15 October): 76.

The Economist. 1990. "Japan's Gangster's: Honourable Mob," (27 January): 19-22.

Emmerson, John K. and Humphreys, Leonard A. 1973. Will Japan Rearm? A Study in Attitudes. Washington: American Enterprise Institute.

Endicott, John E. 1982. "The Defense Policy of Japan," in Douglas J. Murray and Paul R. Viotti, eds., The Defense Policies of Nations: A Comparative Study. Baltimore: The Johns Hopkins University Press.

Enomoto, Jerry. 1984. "The Police: Structural and Cultural Considerations in Comparing Japan and the United States," in George DeVos, ed., Institutions for Change in Japanese Society, pp.230-35. Berkeley: University of California Press, Institute of East Asian Studies.

Farrell, William. 1990. Blood and Rage: The Story of the Japanese Red Army. Lexington, Mass.: D.C Heath, Lexington Books.

Fenwick, Charles R. 1982. "Crime and Justice in Japan: Implications for the United States," International Journal of Comparative and Applied Criminal Justice 6,1 (Spring): 61-71.

Fingerman, Mark E. 1980. "Skyjacking and the Bonn Declaration of 1978: Sanctions Applicable to Recalcitrant Nations," California Western International Law Journal 10,1 (Winter): 123-52.

Fooner, Michael. 1973. INTERPOL: The Inside Story of the International Crime-Fighting Organization. Chicago: Henry Regnery.

Fujita, Hiroyasu. 1988. "Keisatsu-ho 2-jyo no Igi nikansuru Jyakkan no Kosatsu (A Study of the Significance of the Police Law, Article 2)," Hogaku, Vol. 52 (Sendai: Tohoku University): 707-35.

Fujiwara, Akira and Amamiya, Shoichi. 1985. Gendaishi to Kokka Himitsu-ho. (National Security Legislation in Historical Perspective). Tokyo: Miraisha.

Fukui, Haruhiro. 1970. Party in Power: The Japanese Liberal-Democrats and Policy-making. Canberra: Australian National University Press.

Fukunaga, Hideo, ed. 1988. Shinban Gaikin Keisatsu (Patrol Police: A New Edition). Tokyo: Keiseisha.

Fukushima, Shingo. 1972. "Keisatsu to Seiji no Kosaku" ("Overlaps between the Police and Politics"), Shakai Kagaku Kenkyu 24,1: 1-24.
Futo-sosaku-oshu Reraku-kai. 1988. The Gasa (Illegal Search and Seizure Cases). Tokyo: Impact Shuppankai.

Garrison, Ormar V. 1976. The Secret World of Interpol. New York: Pralston-Pilot.

Gelb, Joyce, 1990. "Tradition and Change in Japan: The Case of Equal Employment Opportunity Law," paper prepared for delivery at the 1990 Annual Meeting of the American Political Science Association, San Francisco Hilton, August 30-September 2.

Goto, Motoo et al. 1982. Sengo Hoshu Seiji no Kiseki (The Track Record of Postwar Conservative Politics in Japan). Tokyo: Iwanami Shoten.

Haberman, Clyde. 1984. "Police in Japan: Badges have Lost Their Sparkle," The New York Times (November 5): A2.

Haley, John Owen. 1978. "The Myth of the Reluctant Litigant," The Journal of Japanese Studies 4,2 (Summer): 359-390.

Haley, John O. 1982a. "Sheathing the Sword of Justice in Japan: An Essay on Law without Sanctions," Journal of Japanese Studies (Summer) 8,2: 265-81.

Haley, John Owen. 1982b. "The Politics of Informal Justice: The Japanese Experience, 1922-1942," in Richard L. Abel, ed., The Politics of Informal Justice. Volume 2, pp.125-47. New York: Academic Press.

Haley, John O. 1984. "The Role of Law in Japan: An Historical Perspective," Kobe University Law Review 18 (1984): 1-20.

Hamaguchi, Eshun and Kumon, Shunpei. 1982. Nihonteki Shudanshugi (Japanese Groupism). Tokyo: Yuhikaku.

Harano, Akira and Takada, Akimasa. 1989. "Keisatsu Sosa to sono Ranyo Kisei" ("Regulating the Abuse of Police Investigation"), Hogaka Semina: Sogo Tokushu 36 Keisatus no Genzai: 258-269.

Hatakeyama, Hirofumi. 1984. "Keishokuho Kaisei to Seijiteki Leadership" ("The Revision of the Police Duties Execution Law and Political Leadership"), in Hideo Otake, ed., Nippon Seiji no Soten (Issues in Japanese Politics), pp. 71-126. Tokyo: San'ichi Shobo.

Hatakeyama, Hirofumi. 1989. Kanryosei Shihai no Nichijyo Kozo (Daily Patterns of Bureaucratic Domination). Tokyo: San'ichi Shobo.

Hayashi, Shigeo. 1978. Kokka Kinkyuken no Kenkyu (A Study on the State Authority in Emergency). Tokyo: Banseisha.

Hechter, Michael. 1987a. Principles of Group Solidarity. Berkeley: University of California Press.

Hechter, Michael. 1987b. "Rational Choice Foundations of Social Order," paper presented at the Annual Meetings of the American Political Science Association, September 3-6.

Heishman, William Herbert II. 1990. An Analysis of the Japanese Construction Industry for the 1990s. MA Thesis, Cornell Unversity.

Henderson, Dan Fenno. 1965. Conciliation and Japanese Law: Tokugawa Henderson, D. 1978. "Perspective and Appraisal," in Dan Fenno Henderson and John Owen Haley, eds., Law and the Legal Process in Japan: Materials for an Introductory Course on Japanese Law, pp.702-18. Seattle: University of Washington Law School.

Hidaka, Yoshio. 1989. "Kyokusa Boryoku Shudan niyoru Bakudan-jiken no Gaiyo to Kongo no Hosaku I,II" ("A Survey of Bombing Incidents by Ultra-Leftist Groups and Future Counter-Measures Against Them"), Keisatu Koron (Police Review) (November): 44-50; (December): 62-65.

Hielscher, Gebhard. 1977. "'Ein Leben wiegt schwerer als der Erdball'," Süddeutsche Zeitung (30 September).

Hielscher, Gebhard. 1986. "Japans RAF und 'Zentralkernfraktion': Hervorgegangen aus der studentischen Opposition," Süddeutsche Zeitung (7 August): 10.

Higuchi, Tsuneharu. n.d. Sato Naikaku-ki no Boei Seisaku (Defense Policy in the Sato Administration). University of Tsukuba. M.A. Thesis.

Higuchi, Yoichi. 1979. Hikaku no nakano Nihon Koku Kempo (The Japanese Constitution in Comparative Perspective). Tokyo: Iwanami Shoten.

Hironaka, Toshio. 1955. Nippon no Keisatsu (The Japanese Police). Tokyo: Tokyo Daigaku Shuppankai.

Hironaka, Toshio, 1968. Sengo Nihon no Keisatsu (The Post-war Japanese Police). Tokyo: Iwanami Shoten.

Hironaka, Toshio. 1973. Keibikoan Keisatsu no Kenkyu (A Study of the Security Police and the Public Security Police). Tokyo: Iwanami Shoten.

Hirose, Katsuya. 1989. Kanryo to Gunjin (Bureaucrats and Military Officers). Tokyo: Iwanami Shoten.

Hoffman, Vincent J. 1982. "The Development of Modern Police Agencies in the Republic of Korea and Japan: A Paradox," Police Studies 5: 3-16.

Hogaku Semina. 1971. "Shiho no Kiki" ("Special Issue for 'The Crisis of the Judiciary'") Hogaku Semina (February).

Hogaku Semina. 1980. Gendai no Keisatsu (Contemporary Police in Japan). Tokyo: Nihon Hyoronsha.

Hogaku Semina. 1987. Keisatsu no Genzai (The Present Situation of the Japanese Police). Tokyo: Nihon Hyoronsha.

Homusho. Annual. Kensatsu Tokei Nenpo (Prosecution Statistics Annual Report). Tokyo: Homusho.

Homusho (Homu Sogo Kenkyu-sho). 1989. Hanzai Hakusho (White Paper on Crime). Tokyo: Ministry of Justice.

Hori, Shigeru. 1975. Sengo Seiji no Oboegaki (A Memorandum on Postwar Politics). Tokyo: Mainichi Shimbunsha.

Hori, Yukio. 1983. Sengo no Uyoku Seiryoku (Rightist Forces in Postwar Japan). Tokyo: Keiso Shobo.

Horitsu Jiho. 1975. "Kaisei Keiho Soan no Sogo-teki Kento" ("Special Issue on the Comprehensive Study of a Draft for the Revision of the Penal Law") Horitsu Jiho 47,5.

Hosaka, Kunio. 1986. Shin Keisatsu Kokka Nippon (The New Police State, Japan). Tokyo: Shakai Hyoronsha.

Hoshino, Kanehiro. 1984. "Post-War Law Enforcement: Its Social Impact," in George DeVos, ed., Institutions for Change in Japanese Society, pp.199-23. Berkeley: University of California, Institute of East Asian Studies.

Hoshino, Yasusaburo. 1974. "Keisatsu Seido no Kaikaku" ("Reform of the Police System"), in Tokyo Daigaku Shakai Kaguku Kenkyusho, ed., Sengo kaikaku (The Postwar Reforms), vol.3, Seiji Katei (Political Process), pp.287-350. Tokyo: Iwanamishoten.

Igarashi, Futaba. 1986. "Forced to Confess," in Gavan McCormack and Yoshio Sugimoto, eds., Democracy in Contemporary Japan, pp. 195-214. Armonk, N.Y.: M.E. Sharpe.

Igbinovia, Patrick E. 1984. "Interpol: A Survey of Research Findings," Police Studies 7,2: 112-22.

Iishiba, Seiji. 1990. Soshiki Hanzai Taisaku Manyual (Manual for Operations Against Organized Crime). Tokyo: Yuhikaku.

Inami, Shin'nosuke. 1987a. "'Naimukanryo-teki na mono' no Fukkatsu to 90 nendai Keisatsu no Yukue" ("Revival of a 'MOI' and the Future of the Police in the 1990s"), in Hogaku Semina: Sogo Tokushu 36 Keisatsu no Genzai: 58-65.

Inami, Shin'nosuke. 1987b. "Police Boxes and their Officers," Japan Quarterly (July-September): 295-99.

Inoguchi, Takashi. 1983. Gendai Nippon Seiji Keizai no Kozu (Contemporary Japanese Political Economy). Tokyo: Toyokeizai Shimposha.

Inoguchi, Takashi. 1989. "Kokusaika Jidai no Kanryosei (The State Bureaucracy in the Era of Internationalization)," Leviathan 4: 100-114.

Iokibe, Makoto. 1989. Nichibei Senso to Sengo Nippon (The United States-Japan War and Postwar Japan). Osaka: Osaka Shoseki.

Iokibe, Makoto. 1990. "Senryo Kaikaku no San Ruikei" ("Three Types of Occupation Reforms"), Leviathan 6: 97-120.

Ishii, Shiro and Muramatsu, Michio. 1988. "Nihon Rekishi niokeru Ko-shi" ("The Public and the Private in Japanese History"), Leviathan 2: 7-22.

Ishimura, Osamu, 1987, 1988. "Kon'nichi no Koankeisatsu ni taisuru Kempo-teki Hyoka," (The Present-day Security Police: Its Constitutional Position). Senshu Hogaku Ronshu, vol. 45: 111-52; vol. 47: 105-44.

Ishizuka, Shin'ichi. 1989. "Waga Kuni ni Okeru Gyokei Kaikaku no Rekishi to sono Zenteirikai" ("An Analytical History of Japan's Penal Reform")," Kitakyushu Daigaku Hosei Ronshu 17,1: 1-55.

Itoh, Daiiohi. 1980. Gendai Nihon Kanryosei no Bunseki (An Analysis of the Bureaucracy in Contemporary Japan). Tokyo: Tokyo Daigaku Shuppankai.

Itoh, Hiroshi. 1989. The Japanese Supreme Court: Constitutional Policies. New York: Markus Wiener.

The Japan Law Journal 1, 1: 1-4.

The Japan Times, Daily. Tokyo: The Japan Times.

Jiyuhosodan. 1986. Shimin no Seikatsu to Keisatsu (Citizens' Lives and the Police). Tokyo: Equality Mizuchi Shobo.

JCP. 1980-1990. Seiji Keizai Soran (Japanese Political Economy Annals). Japan Communist Party.

JSP (Kokuminseiji Nenkan Henshu Iinkai). 1961-1990. Kokumin Seiji Nenkan (People's Almanac of Politics). Tokyo: JSP.

Kabashima, Ikuo and Broadbent, Jeffrey, 1986. "Referent Pluralism: Mass Media and Politics in Japan," Journal of Japanese Studies, 12,2: 329-61.

Kabashima, Ikuo. 1988. "Yukensha no Hokaku Ideology to Nakasone-seiji" ("The Conservative-Progressive Ideology Dimension in the Electorate and the Politics of Nakasone)," Leviathan 2: 23-52.

Kabashima, Ikuo. 1990. "Masu Media to Seiji" ("Mass Media and Politics"), Leviathan 7: 7-29.

Kambara, Keiko. 1989. "Japan Battles Rising Crime Wave," The Christian Science Monitor (29 June): 6.

Kamishima, Jiro. 1989. Shinban, Nipponjin no Hasso (The Japanese Way of Thinking: A Revised Edition). Tokyo: Kodansha.

Kaneko, Jinyo. 1975. "Changing Roles of the Police of Japan," Resource Material Series No.10, pp.28-37. Fuchu, Tokyo: United Nations Asia and Far East Institute for the Prevention of Crime and the Treatment of Offenders (UNAFEI).

Kaneko, Jinyo et al. 1987. "Keisatsu no Genzai" ("The Present Situation of the Japanese Police: A Roundtable Discussion"), in Hogaku Semina: Sogo Tokushu 36 Keisatsu no Genzai: 2-26.

Kaplan, David E. and Dubro, Alec. 1986. Yakuza: The Explosive Account of Japan's Criminal Underworld. Reading, Mass.: Addison-Wesley.

Kasai, Akio. 1973. "Some Causes of the Decrease of Crime in Japan," Resource Material Series No.6, pp.134-37. Fuchu, Tokyo: United Nations Asia and Far East Institute for the Prevention of Crime and the Treatment of Offenders (UNAFEI).

Kato, Eiichi. 1980. Nihonjin no Gyosei: Uchino Ruru (The Japanese Style of Public Administration: Its Unwritten Rules). Tokyo: Daiichi Hoki.

Katzenstein, Peter J. 1990. West Germany's Internal Security Policy: State and Violence in the 1970s and 1980s. Cornell University, Cornell Studies in International Affairs, Western Societies Program, Occasional Paper Number 28.

Kawasaki, Hideaki. 1987. "Keisatsu Katsudo to Sosaku-oshu" ("Police Activity and Police Search and Seizure"), in Hogaka Semina: Sogo Tokushu 36 Keisatus no Genzai: 250-256.

Kawashima, Takeyoshi. 1963. "Dispute Resolution in Contemporary Japan," in Arthur Taylor von Mehren, ed., Law in Japan: The Legal Order in a Changing Society, pp.41-72. Cambridge, Mass.: Harvard University Press.

Kawashima, Takeyoshi, 1967. Nihonjin no Ho-ishiki (The Japanese Legal Consciousness). Tokyo: Iwanami Shoten.

Keisatsuseido Kenkyukai. 1985. Keisatsu (The Police). Tokyo: Gyosei.

Keisatsucho. Annual. Hanzai Tokei-sho (Criminal Statistics Annual Report). Tokyo: NPA.

Keisatsucho (Sogo Taisaku Kento Iinkai). 1972. Nanaju Nendai no Keisatsu (1970s Police Policy). Tokyo: NPA.

Keisatsucho. 1973-1990. (1977a, 1980a, 1987a, 1988a, 1989a, 1990a). Keisatsu Hakusho (White Papers on Police). Tokyo: MOF Printing Bureau.

Keisatsucho (Keisatsushi Hensan Iinkai). 1977b. Sengo Keisatsu Shi (A History of the Post-war Police). Tokyo: NPA.

Keisatsucho (Sogo Taisaku Kento Iinkai). 1980b. Hachiju Nendai no Keisatsu (1980s Police Policy). Tokyo: NPA.

Keisatsucho (Bohan-kikaku-ka, Hoan-ka). 1987b. Fueitekiseika-Ho Handbook (Handbook of the Entertainment Business Regulation Law). Tokyo: Tachibana Shobo.

Keisatsucho (Keibi-kyoku, Koan-dai-san-ka). 1988b. Kyokusa boryoku-shudan Hakusho (White Paper on Violent Ultra-Leftist Groups). Tokyo: NPA.

Keisatsucho. 1988c. "Honkakuka Suru Bakudan Toso" ("An Intensification of Bombing Attacks by Radical Groups,") Shoten, no.226.

Keisatsucho. 1988d. "Kokusaitero to Nippon" ("International Terrorism and Japan"), Shoten, no.227.

Keisatsucho. 1989b. "'Tero, Gerira' no Keiko o Tsuyomeru Uyoku" ("Increasing Incidents of Terrorist and Guerrilla Attacks by Rightist Groups"), Shoten, no.230.

Keisatsucho. 1990b. "Kyoaku-ka Shita Kyokusa Boryoku Shudan" ("Violent Ultra-Leftist Groups Turning More Brutal"), Shoten, no.232.

Keisatsukan Jitsumu Roppo (Law and Statute Handbook for Police Officers). 1989. Tokyo: Tokyo Horei Shuppan.

Keizai Koho Center. 1990. Japan 1990: An International Comparison. Tokyo: Japan Institute for Social and Economic Affairs.

Kim, Chin and Lawson, Craig M. 1979. "The Law of the Subtle Mind: The Traditional Japanese Conception of Law," International and Comparative Law Quarterly 28 (July): 491-513.

Kitagawa, Zentaro. 1978. "Theory-Reception: One Aspect of the Development of Japanese Civil Law," in Dan Fenno Henderson and John Owen Haley, eds., Law and the Legal Process in Japan: Materials for an Introductory Course on Japanese Law, pp. 146-56. Seattle: University of Washington Law School.

Koan Chosa-Cho. 1990. Naigai Josei no Kaiko to Tenbo (Retrospect and Prospect on Japan's Internal and External Situation: White Paper of the Public Security Investigation Agency). Tokyo: PSIA.

Kobayashi, Michio. 1986. Nippon Keisatsu: Fushoku no Kozo (Japanese Police: Its Structure of Corrosion). Tokyo: Kodansha.

Kobayashi, Naoki. 1964. Nippon Koku Kempo no Mondi-jyokyo (The Problematic Situation of the Japanese Constitution). Tokyo: Iwanami Shoten.

Kokusai Tero Mondai Kenkyukai. 1989. "Kokusai Tero no Genjo to Taisaku" ("International Terrorism: Present Situation and Counter-Measures"), Keisatsugaku Ronshu (Police Theory) 24,9: 56-77.

Kroeschell, Karl. 1987. "Das moderne Japan und das deutsche Recht," in Bernd Marin, ed., Japan's Weg in die Moderne: Ein Sonderweg nach deutschem Vorbild?, pp.45-68. Frankfurt: Campus.

Kubo, Hiroshi. 1984. Nippon no Keisatsu: Keishicho vs. Osaka-fukei (The Police in Japan: MPD vs. the Osaka Prefectural Police). Tokyo: Kodansha.

Kuby, Ronald and Kunstler, William. 1990. "Political Prisoners in U.S." The Japan Times May 20, p.19.

Kühne, Hans-Heiner. 1973. "Opportunität und quasi-richterliche Tätigkeit des japanischen Staatsanwalts," Zeitschrift für die gesamte Strafrechtswissenschaft vol.85: 1079-1101.

Kühne, Hans-Heiner and Miyazawa, Koichi. 1979. Kriminalität und Kriminalitätsbekämpfung in Japan. Wiesbaden: Bundeskriminalamt.

Kumon, Shumpei. 1982. "Some Principles Governing the Thought and Behavior of Japanists (Contextualists)," Journal of Japanese Studies, 8,1: 5-28.

Kyogoku, Junichi. 1983. Nihon no Seiji (Politics in Japan). Tokyo: Tokyo Daigaka Shuppainkai.

Lehner, Urban C. and Graven, Kathryn. 1990. "Shooting of Mayor Who Faulted Hirohito Puts Japan's Far Right Back in Spotlight," The Wall Street Journal (19 January): A6.

Mainichi, Daily. Tokyo: Mainichi Shimbunsha.

Mainichi. 1986. Saishin Showashi Jiten (The Newest Showa Era Handbook). Mainichi Shimbunsha.

Maki, John M. 1964. Court and Constitution in Japan: Selected Supreme Court Decisions, 1948-60. Seattle: University of Washington Press.

Maruoka, Osamu. 1990. Koan-keisatsu nanbo no monjya (Why Should You Fear the Security Police? A Diary of My Interrogation). Tokyo: Shinsensha.

Matsuhashi, Tadamitsu. 1984. Waga Tsumiwa tsuneni Waga maeni ari (My Sin Has Always Been Before Me). Tokyo: Origin Shuppan Senta.

Matsuhashi, Tadamitsu; Kobayashi, Michio; and Harano, Akira. 1986. "Kono Keisatsu o dosuruka" ("What is to be Done about the Police?"), Sekai (December): 248-65.

Matsumoto, Hitoshi. 1987. Koban no Ura wa Yami (Darkness Behind the Koban). Tokyo: Daisanshokan.

McCormack, Gavan. 1986. "Crime, Confession and Control in Contemporary Japan," in Gavan McCormack and Yoshio Sugimoto, eds., Democracy in Contemporary Japan, pp. 186-94. Armonk, N.Y.: M.E. Sharpe.

McNelly, Theodore. 1975. "The Constitutionality of Japan's Defense Establishment," in James H. Buck, ed., The Modern Japanese Military System, pp. 99-112. Beverly Hills: Sage.

Mendel, Douglas H., Jr. 1975. "Public Views of the Japanese Defense System," in James H. Buck, ed., The Modern Japanese Military System, pp. 149-80. Beverly Hills: Sage.

Meldal-Johnsen, Trevor and Young, Vaughn. 1979. The INTERPOL Connection: An Inquiry into the International Criminal Police Organization. New York: Dial Press.

Metropolitan Police Department Tokyo. 1989. Keishicho. Tokyo: Metropolitan Police Department.

Mikoshiba, Yasuhiro. 1989. "Chukaku-ha no 'Tero, Gerira' ni tsuite" ("'Terrorist and Guerrilla' Attacks by Chukaku"), Koanjyoho 427: 25-35.

Miller, Reuben. 1986. "Acts of International Terrorism: Governments' Responses and Policies," Comparative Political Studies 19,3 (October): 385-414.

Ministry of Justice, 1988. Laws concerning Extradition and International Assistance in Criminal Matters (Translation). Tokyo: Ministry of Justice.

Mitchell, Richard H. 1976. Thought Control in Prewar Japan. Ithaca, NY: Cornell University Press.

Mitchell, Richard H. 1983. Censorship in Imperial Japan. Princeton, NJ: University Press.

Mito, Iwao et al. 1977. "Keisatsu Kokka e no Keisha to Kyuen-undo" ("The Development of a Police State and the Movement to Support Arrested Political Dissenters"), Gendai no Me (October): 166-85.

Mitsudo, Kageaki. 1987. "Shokumu-Shitsumon, Shojihin-kensa" ("Street Ingerrogation and Inspection of Personal Belongings by On-Duty Policemen"), in Hogaka Semina: Sogo Tokushu 36 Keisatus no Genzai: 236-43.

Miyauchi, Hiroshi et al, eds. 1960. Sengo Himitsukeisatsu no Jittai (The Reality of the Secret Police in Postwar Japan). Tokyo: Sanichi Shobo.

Miyazawa, Setsuo. 1985. Hanzai Sosa o Meguru Dai Issen Keiji no Ishiki to Kodo (The Attitudes and Behavior of the First-Line Detectives Concerning Criminal Investigation). Tokyo: Seibundo.

Miyazawa, Setsuo. 1987. "Taking Kawashima Seriously: A Review of Japanese Research on Japanese Legal Consciousness and Disputing Behavior," Law and Society Review 21,2: 219-41.

Miyazawa, Setsuo, 1988. "Social Movements and Contemporary Rights in Japan: Relative Success Factors in the Fields of Environmental Law," Kobe University Law Review 22: 63-77.

Miyazawa, Setsuo. 1989. "Scandal and Hard Reform: Implications of a Wiretapping Case to the Control of Organizational Police Crimes in Japan," Kobe University Law Review 23: 13-27.

Miyazawa, Setsuo. 1990. "Learning Lessons from Japanese Experience in Policing and Crime: Challenge for Japanese Criminologists," Kobe University Law Review 24: 29-61.

Miyazawa, Setsuo. 1991a. Policing in Japan. Albany: SUNY Press.

Miyazawa, Setsuo. 1991b. "The Private Sector and Law Enforcement in Japan," in William Gormley, ed., Privatization and Its Alternatives, pp. 241-57. Madison: University of Wisconsin Press.

Mizoguchi, Atsushi, 1986. "Urashakai no Seijikeizai-gaku (Political Economy of the Underground Society: Yakuza)," Bessatsu Takarajima no. 56: 178-204. Tokyo: JICC Shuppankyoku.

Mizumachi, Osamu. 1982. "Patrol Police in Japan," International Criminal Police Review 37,359: 150-55.

Mizutani, Kiyoshi. 1987. "Keisatsu Chusu no Anbu o miru" ("A Look at the Dark Spots at the Center of the Police)," in Hogaku Semina: Sogo Tokushu 36 Keisatsuno Genzai: 114-19.

Momose, Takashi. 1990. Jiten Showa Senzen-ki no Nihon: Seido to Jittai: (The Pre-war Showa Era in Japan. Its Institutions and Processes). Tokyo: Yoshikawa Kobunkan.

Murakami, Yasusuke. 1985. "Ie Society as a Pattern of Civilization: Response to Criticism," Journal of Japanese Studies (Summer) 11,2: 401-21.

Muramatsu, Michio. 1981. Sengo Nippon no Kanryosei (The Bureaucracy in Post-war Japan). Tokyo: Toyokeizai Shinposha.

Muramatsu, Michio, and Krauss, Ellis S. 1987. "The Conservative Policy Line and the Development of Patterned Pluralism in Japan," in Kozo Yamamura and Y. Yasuda ed., The Political Economy of Japan. vol. 1., pp., 516-54. Stanford: Stanford University Press.

Muramatsu, Takeshi, ed. 1978. Kokusai Tero no Jidai (The Age of International Terrorism). Tokyo: Takagi Shobo.

Murayama, Masayuki. 1980. "A Comparative Study of Police Accountability: A Preliminary Work," unpublished paper, Berkeley, University of California.

Murayama, Masayuki. 1989a. "Patrol Police Activities in Changing Urban Conditions: The Case of the Tokyo Police," unpublished paper, Chiba University (January).

Murayama, Masayuki. 1989b. "Intra-Organizational Control of Patrol Activities in Tokyo," paper presented at the Annual Meeting of the American Society of Criminology in Reno, Nevada (8 November).

Murayama, Masayuki. 1990. Keira Keisatsu no Kenkyu (A Study of the Patrol Police in Tokyo). Tokyo: Seibundo.

Nagamatsu, Yoshisato. 1988. "Ajia-Taiheiyo Chiiki Chian Tanto Kakuryo Kaigi Kaisai" ("A Report on the Ministerial Conference on Security Matters for the Asia Pacific Region"), Keisatsu Koron (September): 45-53.

Naganuma, Akira. 1987. "Keisatsu Zaisei no Check wa nainoka" ("Is There No Check on Police Finances?"), in Hogaka Semina: Sogo Tokushu 36 Keisatsu no Genzai: 92-93.

Naikakuseido Hyakunenshi (A One Hundred-Year History of the Cabinet System in Japan). Volumes 1-2. 1985. Tokyo: MOF Printing Bureau.

Nakamura, Koji. 1974. "The 'Effective Pawns'," Far Eastern Economic Review (18 February): 22-23.

Nakamura, Koji. 1975. "Japan: A Feeling of Helpless Anxiety," Far Eastern Economic Review (15 August): 10.

Nakane, Chie. 1972. Human Relations in Japan: Summary Translation of "Tateshakai no Ningen Kankei" (Personal Relations in a Vertical Society). Tokyo: Ministry of Foreign Affairs.

Nakane, Chie, 1973. Japanese Society. Berkeley: University of California Press.

National Police Agency, 1982. White Paper on Police 1982 (Excerpt). Tokyo: National Police Agency.

National Police Agency. 1987a. White Paper on Police 1987 (Excerpt). Tokyo: National Police Agency.

National Police Agency. 1987b. The Police of Japan 1987. Tokyo: National Police Agency.

National Police Agency. 1988. White Paper on Police 1988 (Excerpt). Tokyo: National Police Agency.

National Police Agency. 1989a. White Paper on Police 1989 (Excerpt). Tokyo: National Police Agency.

National Police Agency. 1989b. The Police of Japan 1989. Tokyo: National Police Agency.

Nickerson, Colin. 1989. "Hirohito's Funeral: Tribute to Japan, Trial for Its Officials," The Boston Globe (20 February): 1,8.

Nihon Kingendai-shi Jiten Henshuiinkai. 1978. Nihon Kingendai-shi Jiten (A Handbook of Modern and Contemporary History in Japan). Tokyo: Toyokeizai Shimposha.

Nihon Seisansei. Honbu, 1989. Katsuyo Rodo Tokei 1989 (Practical Labor Statistics, 1989 edition). Tokyo: Nihon Seisansei Honbu.

Nikkan Keisatsu Shimbunsha. 1989. Zenkoku Keisatsu Kanbu Shokuinroku (National Directory of Senior Police Officials). Tokyo: Nikkan Keisatsu Shimbunsha.

Nikkei, Daily. Nippon Keizai Shimbun-sha.

Nippon Zaigai Kigyokyokai. 1987. Kaigai Anzen Kakuho no tameno Shohosaku (Various Measures to Ensure Security Abroad for Business). Tokyo: Nippon Zaigai Kigyokyokai.

Nishihara, Shigeyoshi. 1987. Yoron Chosa ni yoru Do-jidai-shi (A Contemporary History Based on Public Opinion Surveys). Tokyo: Brain Shuppan.

Nishimura, Haruo and Tsuneyuki Matsumoto. 1963. "Keisatsu ni taisuru Shimin no Taido no Bunseki" ("An Analysis of Citizens' Attitudes towards the Police"), Kagakukeisatsu Kenkyusho Hokoku Bohan Shonen-hen 9,1: 16-32.

Nishimura, Itsuo. n.d. "Extradition: Theory and Practice in Japan and the United States," Cambridge Mass., Harvard University Law School, unpublished manuscript.

Nishio, Baku. 1976. "Shimin Keisatsu wa Mujaki na Meiyu ka" ("Is the Civil Police an Innocent Actor?"), Gendai no Me (May): 218-29.

Nishio, Baku. 1979. Gendai Nippon no Keisatsu (The Police in Contemporary Japan). Taimatsu Shinsho.

Nishio, Baku. 1984. Nippon no Keisatsu (The Japanese Police). Tokyo: Gendaishokan.

Noda, Yosiyuki. 1973. "Far Eastern Conception of Law," International Encyclopedia of Comparative Law. Volume 1, pp.120-36. Tübingen: J.C.B. Mohr (Paul Siebeck).

Noda, Yosiyuki. 1976. Introduction to Japanese Law. Tokyo: University of Tokyo Press.

Novick, Albert. 1989. "Police Use a Variety of Torture Techniques," Yomiuri, August 14.

Obinata, Sumio. 1987. Ten'no-Sei Keisatsu to Minshu (The Police in the Emperor System and Its People). Tokyo: Nippon hyoron-sha.

Odanaka, Toshiki. 1973. Gendai Shiho no Kozo to Shiso (The Contemporary Japanese Judiciary: Its Structure and Ideology). Tokyo: Nippon hyoron-sha.

Office of Strategic Service. 1945. The Japanese Police System Under Allied Occupation. R&A, Report no. 2758. n.p.

Ogata, Yasuo and Ogata, Kaneko. 1987. Kokuhatsu: Keisatsukan Denwa Tocho Jiken (Indictment: The Police Wiretapping Incident). Tokyo: Shin-nippon Shuppansha.

Ogawa, Taro. 1976. "Japan," in Dae H. Chang, ed., Criminology: A Cross-Cultural Perspective. Volume 2, 586-655. New Delhi: Vikas Publishing.

Ohashi, Hideo; Chiba, Nagato; and Matsuhashi, Tadamitsu. 1985. Tatakatta Kanbu Keisatsu-kan no kiroku (A Record of Senior Police Officers who Have Fought against Police Corruption). Tokyo: Origin Shuppan Center.

Oide, Yoshitomo and Shizuo Fujiwara. 1987. "Jyuyo Hanrei Shokai" ("A Review of Major Cases about the Police"), in Hogaka Semina: Sogo Tokushu 36 Keisatsu no Genzai: 388-398.

Oki, Masao. 1983. Nipponjin no Ho Kannen (The Japanese Notion of Law). Tokyo: Tokyo Daigaku Shuppankai.

Oki, Masao. 1984. "Japanese Rights' Consciousness: The Nature of Japan's Judicial System," Look Japan (January 10): 4-5.

Okimoto, Daniel I. 1989. Between MITI and the Market: Japanese Industrial Policy for High Technology. Stanford: Stanford University Press.

Okudaira, Yasuhiro. 1977. Chian Iji-ho Shoshi (A Short History of the Peace Preservation Law). Tokyo: Chikuma Shobo.

Okurasho (Shukeikyoku Chosaka). 1989. Zaisei Tokei (1989 Budgetary Statistics). Tokyo: Ministry of Finance Printing Bureau.

Oono, Masao and Watanabe, Yasuo, ed. 1989. Keiji Saiban no Hikarito Kage (The Bright and Dark Sides of the Criminal Court). Tokyo: Yuhikaku.

Organisation for Economic Co-Operation and Development. 1978. Geographical Distribution of Financial Flows to Developing Countries: Data on Disbursements 1971 to 1977. OECD: Paris.

Otake, Hideo. 1983. "Sengo Hoshu Taisei no Tairitsu-jiku" ("An Axis of Political Cleavage in the Postwar Conservative System"), ChuoKoron (April): 137-51.

Otake, Hideo. 1987. Nakasone Seiji no Ideologi to sono Kokunaiseiji-teki Haikei (The Ideology of the Nakasone Government and the Background in Domestic Politics). Leviathan 1: 73-91.

Otake, Hideo, 1988. Saigunbi to Nashonarizumu (Rearmament and Nationalism). Tokyo: Chuokoronsha.

Packard, George R. 1966. Protest in Tokyo: The Security Treaty Crisis of 1960. Princeton: Princeton University Press.

Parker, L. Craig Jr. 1984. The Japanese Police System Today: An American Perspective. Tokyo: Kodansha International.

Pharr, Susan. 1990. Losing Face. Status Politics in Japan. Berkeley: University of California Press.

Prime Minister's Secretariat Public Relations Office, 1981. Keisatsu ni Kansuru Yoronchosa (Public Opinion Poll on the Police), Prime Minister's Secretariat.

Prime Minister's Secretariat Public Relations Office, 1984. Keisatsu ni Kansuru Yoronchosa (Public Opinion Poll on the Police), Prime Minister's Secretariat.

Prime Minister's Secretariat Public Relations Office, 1990. Keisatsu ni Kansuru Yoronchosa (Public Opinion Poll on the Police), Prime Minister's Secretariat.

Ramseyer, J. Mark. 1985. "The Cost of the Consensual Myth: Antitrust Enforcement and Institutional Barriers to Litigation in Japan," Yale Law Journal 94,3: 604-45.

Ramseyer, J. Mark. 1988. "Reluctant Litigant Revisited: Rationality and Disutes in Japan," Journal of Japanese Studies 14,1 (Spring): 111-23.

Richelson, Jeffrey T. 1988. Foreign Intelligence Organizations. Cambridge, Mass.: Ballinger Publishing Company.

Rinalducci, Ralph J. 1972. The Japanese Police Establishment. Tokyo: Obun Intereurope.

Rincho/Gyokaku OB-kai. 1987. Rincho Gyokakushin (The Provisional Administrative Commission and the Provisional Administrative Reform Council). Tokyo: Gyoseikanri Kenkyu Senta.

Saiko Saibansho. Annual. Shiho Tokei Nenpo (Judicial Statistics Annual Report). Tokyo. Saiko Saiban sho.

Saito, Teruo. n.d. Keisatsucho (National Police Agency). Tokyo; Kyoikusha.

Sakai, Sadao. 1987. Tero no Jidai (The Age of Terrorism). Tokyo: Kyoiku sha.

Sanger, David E. 1989a. "As Hirohito Funeral Nears Security Forces Get Nervous," The New York Times (20 February): A1,A7.

Sanger, David E. 1989b. "Tokyo Goes into Gear, Blimp and All," The New York Times (23 February): A10.

Sankei, Daily. Tokyo: Sankei Shimbunsha.

Sassa, Atsuyuki. 1984 (Original edition, 1979-80). Kikikanri no Nouhau (The Know-How of Crisis Management). Volumes 1-3. Kyoto: PHP Kenkyusho.

Sawanobori, Toshio. 1973. "Hikakuho-teki ni mita Nihon Keiho no Tokushoku (The Japanese Penal Code in Comparative Perspective), in Hiraba, Yasuji and Hirano, Ryuichi, ed., Keiho Kaisei no Kenkyu (A Study of the Penal Code Reform), pp. 20-37. Tokyo: Tokyo University Press.

Sawanobori, Toshio. 1987. "Fueiho Mondai to Keisatsu Katsudo no Genkai" ("The Problem of The Entertainment Business Regulation Law and the Limits of Police Activity"), in Hogaka Semina: Sogo Tokushu 36 Keisatsu no Genzai: 139-49.

Schembri, Anthony J. 1985. "An Overview of the Japanese Police System," The Police Chief 52 (May): 40-43.

Schiller, David T. 1986. "The Economic Implications of Terrorism: A Case Study of the Federal Republic of Germany," TVI Report 7,1 (Summer): 37-40.

Sentaku. 1986. "Naikaku-kanbo" ("Cabinet Secretariat"), Sentaku (August): 126-29.

Shain, I.J. "Cy". 1984. "Recent Trends in Japanese Criminality: Some Comparative Perspectives," in George deVos, ed., Institutions for Change in Japanese Society, pp.224-29. Berkeley: University of California Press, Institute of East Asian Studies.

Shinmura, Izuru. 1955. Kojien (A Japanese Dictionary). Tokyo: Iwanami Shoten.

Shiso no Kagaku Kenkyukai, ed., 1959. Tenko (Apostasy). 3 vols. Tokyo: Heibonsha

Sigur, Gaston J. 1975. "Power, Politics and Defense," in James H. Buck, ed., The Modern Japanese Military System, pp.181-98, Beverly Hills: Sage.

Shiso no kagaku Kenkyukai [Society to Study the Science of Thought], ed., 1959. Tenko [apostasy]. 3 vols. Tokyo: Heibonsha.

Sigur, Gaston J. 1985. "Power, Politics and Defense," in James H. Buck, ed., The Modern Japanese Military System, ed., pp.181-98. Beverly Hills: Sage.

Smith, Malcolm. n.d. "The Internationalization of the Japanese Economy: The Legal Framework," Vancouver, The University of British Columbia, Institute of International Relations and Institute for Research on Public Policy.

Smith, Robert J. 1983. Japanese Society: Tradition, Self and the Social Order. Cambridge: Cambridge University Press.

Smith, Robert J. 1985. "A Pattern of Japanese Society: Ie Society or Acknowledgement of Interdependence?" Journal of Japanese Studies 11,1: 29-45.

Smith, Robert. 1989. "Presidential Address: Something Old, Someting New - - Tradition and Culture in the Study of Japan," The Journal of Asian Studies 48,4 (November): 715-23.

Somucho (Gyosei-kanri-kyoku). 1988. Gyosei Kiko-zu (The Organizational Chart of the Japanese Government). Tokyo: Somucho Gyosei-kanri-kyoku.

Somucho (Tokei-kyoku). 1989. Nihon Tokei Nenkan (Statistical Almanac of Japan). Tokyo: Somucho Tokei-kyoku.

Der Spiegel. 1990. "Japan's Mafia im Aufwind." 45,1 (31 December): 101.

Steiner, Kurt. 1965. Local Government in Japan. Stanford: Stanford University Press.

Steinhoff, Patricia G. 1984. "Student Conflict," in Ellis P. Krauss, Thomas P. Rohlen and Patricia G. Steinhoff, eds., Conflict in Japan, pp. 174-213. Honolulu: University of Hawaii Press.

Steinhoff, Patricia G. 1988a. "What Will the Japanese Red Army Do Next?" unpublished paper, Honolulu, University of Hawaii.

Steinhoff, Patricia G. 1988b. "Tenko and Thought Control," in Gail Lee Bernstein and Haruhiro Fukui, eds., Japan and the World: Essays on Japanese History and Politics in Honour of Ishida Takeshi, pp. 78-94. London: Macmillan.

Steinhoff, Patricia G. 1989a. "Hijackers, Bombers, and Bank Robbers: Managerial Style in the Japanese Red Army,"The Journal of Asian Studies 48,4 (November): 724-40.

Steinhoff, Patricia G. 1989b. "Protest and Democracy," in Takeshi Ishida and Ellis S. Krauss, eds., Democracy in Japan, pp.171-198. Pittsburgh: University of Pittsburgh Press.

Steinhoff, Patricia G. 1991. Tenko: Ideology and Societal Integration in Prewar Japan. New York: Garland Publishing.

Steinhoff, Patricia. n.d. "Deadly Ideology: The Lod Airport Massacre and the Rengo Sekigun Purge," unpublished manuscript, Honolulu, University of Hawaii.

Sterngold, James. 1989. "Japan's Police Use Steel Cages to Subdue Foes of Airport Expansion," The New York Times (6 December): A9.

Suekawa, Hiroshi, ed. 1966. Shiryo Sengo 20 nen-shi: Horitsu (Sourcebook of the Twenty-Year History of Postwar Japan: Law). Tokyo: Nihon Hyoronsha.

Sugai, Shuichi. 1957. "The Japanese Police System," in Robert E. Ward, ed., Five Studies in Japanese Politics, pp. 1-14. Ann Arbor: The University of Michigan Press.

Suzuki, Satoshi. 1987. "Koankeisatsu no Hanzai niwa Me o tsubutta Kensatsu no Ho to Seigi" ("The Legality and Morality of the Prosecutors' Office Decision not to Indict the Criminal Activity of the Public Security Police: The Wiretapping Case of the JCP Executive"), Asahi Journal (11 September): 6-11.

Suzuki, Takuro. 1978. Keisatsu Kisha 30-nen (A Thirty Years History of a Police Newspaper Reporter). Tokyo: Keizaioraisha.

Suzuki, Takuro. 1980. Nippon Keisatsu no Himitsu (The Secret of the Japanese Police). Tokyo: Chobunsha.

Suzuki, Takuro. 1985. Nippon Keisatsu no Kaibo (An Anatomy of the Japanese Police). Tokyo: Kodansha.

Suzuki, Yoshio. 1978. "The United Nations-affiliated Asia and Far East Institute for the Prevention of Crime and the Treatment of Offenders," International Review of Criminal Policy, 34: 75-82.

Tachibana, Takashi. 1975. Chukaku tai Kakumaru. (Chukaku versus Kakumaru) Volumes 1-2. Tokyo: Kodansha.

Tahara, Soichiro. 1979. Nippon no Kanryo 1980 (Japanese Bureaucrats 1980). Tokyo: Bungei Shunjyu.

Tahara, Soichiro. 1986a. Nippon Dai-Kaizo (A Sweeping Reform of Japan). Tokyo: Bungei Shunjyu.

Tahara, Soichiro. 1986b. Keisatsu Kanryo no Jidai (The Age of Police Bureaucrats). Tokyo: Kodansha.

Tahara, Soichiro. 1990. Heisei Nippon no Kanryo (Japanese Bureaucrats in the Heisei Era). Tokyo: Bungei Shunjyu.

Taijudo, Kanae. 1975. "Some Reflections on Japan's Practice of International Law During a Dozen Eventful Decades," Proceedings of the American Society of International Law 69: 64-69.

Taikakai. 1970-1971. Naimusho-shi (The History of the Ministry of the Interior). Volumes 1-4. Tokyo: Taikakai, Harashobo.

Takagi, Masayuki. 1988. Shin Sayoku 30 nenshi (A Thirty-Years History of the New Left). Tokyo: Doyobijyutsusha.

Takagi, Masayuki. 1990. "Seinen-Taishu Undo" ("Youth and Mass Movement"), Chiezo (Contemporary Term Dictionary). Tokyo: Asahi Shimbunsha: 645-50.

Takayanagi, Kenzo. 1963. "A Century of Innovation: The Development of Japanese Law, 1868-1961," in Arthur Taylor von Mehren, ed., Law in Japan: The Legal Order in a Changing Society, pp.5-40. Cambridge, Mass.: Harvard University Press.

Takazawa, Koji ed. 1983. Furemuappu: Tsuchida, Nisseki, Pisukan Jiken no Shinso (Frame up: The Real Facts of Tsuchida, Nisseki, Piece-can Bombing Incidents), Tokyo: Shinsensha.

Takazawa, Koji; Takagi, Masayuki; and Kurata, Keisei. 1981. Shinsayoku 20 nenshi (A Twenty Years History of the New Left). Tokyo: Shinsensha.

Takeda, Mamoru. 1980. "Keishicho Koan Keibi Ryobu no Jittai" ("The Security Bureau and the Guard Bureau in the MPD"), in Gendai no Keisatsu (The Present-Day Police). Tokyo: Nihon Hyoronsha.

Takeuchi, Naoto. 1990. "Dai 11 kai Kokuren Hanzai Boshi Kisei Iinkai no Gaiyo" ("A Summary Report on the 11th Meeting of the United Nations Committee on Crime Prevention and Control"), Sosa Kenkyo 461: 39-49.

Takeyasu, Masamitsu. 1986. "Summary Report on Violent Crime in the Federal Republic of Germany and Responses such as Sentencing Practices," Bulletin of the Criminological Research Department. Tokyo: Research and Training Institute, Ministry of Justice, pp.22-24.

Takigawa, Hiroshi. 1973. Kagekiha Kaimetsu Sakusen (The Operations of Annihilating Radicals). Tokyo: San'ichi Shobo.

Tanaka, Hideo. 1976. The Japanese Legal System: Introductory Cases and Materials. Tokyo: University of Tokyo Press.

Tanaka, Shigeaki. 1987. Gendai Nippon Ho no Kozu (The Design of Contemporary Japanese Law) Tokyo: Chikuma Shobo.

Tashiro, Noriharu. 1985. Nihon Kyosanto no Hensen to Kagekiha-shudan no Riron to Jissen (Changes in Japan's Communist Party and the Theories and Practices of Radical Groups). Tokyo: Tachibara Shobo.

Terzani, Tiziano. 1990a. "Wir sind die Erben der Samurai: Teil I," Der Spiegel 44,26 (25 June): 108-21.

Terzani, Tiziano. 1990b. "Wir sind die Erben der Samurai: Teil II," Der Spiegel 44,27 (2 July): 100-16.

Tipton, Elise K. 1990. The Japanese Police State. Honolulu: University of Hawaii Press.

Titus, David Anson. 1974. Palace and Politics in Prewar Japan. New York: Columbia University Press.

Tokyo-to. 1968-1989. Yosan Gaiyo (An Outline of the Annual Budget). Tokyo: Tokyo Prefectural Government.

Tominomori, Eiji. 1977. Sengo Hoshuto-Shi (A History of Conservative Parties in Postwar Japan). Tokyo: Nippon Hyoronsha.

Toyokeizai. 1984-1989. Seikai Kankai Jinjiroku (Who's Who in Politics and Bureaucracy). Tokyo: Toyokeizai Shinposha.

Tozuka, Hideo. 1973. "Nihon no Shin-sayoku Sho-toha no Keisei to Tenkai: Sono Soshikiteki Keihu ni tsuite no Gaikan" ("Formation and Development of Japan's New Leftist Parties: An Overview of their Organizational Lineage"), Shakaikagaku Kenkyu, 25,1: 57-99.

Tsuji, Kiyoaki, ed. 1966. Shiryo Sengo 20 nen-shi: Seiji (Sourcebook of the Twenty-Year History of Postwar Japan: Politics). Tokyo: Nihon Hyoronsha.

Tsumura, Takashi. 1976. "Konputa Shakai to CR" ("The Computer Society and Community Relation Tactics"), Gendai no Me (February): 102-09.

Tsunakawa, Masao and Handa, Yoshihiro. 1972. rev. 1981. Shokumu shitsumon (Street Interrogation by On-Duty Policemen). Tokyo: Keiseisha.

The 20-Year History of UNAFEI-Regional Co-operation in Social Defence. 1982. Tokyo: United Nations Asia and Far East Institute for the Prevention of Crime and the Treatment of Offenders (UNAFEI).

Uetake, Shintaro. 1987. "Keisatsu-jyoho to Jiken-hodo" ("Police Information and News Reports about Crimes"), in Hogaku Semina: Sogo Tokushu 36 Keisatsuno Genzai: 94-100.

Upham. Frank K. 1987. Law and Social Change in Postwar Japan. Cambridge, Mass.: Harvard University.

Vogel, David. 1990. "Environmental Policy in Japan and West Germany," paper prepared for presentation at the annual meeting of the Weston Political Science Association, Newport Beach, California, March.

Vogel. Ezra F. 1979. Japan as Number One: Lessons for America. Cambridge, Mass.: Havard University Press.

Watanabe, Hisashi. 1989. "Kokusaika suru Keiji Shiho" ("Internationalization of the Judiciary in a Newly Established International Department"), Hanrei Times 708: 27-33.

Watanabe, Osamu. 1985. "Gendai Nippon Keisatsu no Keisei--Kindaika kara Nippon-ka" ("The Formation of the Contemporary Japanese Police: From Modernization to Japanization"), Shakai Kagaku Kenkyu 37,5: 201-38.

Watanabe, Osamu. 1987. "Jyuyo Ronbun Chosaku Annai" ("A Guide to Important Writings"), in Hogaka Semina: Sogo Tokushu 36 Keisatsu no Genzai: 400-415.

Watanabe, Osamu, et al. 1985. Tose Keisatsu Jijyo (The Present Police Situation). Tokyo: Token Shuppan.

Watanabe, Yasuo and Isa, Chihiro. 1989. Yameru Saiban (Sick Courts). Tokyo: Bungei Shunjyu.

Weinstein, Martin E. 1971. Japan's Postwar Defense Policy, 1947-1968. New York: Columbia University Press.

Weinstein, Martin E. 1975. "The Evolution of the Japan Self-Defense Forces," in James H. Buck, ed., The Modern Japanese Military System, pp.41-63. Beverly Hills: Sage.

Weisman, Steven R. 1989. "In Suburbia, Crimes that Seem So Un-Japanese," The New York Times (26 June): A4.

Weisman, Steven R. 1990a. "Japan Enthrones Emperor Today in Old Rite with New Twist," The New York Times (12 November): A2.

Weisman, Steven R. 1990b. "Visitors for Enthronment Press Japan for Support," The New York Times (13 November): A7.

Weisman, Steven R. 1990c. "Japan's Urban Underside Erupts, Tarnishing Image of Social Peace," The New York Times (11 October): A1, A10.

Weisman, Steven R. 1991. "Japan on Guard after Threat by Old Terror Group," The New York Times (29 January): A9.

Westney, D. Eleanor. 1982. "The Emulation of Western Organizations in Meiji Japan: The Case of the Paris Prefecture of Police and the Keishi-cho," Journal of Japanese Studies 8,2: 307-42.

Westney, D. Eleanor. 1987. Imitation and Innovation: The Transfer of Western Organizational Patterns to Meiji Japan. Cambridge, Mass.: Harvard University Press.

Whittemore, Edward P. 1961. The Press in Japan Today . . . A Case Study. Columbia: University of South Carolina Press.

Wolferen, Karel van. 1989. The Enigma of Japanese Power: People and Politics in a Stateless Nation. New York: Knopf.

Wolferen, Karel van. 1990. "Why Militarism Still Haunts Japan," The New York Times (12 December): A23.

Yamada, Hideo. 1986. "Tokyo Summit Oedo Keibi Nikki" ("A Diary of the Activities of the Security and Guard Police Force around Edo (Tokyo) during the Tokyo Summit"), Bungeishunjyu (July): 331-48.

Yamaguchi, Yasushi. 1989. Seiji Taisei (Political Regimes). Tokyo: Tokyo Daigaku Shuppankai.

Yamomoto, Taketoshi. 1989. "The Press Clubs of Japan," Journal of Japanese Studies 15,2 (Summer): 371-88.

Yanaga, Chitoshi. 1935. "Theory of the Japanese State," Ph.d. dissertation, University of California, Berkeley.

Yomiuri, Daily. Tokyo: Yomiuri Shimbunsha.

Yomiuri (Shimbun Osaka Shakaibu). 1984. Keikan Oshoku (Police Corruption). Tokyo: Kadokawa Shoten.

Yomiuri (Shimbun Shakaibu). 1986. Nippon Keisatsu (The Japanese Police). Tokyo: Yomuiri Shimbunsha.

Yoshimura, Katsumi. 1985. Ikeda Seiken 1575 Nichi (The 1,575 Days of the Ikeda Government). Tokyo: Gyosei Mondai Kenkyusho.

Yoshihara, Koichiro, 1976. "Koan Chosa-cho no Kiken na Jittai," (The Dangerous Reality of the Public Security Investigation Agency) Gekkan Shakaito no. 238 (October): 89-93.

Yoshihara, Koichiro. 1978. Boryaku Retto (The Stratagem Archipelago). Tokyo: Shinippon Shuppansha.

Yutenji, Kazumasa. 1989. "Shuyo Kokusai Tero-soshiki to Sho-gaikoku no Kokusai Tero-taisaka" ("Major International Terrorist Organizations and Counter-Terrorist Measures Taken by Foreign Governments"), Koanjyoho no.42: 36-55.

CORNELL EAST ASIA SERIES

For ordering information please write:
CORNELL EAST ASIA SERIES
East Asia Program
Cornell University
140 Uris Hall
Ithaca, NY 14853-7601

9-91/.6M/BB